Mine Eyes Have Seen the Glory

Mine Eyes Have Seen the Glory

A Biography of Julia Ward Howe

By
Deborah Pickman Clifford

An Atlantic Monthly Press Book
Little, Brown and Company   Boston — Toronto

A portion of Chapter 10 appeared in *Vermont
History*, in a different form.

Material from the Howe Papers is reprinted by
permission of the Houghton Library.

Second Printing
T 01/79

Library of Congress Cataloging in Publication Data

Clifford, Deborah Pickman.
    Mine eyes have seen the glory.

    "An Atlantic Monthly Press book."
    Includes index.
    1. Howe, Julia Ward, 1819–1910 — Biography.
2. Authors, American — 19th century — Biography.
I. Title.
PS2018.C55   818'.4'09 [B]   78-10379
ISBN 0-316-14747-8

ATLANTIC–LITTLE, BROWN BOOKS
ARE PUBLISHED BY
LITTLE, BROWN AND COMPANY
IN ASSOCIATION WITH
THE ATLANTIC MONTHLY PRESS

Designed by Janis Capone

MV

*Published simultaneously in Canada
by Little, Brown & Company (Canada) Limited*

PRINTED IN THE UNITED STATES OF AMERICA

For Nicholas

Mine Eyes Have Seen the Glory

Prologue

One day Julia Ward Howe's daughter Laura, having lost her way on a back road in Maine, stopped at a farmhouse to inquire the way. The door was opened and a smiling face greeted her. "I know who you are!" the woman exclaimed. "You're the daughter of the Queen of America."

It was May 30, 1888, and rain had fallen on the city of San Francisco all that Memorial Day, spoiling the picnics but not the spirits of those determined to enjoy the parades and other ceremonies. The holiday atmosphere prevailed well into the evening, when a great crowd assembled in the Grand Opera House for the last of the day's celebrations: the Literary Exercises. Here out of the rain great monuments of lilies and English ivy greeted the men and women in evening dress who streamed in through the front entrance. There were flowers everywhere. Clusters of blossoms were tied "in fanciful design" across the front of the boxes. The backdrop of the stage consisted of a ship made entirely of evergreens, carnations, roses and bright-colored geraniums. On the stage itself three tall vases filled with flowers stood like sentinels across the footlights and behind them a row of dignitaries faced the audience. In the middle of the row, seated in a velvet armchair, was a small elderly woman dressed in black satin, with a white shawl over her shoulders and a lace cap on her head.

3

After the overture had been played and the opening prayer read, the speaker of the evening, Henry C. Dibble, welcomed everyone "to this festival of loyalty," a sentiment which he said had been destroyed by the Civil War but which was now being kept alive by the celebration of Memorial Day and "the singing of patriotic songs such as 'The Battle Hymn of the Republic.' " The speaker then informed those assembled that "the noble woman who penned these lines is in our midst tonight." Julia Ward Howe — for the little lady in black satin was indeed she — rose and bowed her head in graceful acknowledgment of the cheers from the audience. According to a reporter from the *Daily Examiner,* the speaker then went on to pay "a glowing tribute to the lady," concluding with the words, "May your hearts be inspired by those acts of love and loyalty which inspired the volunteers, saved the Union and abolished slavery."

Later in the evening after various poems had been recited — "Blossoms for the Brave" was one — and various songs sung, including "The Star Spangled Banner," Mrs. Howe was once more introduced, this time by General Salomon, who spoke of the honor accorded both the Grand Army of the Republic and the city of San Francisco by the first visit to California of this distinguished woman. He then presented her "on behalf of the people of this city" with two handsome bouquets, and immediately someone in the audience proposed "three cheers and a tiger" for Mrs. Howe, which, according to the reporter from the *Examiner* were "given with a will." Round after round of applause accompanied the waving of handkerchiefs as Julia Ward Howe again stood in quiet acknowledgment. When the cheers had died down she spoke briefly. Her soft yet resonant voice could be clearly heard by everyone in the house as she declared that she had come to the Literary Exercises "with a thrilled heart." Her few words were greeted with more cheers and more waving of handkerchiefs, which ceased only as the First Artillery Band broke into the opening chords of "The Battle Hymn of the Republic." A lone singer's voice then filled the hall:

Mine eyes have seen the glory of the coming of the Lord:
He is trampling out the vintage where the grapes of
      wrath are stored;
He hath loosed the fateful lightning of His terrible
      swift sword:
His truth is marching on.

With the completion of the first verse the great audience rose spontaneously and joined in the chorus:

Glory, glory, hallelujah! Glory, glory, hallelujah!
Glory, glory, hallelujah! His truth is marching on.

All five verses of the hymn were sung, with the audience joining in the chorus at the end of each. That night Julia Ward Howe noted in her diary, "It was a splendid tribute."

5

1

Wards and Cutlers

I was born 'neath a clouded star
More in shadow than light have grown;
Loving souls are not like trees
That strongest and stateliest shoot alone.
— Julia Ward Howe, "Salutory"

Julia Ward Howe's earliest recollections were of a tall brick house facing Bowling Green, the oldest city park on Manhattan Island. Her father, Samuel Ward, a partner in the banking offices of Prime & Ward, had bought one of the seven lots facing the Green in 1821, when Julia, the third child and only daughter, in what was then a family of four, was a year and a half old. Six houses were erected on the plot of land where first a fort and later the Government House had stood. The Wards' was in the middle of the short block with two nearly identical dwellings flanking it. All six were narrow and deep, with four stories and a view from the back windows of the Battery and the harbor beyond. From the front one looked northward across the Green and up Broadway, then the most fashionable avenue in the city. By the end of 1821 the four little Wards, their parents and various servants were able to move into Number 5 Bowling Green, where the children divided their time between the nursery on the top floor and Battery Park. The Battery had served the city of New York since the Revolution as a playground, village green and parade

6

ground for soldiers. Here also vessels of every sort could be seen, from the Liverpool packets, which now made regular runs across the Atlantic, to the little market craft that sailed up and down the coast and along the inland waterways.

The view from the Battery had not always been so full of activity. Only a few years earlier the War of 1812 had brought shipping in New York Harbor almost to a standstill. Vessels rotted at their moorings, while bankers and merchants fretted in their countinghouses. By 1821, however, the hardships of war were all but forgotten and merchants could proudly boast that the value of New York's trade had greatly surpassed that of its principal rivals, Boston and Philadelphia.

The population of the bustling little city was growing as fast as its wealth. In the early 1820's nearly ten thousand people a year were coming to New York to seek their fortunes. The great majority of these newcomers settled in the already overcrowded tenements of the Lower East Side. Here, with little or no sanitation, often living in converted warehouses or shacks, the poor crowded together in windowless rooms, while to the north and west of them the well-to-do occupied the handsome houses west of Broadway or those around Gramercy Park and Union Square. Citizens of more modest means lived east of Broadway below Fifteenth Street in a section containing solid rows of dwellings and shops, some of brick and others of wood. Here lived the skilled factory workers, the owners of small shops, and the clerks and bookkeepers employed by the wealthy merchants and bankers of the city.

No matter where one lived in New York then, the noise and bustle were overpowering. A visitor in 1824 described the "everlasting clatter of carriage wheels . . . the stunning clamour of ten thousand side-mouthed bells, scavengers and travelling hucksters, re-echoing from corner to corner."[1] Buildings were constantly being torn down and others put up in their places. In 1824 alone more than sixteen hundred dwellings of various sorts were built, extending the city limits north along Broadway. New York was not only noisy but dirty. Rubbish and dust filled the streets and as late as 1842, Charles Dickens noted with disgust the large number of swine, gaunt, unwholesome-looking scavengers, that wandered the streets.[2]

Julia Ward and her brothers and sisters were undoubtedly shielded from the uglier aspects of city life. Twice a day on fine days they and their nurse took a walk in Battery Park and joined the other children with their balls and skipping ropes. Their mother would often sit in the parlor window of the house and watch them, loving, as she said, the sight of the "lively groups of children and their nurses taking their daily promenade."[3] Mrs. Ward would rarely join her children on their walks, for every spring since her marriage in 1812 she had been subject to flare-ups of tuberculosis and forced to spend much of her time in bed or in one of the parlors downstairs.

By 1821, the year the Wards moved into the house on Bowling Green, Mrs. Ward, even though she was still in her middle twenties, had lost her youthful freshness. The weakness caused by both illness and childbearing had left her thin and pale with sunken eyes and cheeks. Only nine years before, in January 1812, when she had first met Samuel Ward, Julia Cutler had been a lovely brown-haired, dark-eyed girl of fifteen, whose gaiety, charm and intelligence had completely won over the serious young banker.

She had been born and brought up in Jamaica Plain, Massachusetts, where her mother, the widow of Benjamin Clarke Cutler, still lived. Sarah Mitchell Cutler, a South Carolinian by birth, came of a wealthy, plantation-owning family in Charleston. She had once been considered an "elegante" of Southern society and remembered with pleasure an evening in her youth when George Washington had crossed the ballroom floor expressly to speak to her.[4] The niece of Francis Marion, the Swamp Fox, Sarah Cutler prided herself on her Huguenot ancestry. She

8

was first married at the age of sixteen and moved to Georgetown, where she was left a widow four years later. Her second husband, Benjamin Clarke Cutler, whom she married in 1791, has been described as a "genial handsome man much given to hospitality."[5] But when he died in 1810, he left his widow with five children, an old drafty house in Jamaica Plain and the promise of various legacies, but little money for immediate needs. Sarah Cutler, whose chief talents were a lovely voice and a passion for literature, found poverty difficult, but with the help of various relatives she managed somehow.

Of the three Cutler girls, Julia was apparently the best educated. At the age of six she had been sent down to New York to attend Mrs. Isabella Graham's school on Bowling Green, right across the park from where she later lived as a married woman. She must have been the youngest or one of the youngest pupils in the school, for she slept in the same bed with "Grandmamma," as she called Mrs. Graham, and her particular playmates were Mrs. Graham's two granddaughters. But she was apparently a good student, and Grandmamma's only complaints about her pupil concerned her rather moody disposition.[6]

Why Julia Cutler was sent away to school at such a tender age is nowhere explained, but she could hardly have been left in better hands, at least in her mother's view. Isabella Graham, who was known for her piety, had an excellent reputation as a schoolmistress. Born in Scotland and reared in the stern tradition of Scottish Presbyterianism, she had come to New York in 1789, an impoverished widow with three unmarried daughters. A number of influential persons had helped her found the school on Bowling Green.[7] Mrs. Graham probably felt more concern for the souls than the minds of her pupils, for she eventually abandoned her school to devote her time to philanthropy. In 1797 she founded one of the earliest charitable associations in the United States, the Society for the Relief of Poor Widows with Small Children. Her evangelical piety, with its emphasis on the need for regeneration and good works, left a permanent mark on Julia Cutler as it did on so many of her pupils.[8] Grandmamma remained as important to Julia as any member of the Cutler family, and perhaps her influence, through Julia, extended to the next generation. Julia Ward Howe would herself fall for a time under the spell of Calvinism, and in later life, long after she had grown away from the stern religion of her parents, she would devote herself to many of the great reform movements of the nineteenth century, whose origins can be traced to the good works of men and women like Isabella Graham.

When Julia Cutler's schooling was finished, she returned to Jamaica Plain, but not for long. In the winter of 1812 she and her older sister, Eliza, were brought down to New York by their mother in the hope that a winter in the city would find them both husbands. Mrs. Cutler installed the girls in a boardinghouse. This was not as unusual as it may at first sound: "respectable" boardinghouses were regarded as excellent places in which a girl of good family could make a suitable match.[9] Having been assured that the two Ward brothers who were staying in the same house were already spoken for and that Mrs. Graham would keep an eye on the two girls, Sarah Cutler returned to Jamaica Plain leaving her two daughters to fend for themselves.

As it turned out, neither of the Ward brothers, Samuel and Henry, was engaged and it was not long before the former had made up his mind that Julia Cutler was the wife for him. Poor Eliza, although lively and witty enough, did not provide much competition for her sister. She suffered both from poor teeth and hairy moles on her face and there were those who found her personality rather overpowering. But she was a warmhearted and good-natured young woman, and would eventually marry when she was well into her thirties.

Julia was pleased with the attentions shown her by the tall, serious Mr. Ward in the boardinghouse parlor. In fact, Samuel Ward was a very eligible bachelor with excellent prospects but he was some ten years Julia's senior and so very grave in manner that she could not think of him as a beau; he seemed more like an uncle or a father.

The Wards were an old and respected Rhode Island family, who had emigrated to America from England during the Restoration. Samuel's father, Colonel Samuel Ward, had fought in the Revolution under General Washington. When he retired from the army at the age of twenty-one (he was already possessed of a wife and several small children), he found the prospects in Newport poor and decided to try his fortune as a merchant in New York. He proved to be only moderately successful as a businessman: he enjoyed the good things in life too much ever to devote himself wholeheartedly to his work. Consequently, when his fifth son and namesake reached the age of fourteen it was decided for financial reasons that instead of being sent to college, young Sam would be apprenticed to a banking firm as a clerk. In some respects this was a wise choice. Sam was an intelligent, hard-working boy with a good head for figures, and grew up to be one of the most successful private bankers, and one of the richest men, in New York. But Sam would always regret that he had never gone to college, and like so many parents whose own schooling had been necessarily limited, he would place great emphasis on giving his own children the best education possible.

At twenty-five, Sam considered himself prosperous enough to provide for a wife and family, so when he first met the pretty and cultivated Miss Julia Cutler in the early winter of 1812, he was ready to fall in love. In late January, only a few weeks after the two Cutler girls had been installed in their lodgings, Sam handed Julia a note asking for her hand in marriage. She was completely taken by surprise and apparently offended him by the look of astonishment that crossed her face as she read his letter. She explained her bewilderment to him a few days later: "I take up the pen, but how shall I address you, now all that sweet intercourse of father and daughter has fled between us." She pleaded that she was too young "to take such an irretrievable step."[10] Julia's mother, hearing of Mr. Ward's proposal, urged her daughter to accept. The successful young banker of excellent character seemed the perfect match for Julia, whose own financial prospects might be very poor, but whose background and up-bringing, according to her mother at least, were impeccable.

In March, two months after receiving Samuel Ward's proposal, Julia Cutler was back at home in Jamaica Plain still unde-cided, although she was under even more pressure from her mother to accept. In her letters to Mr. Ward she thanks him for his "continued declarations of attachment" but begs him not to think her "capricious."

> You cannot perhaps conceive of my feelings at the moment, because you can never have felt them, what agony, how many and various are the feelings that tear at once this almost lifeless bosom — yet it is all perfectly natural, for be assured I do not harbor a doubt of my happiness hereafter, or I never should have gone thus far with anyone that I did not know to be perfectly calculated in *every way* to promote as far as lay in the power of mortal, my felicity on *earth*. . . . The conflict will I hope soon be ended, and then I will write you my final deter-mination.[11]

Sometime during the first week of September, Julia agreed to marry Samuel Ward. The wedding took place on October 12, 1812, in Boston, and after returning to New York the young couple settled in a little square house on Marketfield Street, not far from Bowling Green and Battery Park. The marriage from the start was an extremely happy one. Mr. Ward's somber and serious side was enlivened by his young wife's gay and even frivolous nature, and she for her part profited from his fatherly, yet loving attentions. Both husband and wife shared a love for literature and Samuel soon grew to enjoy the numerous parties of that first winter in the Marketfield house as much as Julia did. But the constant round of entertainment soon proved too much for her health, and in March of 1813 she suffered the first of what were to be annual flare-ups of tuberculosis. She was so ill that for five days and nights her husband did not change his clothes while he and Eliza kept a constant vigil at her bedside. Within a few weeks Julia was better, and after a summer of traveling and a long visit with her father-in-law on his farm in Jamaica, Long Island, she appeared entirely recovered.

The Wards' second winter in the Marketfield house was quieter than the first, as they were expecting their first child in late January. A boy was born on January 28, 1814, and was named Samuel after his father and grandfather. He was a good healthy baby and his mother appeared to be recovering beautifully until six weeks or so after his birth, when she once more suffered a flare-up of tuberculosis. This time the illness was so severe that Julia thought she was dying. Overcome by agonies concerning the fate of her soul, for days she suffered a spiritual torment that far surpassed her physical sufferings. If only God would allow her to live, she promised that henceforth she would abandon the parties and balls and other frivolities that had so occupied her mind and her time during the first months of her marriage, and would devote herself entirely to prayer and good works. In the midst of these torments she asked that Mrs. Graham be allowed to come and see her, for she could think of no one but "Grandmamma" who could bring her spiritual comfort. Mrs. Graham, now a woman of seventy-one, no longer had the strength for active philanthropic work and was spending the last months of her life (she died of cholera the following July) in prayer and meditation. But she was glad to come and sit by the bedside of an especially dear pupil and help her to pray and renounce her frivolous ways. It pleased Mrs. Graham to encourage this good but undisciplined girl to dedicate her life to Christ and the welfare of the unfortunate.

Julia Ward for a time did give up all fashionable entertainments, and wrote her mother that she was sending Eliza her white crepe dress and all the rest of her finery "that will no longer be useful to me."[12] The tuberculosis symptoms returned each spring despite her pious intentions, and eventually Julia allowed herself to enjoy what sociability her health would permit. But she did devote the remaining years of her life to good works. Not having the strength to visit the poor in their homes, as Mrs. Graham had done, she donated food and clothing to her neighbors in nearby slums and was active in securing contributions from her friends for the Society for the Promotion of Industry Among the Poor, one of Grandmamma's philanthropic organizations founded the year before her death.[13]

Despite her deteriorating health, Julia Ward continued to produce one baby after another. After a miscarriage in 1815, a second child, a girl named Julia after her mother, was born in January of 1816. A second boy, Henry, made his appearance in 1818, and the next year, in May, little Julia died of whooping cough. Two weeks later, on May 27, another girl baby was born, and was also named Julia. Marion, the third son, arrived in the summer of 1820, and two more girls, Louisa and Annie, were born after the family moved into the Bowling Green house in 1821.

From the moment of birth a middle- or upper-class girl brought up in nineteenth-century America was likely to find herself in a world of women. Her brothers might share this world for a few short years, but then they would be off to school or work. Girls for the most part stayed at home and learned from their mothers and other female relatives the skills necessary for their future as wives and mothers. Birth, marriage, illness and death, as well as lesser domestic joys and sorrows, brought women together, and their shared experiences necessarily created close bonds between them. On the other hand, relations with men were often stiff and formal; fathers were rarely around enough to provide much companionship for either their wives or their daughters. Samuel Ward, for all that he was a loving husband and father, spent long hours in his office, and his wife had come to depend for companionship on her children and on her two sisters, Eliza and Louisa, who often spent months at a time in the house on Bowling Green. Even the oldest Ward boy, Sam, was not around a great deal. His parents, thinking the city air disagreed with him, had sent him off to his grandfather Ward's farm in Jamaica, Long Island, where he stayed most of the time until he was old enough to go away to school. Julia was therefore the oldest child at home and her mother's almost constant companion.

Unlike the first Julia, who had been sweet and gentle, this child was temperamental and high-strung. She was in fact difficult to bring up and would have been the despair of her mother had it not been for her warmhearted nature and her precocious remarks, which never failed to make her parents laugh. Of all the Ward children she was the most like her mother. The two shared a warmth and a vivacity which the family always ascribed to Grandmother Cutler's Huguenot ancestry (the Roundhead forebears of the Wards apparently lacked these qualities). But Mrs. Ward recognized in her oldest daughter her own moodiness and impulsiveness. Julia had a temper to match her red hair and this, together with the similarity in their natures, meant that mother and daughter sometimes found life together to be difficult. One summer day when Mrs. Ward and the children were staying alone at Grandpa Ward's farm in Jamaica, Julia was so incorrigible that her mother was forced to spank her. "At the sight of the rod," Mrs. Ward wrote her mother, "she screamed herself almost to death . . . trembling as violently as if she had an ague, all the time I whipped her." Mrs. Ward herself was so ill as a result of this emotional encounter that she could not eat for several days.[14] But Julia could be affectionate and very charming when she wished. After a visit to the Cutlers in Jamaica Plain when Julia was about three, Mrs. Ward

15

reminded her of her promise not to forget Grandma Cutler. "How could I forget her!" Julia admonished her mother in an indignant tone. "How can you say so! I shall never forget her."[15]

Every summer Mrs. Ward and the children would leave the city. Sometimes they would stay with Grandpa Ward in Jamaica, sometimes they would go to the Jersey shore. But Mrs. Ward preferred above all else to travel. For some reason travel seemed to have a marvelous effect on her health, and the quantity of letters she wrote her husband from places as far away as Savannah or Niagara Falls indicate that she managed to see a good deal of America during the few short years of her married life.

In the spring of 1824 Mrs. Ward was pregnant for the eighth time and suffering from her usual flare-up of tuberculosis, when her husband decided to rent her a house for the summer in Bloomingdale, a country suburb in what is now the upper West Side of Manhattan. Julia remembered that summer as a particularly happy time. She recalled lessons with her brothers "in a lovely green bower," and walks with her mother in the garden. She remembered "much mysterious embroidering of small caps and gowns, the purpose of which I little guessed."[16] The family returned to town in early November, just in time for a little girl to be born. But their happiness was soon shattered. Three days after Annie Ward's birth, Mrs. Ward succumbed to puerperal fever and died.

The family was plunged into grief. Samuel Ward was so heartbroken that for a long time he refused even to see the child whom he thought had caused his wife's death. The house on Bowling Green with all its painful memories was quickly sold and the poor widower and his six children moved out to Bond Street off Upper Broadway, where they took up residence at Number 16.

Samuel Ward's twelve years of marriage to a woman whom he adored and often spoiled had been the happiest period in his life. The shock of losing her, compounded by his innate seriousness, cast a permanent shadow over him and it was not surprising that he turned to religion for consolation. His wife in the years before her death had tried to convince him of the necessity of dedicating his life to God. As a Low Church Episcopalian he was a faithful enough churchgoer and observed all the external pieties, but Julia urged a deeper commitment, one that stressed the evangelical belief in the depravity of man and his inability to attain salvation except through God's grace. She recommended books for him to read and assured him that "religion would operate so powerfully on his mind" as to "transform him completely" and make him "happy in spite of every event."[17] Perhaps she knew then that she would not live much longer, and understood only too well how desolate he would be without her.

Religion did indeed prove a consolation to the bereaved husband. As Julia had called in Isabella Graham in her hour of spiritual crisis, Samuel Ward now asked his brother-in-law Benjamin Cutler, who was an Episcopalian clergyman, to help relieve his mental anguish. Ben Cutler was also a Low Churchman, as were most Episcopalians in America in the early nineteenth century, but he was particularly noted for his saintliness and piety and had the reputation of being a true evangelical. Samuel Ward had helped to found a mission church on Vandewater Street in New York City and he persuaded Ben Cutler to come down from Quincy to become its pastor.[18] Having his brother-in-law nearby was indeed a source of spiritual comfort to the widower, who now plunged into his work for the church as well as the bank with more vigor than ever. Nor were his labors simply confined to these institutions. A founder of both New York University and the Stuyvesant Institute (an association of learned men in New York City), he was also a generous supporter of both Columbia College and Kenyon College in Ohio. Those who worked with him in these various enterprises recalled that he combined a stern manner with an "almost feminine kindness of feeling."[19]

The intensity of his labors both for his firm and for good

works by no means meant that he neglected his children. On the contrary, he now felt that he must be both father and mother to his lively brood, and no expense was spared to provide them with the necessary comforts and the best education. Aunt Eliza came down from Jamaica Plain to take over the running of the household. But it was the father, not the aunt, who looked after the spiritual and mental welfare of the six children. He was determined that they would have the education he had lacked.

At first the young Wards were taught at home by nurses and governesses. French, literature, music and the Bible were all part of the nursery curriculum and Julia remembered speaking French before she could read or write. By the time the Wards had moved north to Bond Street, young Sam was already away at school in Northampton, Massachusetts. Round Hill was probably the most progressive school in the country, and Joseph Cogswell, its founder, was a great friend of Samuel Ward's. Cogswell had developed his educational theories after a visit to Germany, and it was his belief that school should develop the whole person. Samuel Ward agreed with him. At Round Hill, mathematics, English and modern languages were taught, as well as the classics. Each pupil was instructed individually and advanced on his merits. Sam was sent to school when he was nine and Henry and Marion eventually followed him. But there was no school like Round Hill for girls, and in any case Mr. Ward's liberal ideas on education were not quite so liberal when it came to his daughters.

Beginning in the early nineteenth century a limited but formal education was regarded as a suitably genteel and womanly aspiration. Female seminaries sprang up all over the Northeast, not to train girls for work outside the home (although teaching was considered an admissible occupation for those in financial straits), but to prepare them for the responsibilities of motherhood and the rearing of future citizens. The academic curriculum was usually limited to a smattering of history, literature and languages and to large doses of moral philosophy. Science and mathematics were considered beyond the scope of the female mind. Even such leading educators as Emma Willard, who taught her girls not only mathematics and science but geography as well, placed great emphasis on the importance of the domestic role. Here and there a girl managed to acquire a learning comparable to that of an educated man, but she was a rarity, and her achievement usually depended on a father who was willing to provide the necessary instruction. Even those parents who encouraged their daughters' education made it quite clear that learning was meant to contribute to a woman's domestic felicity and not encourage her to cherish thoughts of independence and personal ambition.

Julia Ward went to school at the age of nine, when she was allowed to attend Miss Catherine Roberts's Day School for Young Ladies on Wabash Street. She found the experience rather disappointing. The girls were expected to do little except memorize long passages of Paley's *Principles of Moral and Political Philosophy* and other such works. Next, she attended Miss Angelina Gilbert's school, which was on Bleecker Street just around the corner from the Wards' house. This was a bit more satisfactory. Julia began to study Italian and was even allowed to read a chemistry textbook. But after seven or so years of formal education, she decided that she really preferred to study at home, which was no wonder, since her father was ready to provide her with the best private tutors to be found in the city of New York. The fact was that Miss Gilbert did not really care if the graduates of her school knew anything or not.

Julia's fondness for music, which began early and which was to be one of the passions of her life, may have persuaded her father to take her, when she was about seven, to hear *The Barber of Seville,* then being performed by an Italian company in New York. Undoubtedly this was the Garcia Troupe, which first brought opera to New York in 1825, and it is possible that Julia was present at the opening night on October 20, when they performed the Rossini work. In any case, she was only allowed one more trip to the opera before her father, overcome by his recently adopted religious scruples, put an end to all theatrical entertainments. Yet he had no objection to music, even dancing, at home. The best voice, piano and dancing instructors in New York taught the Ward children. Music was the favorite family pastime. Julia both played the piano and sang. She loved to play duets with Sam, and when he and Henry were home the three often sang together. Occasionally, Mr. Ward would take Julia to a concert — unlike the opera, concerts were approved. Julia was especially fond of Handel's oratorios, particularly the *Messiah*. But her enjoyment was often "succeeded by a reaction of intense melancholy," a reaction so strong that she half dreaded going in the first place.[20] Her father, too, was disturbed by the effect on his impressionable daughter and undoubtedly welcomed the long intervals between performances.

Mr. Ward's disapproval of opera did not manage to quench Julia's love for the drama, and though he also prevented her from going to plays he did not seem to object to her putting on her own. Her first play, "The Iroquois Bride," written shortly after she had learned to read, was inspired by a book she had found in her father's library. Julia, of course, was the bride; her younger brother Marion played the lover. In the final scene the two children climbed up on a stool which served for a rock and stabbed one another. The grown-ups in the audience apparently were not pleased with the immoral tone of Julia's first dramatic effort: "The Iroquois Bride" was permanently removed from the nursery repertoire. But many other dramatic pieces soon took its place.[21]

For all his concern for the spiritual welfare of his children, Samuel Ward found it difficult to protect them from what he must have considered the unfortunate influences of some of their relatives, a good many of whom lived right down the street. Colonel Ward, for instance, the banker's father, had recently moved into 7 Bond Street with his two sons John and Richard.

The colonel had never taken any particular interest in religious matters and in the eyes of his son Samuel was rather too dependent on his wine and cards. John Ward, a New York broker, lacked his older brother's financial principles and enjoyed playing the stock market. At the same time he had an excellent reputation among New Yorkers for the quality of food and wine served at his table. Another brother, Henry, who lived at Number 23, loved music and dancing, and a fourth, William, was reputed to be rather too fond of Madeira. When, several years after his wife's death, Samuel decided to take up the cause of temperance, his relatives were understandably horrified to hear that he had emptied his whole cellar of its store of vintage wine and not one of them could profit from his conversion.

The various Ward gentlemen did their best to liven up the rather drab existence of their nieces and nephews at Number 16. There was much visiting back and forth between houses and every Sunday the whole family would gather at Uncle Henry's for tea. After tea came music and dancing, with Uncle Henry tirelessly playing waltzes and polkas. These boisterous relatives made Samuel Ward's efforts to shield his children from the frivolities of life very difficult.

In the fall of 1829 an event occurred which did much to ease the sober atmosphere at Number 16. After a long and stormy courtship Aunt Eliza and the Wards' old friend and family doctor, John Francis, decided to get married. The wedding took place on November 16, and because Eliza had promised to stay and care for her nieces and nephews until they were grown up, the couple moved into an apartment set aside for them in the Ward house. John Francis, a man of eclectic tastes with a broad sense of humor, was probably attracted to Eliza as much for her sharp wit as her generous nature. Although her looks had been improved by a set of false teeth and the removal of the hairy moles from her face, she was still no beauty. The doctor himself had a ruddy complexion and a quantity of fine curly hair. A man of enormous energy, he combined an extended medical practice with numerous civic, artistic and philanthropic enterprises.

His circle of friends was large and admiring, and with his addition to the household the Ward parlors were often filled with actors, writers and artists of various sorts. Dominik Lynch, who was a singer of English ballads, and according to Dr. Francis, the arbiter of the city's musical life,[22] was a frequent visitor, and Julia remembered his singing with delight: "His voice, though not powerful, was clear and musical, and his touch on the pianoforte was perfect." She remembered creeping under the instrument to hide her tears when she heard him sing the ballad "Lord Ullin's Daughter."[23] Edgar Allan Poe was another intimate of Dr. Francis's. He once described the doctor's conversation as a "sort of Roman Punch made up of tragedy, comedy and the broadest possible farce."[24]

The same year the Francises were married, Sam came home from the Round Hill School to attend Columbia College. After his many years of absence from home, Julia hardly knew her eldest brother. If Sam was not as close a companion as Henry, he had always been her childhood idol, perhaps precisely because he had not been around enough to torment her. In any case Sam at fifteen was a charming and gifted boy. Possessed of bright blue eyes and a winning smile, he of all Julia's brothers and sisters shared her lively wit and love of fun and laughter. And like her, he was an eager and able student. He had passed the entrance examinations for Columbia with ease and later finished college in two years. But, as George Bancroft, a teacher at Round Hill, told Mr. Ward, the ease with which learning came to Sam made him overconfident.

Julia was delighted to have Sam home, but she also soon grew very jealous of the freedom her older brother enjoyed. She had already noticed that at school the other girls were freer to go about than she was; they went to Monsieur Charnaud's dancing classes and were allowed to visit one another's houses. Now she saw her brothers coming and going virtually as they pleased, and longed for some friendships and fun of her own. Julia naturally took for granted all the comforts and advantages with which she was provided. Her father, as she said later, "demurred only at expenses connected with dress and fashionable entertainment. He had always disliked and distrusted the great world."[25] She begged to be allowed more freedom, both to visit friends and to have them visit her. "I seemed to myself like a young damsel of olden time, shut up within an enchanted castle. And I must say that my dear father, with all his noble generosity sometimes appeared to me as my jailer."[26]

Young Sam sympathized with his sister's predicament and once had a rather heated argument on the subject with their father.

"Sir," Sam accosted his father, "you do not keep in view the importance of the social tie."

"The social what?" Mr. Ward inquired.

"The social tie, sir."

"I make small account of that," his father retorted.

"I will die in defense of it!" Sam exclaimed.[27]

As it happened, Julia's enforced isolation had the effect of making her withdraw into herself. She turned to books instead of people and allowed "fiery feverish dreams" to fill her mind. "In the large rooms of my father's house I walked up and down perpetually alone, dreaming of the extraordinary things I should see and do. I now began to read Shakespeare and Byron and to try my hand at poems and plays."[28] Such daydreams appealed to her far more than her schoolwork. At the age of eleven she handed in a collection of poems to her teacher instead of the prose composition that had been assigned, and was rebuked for being overambitious. She persisted nonetheless, and by the age of fourteen she had succeeded in having several poems published in the New York *American*.[29]

Julia received the most encouragement for her literary ventures from her brother Sam. During his vacations from school they had composed plays together, and Sam shared his sister's love of poetry. Her father, who had ignored his wife's efforts to write poetry and who even refused to read the poems she managed to publish in the year before her death, was not likely to give much encouragement to his daughter's literary aspirations.[30] And Sam, whose chief interests were mathematics and literature, was expected to follow his father's profession. Banker Ward would tolerate no opposition to his plans for his son's future. When Sam graduated from Columbia, he was seventeen and full of energy and a desire to see the world. Somehow the prospect of spending the rest of his days in a banking firm was hardly appealing. While higher mathematics, particularly astronomy, fascinated him, the mathematics of the countinghouse bored him. He did manage, though, to persuade his father to allow him to postpone the start of his banking career so that he might spend a winter in Boston studying under Nathaniel Bowditch, the highly respected mathematician, and when he was through he succeeded in further delaying his entry into the bank by accepting a position on the examining board at West Point.

The spring Sam was at West Point was also the year of the terrible cholera epidemic. By 1832 the population of New York had swelled to three hundred thousand. The city limits were rapidly extending northward; Washington Square, once a potter's field, was becoming a charming residential section and Greenwich was no longer a village. Further north were farms, occasional country seats and the peaceful hamlets of Chelsea, Bloomingdale, Harlem and Manhattanville. The great majority of the inhabitants were still concentrated in the southernmost tip of Manhattan. The well-to-do for the most part lived west of Broadway but they were moving northward, some as far as Bond Street, where Samuel Ward had recently purchased a large property. East of Broadway on the Lower East Side conditions had worsened. In 1832 alone, thirty-two thousand immigrants crowded into the already overfilled slums, depleting further the inadequate water supply and adding to the appalling sanitary conditions.[31]

On June 15, 1832, Philip Hone, the noted diarist, mentioned in his journal the arrival of the Albany steamboat with alarming news:

> The cholera, which has of late been the scourge of the eastern continent, has crossed the Atlantic and made its appearance in Quebec and from thence travelled with its direful velocity to Montreal. It was brought to the former city in a vessel . . . with a cargo of Irish immigrants of whom many died on the passage. . . . There can be little reasonable ground to hope for our exemption in New York from this dreadful scourge. It must come and we are in a dreadful state to receive it. The city is in a more filthy state than Quebec and Montreal, and I do not know a European city which is more so.[32]

Hone's fears were realized: cholera struck New York early in July, hitting the poor the hardest, and at its height, the epidemic caused nearly one hundred deaths a day. Before it was over, 3,527 — over one percent of the population — had been killed by it, and about one-third of the citizens had fled the city.[33]

The young Wards were among the fortunate who were able to leave. Earlier that spring they had all suffered from whooping cough, and before anyone was even worried about cholera Grandma Cutler had persuaded her son-in-law of the advisability of a change of air. Consequently they were shipped off to Newport to spend the first of many summers with Grandma Cutler and Aunt Eliza.

Newport had once been a flourishing seaport, ranking not far behind Boston and New York. An essential link in the triangular trade, it had shipped molasses up from Jamaica and made it into rum, which was carried to Africa and traded for slaves. The slaves were then taken to Jamaica where they in turn were traded for more rum. The British occupation of Newport Harbor during the Revolution had brought this commerce to a standstill, and when Sarah Cutler first rented rooms at Bailey's farmhouse several miles outside Newport at the Third Beach, the town had a lonesome and deserted air. Once-handsome houses were old and shabby, grass grew in the streets, and only a few of the public buildings were kept painted. But Newport had already begun its slow climb to prosperity of a different kind. Summer visitors, not commerce, would cause the old houses to be painted and new houses to be built.

The history of Newport as a resort began in the summer of 1784, when a packet from Charleston docked in the nearly deserted little harbor. On board were a number of South Carolina planters and their families who had sailed north to escape the fever-ridden heat of the Charleston summer. Finding the climate in Newport a pleasant one and the inhabitants of the town hospitable, they stayed until October. The Southerners returned the following summer, and before long a season in Newport became the accepted routine of quite a number of Charleston families. Since she was a Charlestonian herself, it was only natural that Grandma Cutler should choose Newport as the place in which to spend her summers, and for some time she had been trying to persuade her son-in-law to send his children to her.

The children were of course delighted to leave the restricted life of the city behind them. At Jacob Bailey's farmhouse they slept on corncob mattresses, ate lots of good plain food, and spent their days on horseback or at the beach, where Julia had to wear a thick green veil to protect her delicate complexion. Grandmother Cutler liked to have as many of her family under her roof as possible, so there were always plenty of cousins around to play with, including the five sons of her youngest daughter, Louisa McAllister. Samuel Ward was far too busy at the bank to spend the summer on the beach, and in any case by mid-July it would have been impossible for him to join his children even if he had wished to: the authorities had forbidden boats from New York to land their passengers on the Newport docks. Grandpa Ward also stayed in the city and fell victim to the cholera in the early fall when the disease appeared to have run its course.

Shortly after the colonel's death the quarantine on travel to Newport was lifted, and Mr. Ward, accompanied by those members of the family who had remained in the city, went up to Newport to see his children and bring them back to town. Young Sam, now eighteen, had finished his assignment as an examiner at West Point and had been offered an assistant professorship in mathematics there. He too was in Newport, but dreaming of Paris, not the Academy. By citing his ignorance of military engineering he hoped to persuade his father that he needed further training in mathematics before he could accept any such post. Besides, the additional training would surely be of use to him when he went to work at the bank. Mr. Ward was skeptical of his son's scheme but eventually gave in, and on October 29, Sam sailed for France, ostensibly to continue his studies. There he was to remain for four years, and while he did work hard during his first winter, much of the rest of his time he devoted to good food and good companionship, tastes which he was able to indulge because his father — uncharacteristically perhaps — had given him an unlimited letter of credit. Much of the correspondence between father and son concerned Sam's profligate habits (he worked his way through some $16,000), and he had picked up enough French ways so that Mr. Ward had to chide him for sending Julia a letter with "too much Paris frippery and froideur about it." When writing to children, Mr. Ward explained, one should put oneself "in the place of a parent, and write in reference to their moral improvement."[34] Sam had little taste for the subject of moral improvement, but while he was away he continued to write his sister, encouraging her in her studies and her literary ventures. For the next four years, while he was in Europe,

27

the time would pass quietly enough for Julia. She continued her daydreaming and applied herself more or less diligently to her schoolwork with only Newport summers and occasional family parties breaking the otherwise sober regime of the Ward household.

New York Girlhood

The false romance of the time made a tyrant to a childish imagination of the best and kindest of parents.

— Julia Ward Howe, Diary,
May 1, 1891

By the time Julia was sixteen, her family had moved out of 16 Bond Street into a new house not far away at the corner of Broadway. The household by now had grown very large indeed. Besides Samuel Ward and five of his children (Sam was still away in Europe), there were Dr. Francis and Aunt Eliza, who now had four children of their own. Numerous relatives came and went, including Grandma Cutler, a frequent visitor; and of course there were the servants and tutors of various sorts who accompanied a family of rank and standing in New York.

When Samuel Ward first moved to Bond Street in the late 1820's, his friends told him that he was leaving town, and indeed Bond Street was then so remote that the houses of Manhattan were barely visible across the fields and trees. Even in 1835, Bond Street marked the city limits on the north and most of the Wards' friends still lived down near the Battery. The new house was thus not constrained by its surroundings, and it was large even by the standards of New York. Known familiarly as "The Corner," it was built of brick with white columns flanking the front door.

On the ground floor were three large rooms and a small study. In the red room — so called because of the color of its silk curtains — the family ate its meals; in the blue room they received their visitors; and the yellow room (in Julia's recollection it was "thrown open only on large occasions") served as a drawing room. But in it were also to be found Julia's desk and piano, and she was "allowed to occupy it at will."[1]

All three of these large downstairs rooms contained marble fireplaces carved by Thomas Crawford, the young sculptor who later designed the pediments and bronze doors of the Senate wing of the Capitol. At the back of the house along Broadway, Samuel Ward had added a wing that housed the first private picture gallery in New York, and for this he had commissioned Thomas Cole, the pioneer of the Hudson River School, to do a series of allegorical paintings. Here also, on young Sam's return from Europe, a library was built to house the quantity of books he had brought back with him. In the basement was an office for Uncle John Francis, and in the attic, a cupola with a telescope. It was, in short, a house that lacked little or nothing, and Samuel Ward hoped to make it such a self-contained world that his children, and especially his daughters, would have little need or desire to leave it.

Breakfast at The Corner was at eight in the winter and half past seven in the summer. After breakfast Julia would retire to the yellow room. Here she would have Louisa or Annie tie her to her chair so that she would not be tempted to leave her desk until her morning studies were completed. Accustomed to self-analysis like all good evangelical Christians of her day, Julia knew that she was studious only "by fits and starts,"[2] and to have herself physically confined in this way seemed perfectly natural to one whose whole upbringing emphasized self-discipline and the virtue of hard work. By the time the Wards had moved into The Corner, Julia's formal education was at an end, but she did attend a few classes at a nearby private school. Other studies she pursued at home with private tutors. She now "began to feel the necessity of more strenuous application."[3] She had begun to study Italian at the age of fourteen with the son of Lorenzo da Ponte, Mozart's old librettist. She was also anxious to learn German and was therefore delighted when Joseph Cogswell, her brothers' old headmaster, came to live with the Wards for several months. The Round Hill School had closed for financial reasons and Samuel Ward, who had done his best to support the school, was only too happy to offer Cogswell a place to live until his future was settled. Cogswell had been one of the first Americans to study in Germany,[4] and now he helped Julia start on the language. She made rapid progress and it was not long before she was reading the works of Goethe and Schiller.

In addition to languages Julia's other studies included history, geometry and, of course, the Bible. The habit of reading a passage from Scripture every day was one she kept for the rest of her life, and while she was young and still very much influenced by her evangelical upbringing, she regarded the Bible as "the true passport to salvation." She then read it morning, noon and night, and her "young imagination gloried in the vision of psalms & thrones & white robes."[5] As a little child she had slept with the Bible under her pillow for protection against the devil. Her earliest poems reflected this evangelical mood, bearing such titles as "All Things Shall Pass Away," "Redeeming Love" and "My Heavenly Home." One of the earliest, entitled "Morning Hymn," she wrote during her first summer holiday in Newport. It concluded with the following verse:

> Let thy assistance, Lord, be given,
> That when life's path I've trod,
> And when the last frail tie is riven,
> My spirit may ascend to heaven,
> To dwell with thee, My God.[6]

31

When Julia's morning studies were over she turned to music. A Mr. Boocock gave her piano lessons, but Julia was also now studying singing with Signor Cardini.[7] Perhaps it was Cardini who trained her voice so well that even at the age of ninety she could be heard with ease across a crowded auditorium. Despite her apparent talent, Julia never took her musical training very seriously. "I do not think that I shall ever consider music as a serious occupation instead of a recreation,"[8] she told her father when she was eighteen. Her real avocation was literature, and it was her ambition to be a great writer that kept her at her studies morning after morning. Later she admitted that she could not really account "for a sense of literary responsibility which never left me." Women writers were not very numerous in those days, and she remembered that it was difficult for a girl student to "find that help and guidance which were necessary in order to attempt a career in literature."[9]

Julia later claimed that her father had taken a "certain pride" in her literary accomplishments, although the passage of time may have softened his attitude in her mind. Certainly he approved of her efforts in both music and languages since he had no hesitation about hiring the best teachers for her, but he surely wished that his eldest daughter would take more of an interest in household matters. Julia was not domestic then, and never would be, but her relatives would sporadically try to reform her. Uncle John apparently resented the time she spent on books and music, and once gave her a bolt of fine cloth, hoping she would learn the art of dressmaking. When Julia published her first serious work, a translation of Lamartine's "Jocelyn," he showed her a favorable review of it in a newspaper saying, "This is my little girl who knows about books and writes an article and has it printed, but I wish she knew more about housekeeping."[10]

There were, however, a number of people who encouraged Julia to pursue her literary ambitions. Her translation of Lamartine appeared in the *Literary and Theological Review,* which was edited by Leonard Woods, a conservative clergyman who was also a friend of Samuel Ward's. Charles King, the brother of one of her father's partners, edited the New York *American,* in which her first poems were published. Her most valuable support came from Joseph Cogswell, who helped her "with the style and arrangement" of her Lamartine translation, for which, she later recalled, she received a good deal of critical acclaim.[11] Within the Ward household young Sam was her greatest ally. He saw no reason why a girl, especially a girl as gifted as his sister, should not pursue a literary career.

When her studies and practicing had been completed for the day, Julia was free to do as she wished until dinnertime, which was at four. Her greatest pleasure, since she was discouraged from leaving the house except for an occasional drive with her sisters, was to go into Sam's new library and lose herself in one of the hundreds of volumes of German, French and Italian literature that filled the shelves. Joseph Cogswell had already introduced her to the works of various German authors and she had read some Byron, but it was in her brother's library that she found Victor Hugo, Balzac, George Sand and other European writers of the day. Sam encouraged her to read anything she wished, and Julia later remembered that the "sense of intellectual freedom" this reading gave her was "half delightful, half alarming." Her father appears to have known amazingly little about the books his daughter was reading and surely would have disapproved of most of them. Once, after perusing an English translation of Goethe's *Faust,* he came to her and said, "My daughter, I hope you have not read this wicked book!"[12] Julia's reply was not recorded. She had in fact read a great many books her father considered "wicked," and their effect on an overprotected, imaginative girl in her late teens could only have been to intensify those "fiery, feverish dreams" to which she had always been prone.

Food at dinner was plentiful but plain: probably meat and vegetables with a pudding or a pie for dessert. After Samuel

Ward took up the cause of temperance no wine was served. This did not bother Julia particularly, but it did upset her brother Sam, who was to become famous for his knowledge of good wine. Julia sat next to her father at the dining room table. Often in a gesture of affection he would take one of her hands in his and hold it throughout the meal, apparently oblivious of how difficult this made eating for both of them. Tea was served at seven-thirty, usually without meat but with an abundance of cakes. Afterward the family would gather in front of the fire in the blue room. Here the girls did needlework while the men talked or read aloud. Sometimes they sang and danced. Occasionally they would all go out to a concert or a few friends would be invited for a sober dinner party.

The only relief from this confining regime came in the summer. Ever since 1832, when they had been shipped off to Newport to stay with Grandma Cutler, the Ward children had returned to Bailey's farmhouse for the summer months. Then in the summer of 1836, having succumbed to the charm of the little seaport, Samuel Ward purchased a large clapboard "cottage" on the corner of Bellevue Avenue and Catherine Street. It was here that young Sam was reunited with his father and his sisters when he returned from his four years in Europe. Immediately, he noted the changes that had taken place since he had left. Julia was now a young woman of seventeen, short in stature, with a well-rounded figure set off by a becomingly slim waist. "Julie," or "Jolie Jule," as her family called her, with her red hair and cream complexion, was not pretty in a conventional way, but her looks certainly attracted attention. She was "pert, strong-minded, vivacious," Sam wrote, "but inclined to be moody," while Louisa, now thirteen, was "proud" yet "warmhearted," and ten-year-old Annie, "gentle and affectionate." His father, who was enjoying a brief vacation, appeared reserved and careworn, but happy to have his eldest son once more safely under the family roof.[13]

Julia was very happy to have Sam home. Not that she wasn't enjoying herself: the relaxed atmosphere of Newport encouraged Mr. Ward to give his girls a little more freedom. Although the social life of the town was then very restrained in contrast to what it would become in several decades, Julia found it very exhilarating. She wrote Sam shortly before his arrival that Newport was quite full of people, "visitors flocking from every direction to cool themselves in its breezes, fogs and waves. The houses swarm with straw hats and canes; the beach with nankeen tights, life-preservers, oilcloth caps, bathing dresses — red, blue, green, purple. . . . There are sailing parties, walking parties, fishing parties, riding parties, dancing parties — all kinds of parties."[14] Julia, of course, could not go to dances but she asked Sam to bring her guitar with him when he came from New York. They might not drink but at home they could sing and dance all they liked.

Julia grew more attached to Newport every year. Late in the summer of 1837 she wrote her father that "the beaux are all gone, so that we are quite deserted. I cannot imagine why they all run away from this lovely spot, lovelier now than ever."[15] Sometimes a bittersweet feeling would overtake her.

> I walked on the beach yesterday at sunset. It was beautiful, and awakened many pleasing associations of former days. I have spent some of the happiest hours of my life there, and as I sat upon the rocks, enjoying the sublimity of the scene, every wave as it dashed upon the shore seemed to tell a tale of days that will return no more. I know not why there is such a melancholy feeling attached to the remembrance of past happiness, except that we fear that the future can have nothing so bright as the past.[16]

In fact Julia would spend most of the summers of her long life in or near Newport and she came to think of it as more her home than either New York or Boston.

It was in Newport that Julia had her first beaux, although a number of tutors and other bachelors, who at one time or another passed through The Corner, were known to have lost their hearts to her. Among her earliest loves was a young harpist who came occasionally during the winter she was fourteen to play trios and quartets with the Ward children. One afternoon Signor Cardini suggested that she should sing some Rossini arias with the harpist as her accompanist. For Julia this was a supremely romantic moment and four years later she claimed that she could still remember his "large, deep, speaking blue eyes and sweet yet melancholy smile. . . . When he played his face was lit up with a lofty and impassioned expression, and as he bent over his harp I thought he looked truly inspired."[17] They saw one another again several times but Julia's father apparently became disturbed by the effect the harpist was having on his susceptible eldest daughter and asked the young man not to return. Even Joseph Cogswell was apparently in love for a time with his clever pupil, although there is only the vaguest evidence for this.[18]

In Newport when she was eighteen, a middle-aged sea captain, who was employed by her father, handed her a visiting card in the garden of the Ward cottage. On it was inscribed the chaste pledge *"Russell E. Glover's* heart is yours."[19] What her reaction was we do not know, although it is unlikely that she gave the unfortunate Captain Glover any encouragement.

Back in New York Mr. Ward's strict rule, forbidding any entertainment for his daughters except under the roof of The Corner, was in effect once more. The wineless formal dinners, few and far between, were hardly lively affairs. But once, when Julia was nineteen, she and her three brothers, Sam, Henry and Marion, did manage to trick their father into giving a party for them. The whole idea was Julia's, and she insisted on taking full responsibility for the consequences. She and her brothers drew up a list, invitations were sent out, and the best caterer in New York was hired. Mr. Ward was told that a few friends were being invited for the evening, nothing more. When the guests had all arrived, he came downstairs to find the cream of New York society assembled in his parlor. He showed no surprise, and greeted everyone as cordially as though he had invited them himself. Meanwhile, poor Julia, overcome with the thought that she had deceived her father, could think of nothing but what he would say when it was all over. When the last guest had departed, Sam and Henry insisted on speaking to their father for her. "No," protested Julia, "I must go myself." She found her father not the least bit angry. He merely remarked that her idea of a few friends was rather different from his own.[20]

Julia did not mention the subject of parties again, but the moodiness her brother Sam had observed increased, and she spent more and more time in her room alone, writing poetry and brooding over her father's mistreatment of her. Sam and Henry were both worried about their sister. One summer Mr. Ward decreed that Julia should keep him company in New York, where he could keep an eye on her, instead of going to Newport with her sisters. Sam wrote him:

> Poor Jule. You always expect too much of her in desiring that she should not only obey you but be happier in so doing than in following up certain wishes of her own. You began her education, dear father, late in the day. She had been left entirely to herself and to other influences until one morning you woke up and finding her old enough to get into mischief took her exclusively under your wing. You did not perhaps see that certain opinions and tastes had already formed and hardened. The wax had in some cases become marble . . . Julia writes all day and half the night . . . She is murdering herself. Yet she is forced to do this. In the tedium and heat of a large solitude her restless mind must be at work.[21]

In 1838 Julia got a taste of the freedom she had been missing. Her brother Sam became engaged to Emily Astor, the granddaughter of John Jacob Astor, then the richest man in New York. Mr. Ward allowed her to attend a dinner given by the Astors for Sam and Emily, and here she got her first real glimpse of New York society. From that time until the wedding there was a good deal of visiting back and forth between the Astors and the Wards. William B. Astor, Emily's father, was a solemn, humorless man, intent only upon moneymaking, but his daughter Emily was vivacious and fun-loving. She and Julia quickly became friends and were happy to discover that they both loved music. Emily's grandfather, old John Jacob, was delighted with Sam, and enjoyed listening to the three of them, Sam, Emily and Julia, singing old German folk songs that Sam had learned in Europe. The gouty old gentleman would sit in an armchair near the piano, listening, sometimes even joining in himself.

Julia and Louisa were both in the wedding. "I was the first bridesmaid," Julia wrote Henry, who was at that time in Paris. She found the whole affair exhilarating; her head swam with visions of "pearls, diamonds, silks, satins and laces." When supper was announced at ten o'clock she found herself seated "at a table which resembled some of the entertainments in the Arabian nights."[22] After the wedding Sam and Emily came to live at The Corner until their own house at 32 Bond Street was ready for them. At last Julia was free to go to parties as long as Emily, now a married woman, agreed to be a chaperone. The next two years were among the happiest Julia had known. Even Mr. Ward was affected by the presence of the gay young couple. He was working harder than ever at the bank, but on Sunday afternoons, when the whole Ward family gathered as usual for tea at Uncle Henry's, he was as eager as anyone to join in the singing and dancing, and when it was time to go home it was he who was the most reluctant to leave.

Friends of Sam's and Emily's came often to The Corner, and among them was the young poet Henry Wadsworth Longfellow, whom Sam had befriended during his stay in Europe. Julia took an immediate liking to this particularly delightful friend of her brother's. Despite his slight build, Longfellow was unquestionably attractive; his clear complexion and bright chestnut hair accompanied a lively mind and a most cheerful disposition. He and Sam Ward had much in common. Both found life challenging and pleasurable; both were of a scholarly nature, gifted in languages and thoroughly familiar with the classics; both wrote poetry and certainly both liked to talk. It was not long before Julia was showing Longfellow her own verses; she was eager and grateful for his kindly criticism. He, in turn, introduced her to *Beowulf,* and she immediately went out and bought an Anglo-Saxon grammar so she could read it in the original herself.

But this happy interlude soon came to an end. Samuel Ward began working even longer hours after the Panic of 1837 struck New York. He was a fiscal conservative who had long been disturbed by President Andrew Jackson's monetary policy. He had strongly denounced Jackson's removal of the public deposits from the Bank of the United States in October 1833, considering it an act that was as illegal as it was outrageous. There was, in fact, no question that the destruction of the Bank of the United States was in part responsible for the wave of inflation and speculation that overran the country in the mid-1830's. Real estate values soared in New York and trading on the stock market reached dizzying heights. Meanwhile, the Specie Circular of 1836, an attempt by Jackson to curb the use of paper money in land sales in the West, had considerably limited the supply of gold held by banks in the East. Thus when the panic came, the already depleted supply of specie in New York banks was in danger of disappearing entirely. Even Prime Ward & King (the firm had added a partner) was threatened with ruin when the British closed their accounts there. One of the partners was therefore dispatched to London to secure a sterling loan. James Gore King's mission was successful and the five million pounds in gold that he succeeded in borrowing were distributed among the various banks in the city. Specie payments in New York resumed once more, but Samuel Ward's efforts to save his city had cost him his health.[23] He went to Newport to recuperate from the crisis and never really mended. By the summer of 1839 it became obvious that the end was near. In November he died, leaving behind him his six children and an estate estimated to have been worth about six million dollars.

Julia later recalled "the desolate hush which fell upon our house when its stately head lay, silent and cold, in the midst of weeping friends and children." Whatever disagreements and dissensions there may have been among the orphaned children quickly dissipated, and the six were drawn together "in a bond of common sorrow."[24] It was to her brother Henry that Julia now turned for comfort and consolation. Although he was as full of fun as any of the Ward brothers and sisters, the serious side of Henry's nature ran deeper than Sam's, and it was natural that Julia should seek out him rather than her eldest brother. Sam himself had come to rely heavily on Henry, whose business sense and dedication to the world of banking far exceeded his own. What a blow it was, therefore, to both Sam and Julia, when less than a year after the death of their father, Henry succumbed to an attack of typhoid fever. Many years later Julia recalled that the death of this beloved brother had almost killed her. The two had become particularly intimate in the months after their father's death, and while Henry was sick Julia never left his bedside. The progress of the disease was swift and the family had scarcely become aware of the seriousness of his condition before he was dead. Julia remembered the time that followed this terrible loss as "without light or comfort."[25] Poor Sam's sorrow was soon compounded by the death of his young wife and baby son in the winter of 1842, and consequently he could be of little comfort to his sister.

Faced with the deaths of so many who had been close to her, Julia turned again to religion for solace. The loss of a number of relatives in quick succession was by no means unusual in the early nineteenth century, when death and disease were common occurrences, and to some degree explained the deep need people had for religious consolation. New York was at that time in the midst of an evangelical revival, and Julia was persuaded by a friend to attend some meetings. As in revivals today, the preacher would seek to convince the unrepentant of their need for conversion. The sinner must be overwhelmed by a sense of personal guilt and he must truly repent his misdeeds. Then he would experience an all-pervading sense of joy at being born again and at having entered into a new and deeply personal relationship with God.[26]

Julia did not, unfortunately, experience the joy of conversion. The evangelical doctrines only came home to her with greater force, emphasizing as they did the sinfulness of man's nature, and she suffered what she described in her diary as "a season of religion (or irreligion), melancholy, and of irrational despair."[27] She was also wracked by pangs of guilt for the way she had treated her father. How much he had done for her and yet how little she had appreciated his solicitude! Although he was dead, perhaps she could in some sense repay him for his care by seeking to continue in his family the ways that would have pleased him. She was now the oldest member of the household and she forced her newfound evangelist creed on the younger members of the family. She became for a time the image of her father in the severity of her rule and her solicitude for the spiritual welfare of her younger brothers and sisters. Only cold meat was allowed on Sunday. Uncle John christened this uninviting meal "Sentiment." Hot tea, which was permitted on Sunday evenings, was known as "Bliss" and Julia herself, who in happier times had been known as "Jolie Jule," was now referred to by her brothers and sisters as "The Old Bird."

At the same time Julia poured out her misery in poems, melodramatically spurning the fellowship of all humankind in her anguish over the death of her brother Henry:

But men are spectres to me now,
I know how false, how foul they are,
And I would find thee to my brow,
A spell of hope, a morning star;
Then on thy swift sped way look back;
And mark the light upon thy track.

Alas! their words do mock me so,
I shun their touch, mistrust their gaze;
For they have wrought me much of woe,
And blighted o'er my early days,
Until their kindness seems to me
More fearful than their cruelty.[28]

Julia must indeed have been hard to live with if these misan-thropic sentiments were at all representative of her true feelings toward her sisters and other kindly relatives. To accuse them of having wrought her "much of woe" and of blighting her youth was surely no more than a desperate attempt to find some living cause for her present misery.

One of the basic principles of evangelism demanded that the regenerated Christian live his life in a practical sense. Having experienced conversion himself he must now seek to convert others. This led to the formation of various voluntary societies for reformatory, benevolent or missionary purposes. Since church work had traditionally been considered a suitable female occupa-tion women were not only permitted but encouraged to partici-pate in these activities. Tract and missionary societies were com-mon in the early decades of the nineteenth century and by the 1830's and '40's female societies to curb prostitution, promote temperance and foster the abolition of slavery were prevalent in the northeastern state. All but the last were considered "wom-anly" concerns. Julia's mother had belonged to a benevolent soci-ety, and now Julia followed her example. Going into the slums of the lower East Side she distributed religious tracts among the poor. "For the first time I saw a true picture of the neglected children of the poor — pale and wan, barefoot and ragged, with uncombed hair and unwashed faces, and here and there with eyes diseased or sores bound up. And I saw that among the wretched even childhood is shorn of its beauty."[29]

During this time Julia allowed herself to continue the most serious of her studies, but for the moment she put aside her ambitions to be a great writer, knowing that it was her Christian duty to avoid indulging in such worldly and therefore unfeminine dreams. She also remembered her father's disapproval of certain modern authors, and now she carefully avoided Sam's books. Her sense of guilt at having so often disobeyed her father, combined with the intellectually inhibiting tenets of evangelism, led her to regard the works of authors like Balzac and George Sand, as well as Goethe and Byron, as profane and unsuitable.

Julia Ward could not, however, remain miserable forever. Gradually even her anguish over the deaths of her father and brother eased. Her sense of humor, her high spirits, and above all her intellectual curiosity and literary ambition eventually reasserted themselves, and her preoccupation with sin and sorrow slowly disappeared. Near the end of the two-year period of mourning for her father she found herself rereading Milton's *Paradise Lost.* She saw "the picture of an eternal evil, of Satan and his ministers subjugated indeed by God, but not conquered, and able to maintain against him an opposition as eternal as his goodness." This she had seen many times before, but suddenly, she wrote, this vision "appeared to me impossible, and I threw away, once and forever, the thought of the terrible hell which till then had always formed a part of my belief." With this questioning of the cold, repressive doctrine of Calvinism, Julia's evangelical enthusiasm gradually faded away. As she herself admitted, she began to feel the need for "vanity, amusement and other study. Then I turned against my New Testament and said, I know you all by heart!" Later she would again take up the

Bible, this time it would be not "in the light of enthusiasm but of common sense and experience."[30] She was, in other words, moving away from the evangelical faith of her parents, which stressed both Biblical and ecclesiastical authority as well as the innate depravity of man, toward a more liberal Christianity, which believed that human nature, though by no means perfect, was inherently capable of reforming itself and possessed considerable powers of conscience and reason.

During the time following the deaths of her father and brother Julia received much advice and comfort from her one good friend outside the family circle, Mary Ward of the Boston Wards. The two Ward families (they were not related) had met in Newport the summer before Mr. Ward's death and Mary not only became intimate with Julia but engaged to Henry as well. It was therefore natural that after Henry died both girls would wish to share their sorrow. Julia sent Mary many of the poems written in the months immediately following her brother's death. By the time she sent them she had already recovered from the worst of her grief and was spurning the most morbid of her religious thoughts, and Mary wisely pointed out that Julia's poems no longer represented her true self. They "would not universally interest, because they express but a very partial view of the truths of our religion and that one of a stern, painful, ascetic character to which the whole spirit of the time is opposed." She reminded Julia that the verses were "the exact impress of the religious views which you entertained one year ago, which were ever painful to behold," that her mind at the time had been "excited" and "deeply suffering" and had consequently seized hold of religion "almost as a scourge and penance. . . . This is not your religion; in an excited state of mind you strove to make it so, but nearly lost your reason in the attempt."[31] Mary at least understood the suffering her friend had endured. She also knew that the time had come for Julia to place all that behind her and begin again.

Julia had been making several trips a year to visit Mary in

Dorchester and it was while returning from one of these that she first met a man whose writing and philosophy were to have a tremendous effect on her own thinking. On the train with Mary, staring out at the bleak winter landscape that stretched from Boston to Providence, she found herself being introduced to Ralph Waldo Emerson. As she later remembered the episode, she was horrified by the thought of finding herself face to face with the man whose transcendentalism represented the very kind of "radical" thinking she had been taught to distrust. "I do not wish to meet the wicked man!" she cried out in dismay to Mary, but despite the awkwardness which must have followed this outburst, Mary persisted, and almost immediately Julia's feelings toward Emerson began to soften. In the tall, thin man with blue eyes and a quiet smile Julia noticed a "gentle, ethereal quality which belied his reputed wickedness." She warmed to him even more later on in the day. The train had stopped for some time at a way station, and she caught a glimpse out the window of Emerson walking up and down the platform with a small child on his shoulders. She had thought the "great Transcendentalist" was a man "very remote from common human sympathy but this action on his part could not but impress me as most kind and humane."[32]

The trip from Boston was delayed by a blizzard, which forced the weary travelers to spend the whole of the following day aboard the steamer that ran from Providence to New York (there was then no train connecting the two cities). The delay did have the advantage, however, of giving Julia a further chance to talk to her new acquaintance. Emerson, a man of few words, was a patient listener. He sat quietly while this earnest young woman expounded her views on religion and philosophy. Trying to impress him with her thinking, she spoke at length on the great powers of Satan, and when she had finally completed her discourse his only comment was, "Surely the angel must be stronger than the Demon."[33]

The two years of mourning for Mr. Ward were over by the winter of 1841–1842 and Julia and her sisters began once more to go to balls and parties. The three Ward girls had continued to live at The Corner, where their Uncle John Ward had moved in to keep an eye on his nieces after the death of his brother. (Aunt Eliza and Uncle John Francis had long since moved out into a house of their own.) With the girls now free to go out, the poor man began to find his role as a guardian a difficult one. He was suffering very badly from gout, and the endless procession of what he considered to be rather worthless young men, who trooped in and out of The Corner, was somewhat more than he could stand. "The Old Bird" was "Jolie Jule" once again, and Annie, the youngest, who was now seventeen, found the guardianship of her eldest sister less restrictive. When she asked Julia for permission to go to Washington, where she had been invited to several parties, Julia consented with cheerful reluctance: "Annie, you hadn't ought to go to parties, but if you do, look as pretty as possible."[34] In fact, "The Old Bird" enjoyed dances as much as her sisters. She could not seem to help enjoying herself. Years later, one of her children was told by an old friend of Julia's: "My dear, Louisa had her admirers, and Annie had hers; but when men saw your mother they just *flopped*."[35]

During the winter of 1842 Julia and her sisters moved out of The Corner, which was subsequently sold, and went to live with their brother Sam. Since his wife's death the winter before, he had been living all alone at 32 Bond Street, having put his little daughter Maddie under the permanent care of her Astor grandparents. It must have cheered Sam up considerably to have his three pretty sisters under his roof, a good excuse to give parties once more. Being naturally sanguine Sam had quickly recovered from his own sorrow.

One of their frequent visitors was Charles Sumner, the young Boston lawyer whom Julia had met the winter before while she was staying with Mary in Dorchester. Little about this boyish, slender man in his early thirties suggested the inflexible, morally righteous reformer of the 1850's. Accompanying him was Cornelius Felton, a young professor of Greek at Harvard who was thoroughly taken with Julia. "I am astounded that all the unmarried men are not piled up at her feet!"[36] It was Felton who christened Louisa, Annie and Julia the "Three Graces of Bond Street."[37] Julia, for her part, found all of Sam's Boston and Cambridge friends delightful; to her they seemed much more witty and fun than most of the fashionable young New Yorkers whom she was beginning to meet at balls.

Julia saw a good deal of Sam's Boston and Cambridge friends on her frequent visits to the Wards in Dorchester. Indeed she found herself moving easily into the upper reaches of Boston society. George Ticknor, the urbane scholar who ruled Beacon Hill from his library at 9 Park Street, had been a friend of her father's. It was well known that Ticknor's approval of someone — and he apparently approved of Sam and Julia Ward — ensured acceptance by the remainder of Boston society. Consequently Julia found herself being treated as a "petted visitor" from New York and invited to an endless round of balls and evening parties. Longfellow, who was in the habit of informing Sam in New York about his sister's activities in Boston, gave frequent reports of a visit she made in the winter of 1842: "Your sister Julia is very well. I met her last evening at Mrs. Wm Appleton's — the evening before at Mrs. Eliot's — neither of these parties — only a chance medley of friends and, — strangers." He assured Sam that Julia was "enjoying herself much in Boston, and making many friends and admirers. . . . Park Street was never more brilliant than now."[38]

Julia was not content, however, with confining herself to the company of the socially respectable. Boston in the 1830's and 1840's was full of people entertaining all sorts of strange new ideas, ideas which Julia had already begun to discover in Sam's European books. It was true that Ticknor and his friends had originally been responsible for introducing some of these transatlantic ideas to America, but now they found themselves appalled by what was happening when European Romanticism fed into American transcendentalism. Ticknor was ready to accept Romanticism as an ingredient of the new national literature he and his friends were trying to foster, but he drew the line at divorcing literature from religious orthodoxy, and in 1840 he referred to the "tendency in a few persons among us to a wild sort of metaphysics, if their publications deserve so dignified a name."[39] He was referring, of course, to men like Emerson and William Ellery Channing. In their rebellion against both religious and literary formalism, they were creating the truly American philosophy of transcendentalism, which emphasized among other things the innate goodness of man, the presence of God in all nature, and the power of human intuition to reform both man and society.

Samuel Ward would have shared his friend Ticknor's disapproval of such revolutionary ideas but his daughter was quickly losing her fear of these New England radicals. In a letter to her sisters in which she assured them that she had had "hardly the least dash of transcendentalism, and that of the very best description,"[40] she told of having heard Emerson lecture and of his having been kind enough to repay her interest with a call. She had also been fortunate in hearing one of the last sermons of the great Unitarian preacher William Ellery Channing, and took comfort in his emphasis on divine love rather than on divine judgment. Julia also met Margaret Fuller, the editor of the transcendentalist journal *Dial,* and a close friend of Emerson's. The occasion was one of Miss Fuller's famous "conversations," held at Elizabeth Peabody's West Street Bookshop in Boston. Julia quickly came to admire Margaret Fuller above all other women, and although she would never defy convention to the degree Miss Fuller did, she nevertheless adopted her as a model for her own

life and many years later wrote a short, sympathetic biography of
this remarkably courageous and intelligent woman. While Julia
was in Boston she took the opportunity to show Miss Fuller some
of the poems she had written shortly after her father's death.
Surprised at the intensity of thought and feeling that Julia's
verses revealed, Miss Fuller found it hard to believe that they
could have been written by the sheltered young woman she had
just met. "It had not yet pervaded her whole being, though I can
recall something of it in the steady light of her eye. . . . I saw in
her taste, the capacity for genius, and the utmost delicacy of
passionate feeling, but caught no glimpse at the time of this
higher mood."[41] It is unclear which of Julia's poems Margaret
Fuller read. Perhaps they were the same ones that Mary Ward had
thought unsuitable for publication. In any case Julia was looking
for other opinions and Miss Fuller was encouraging. Some of
Julia's poetry had already appeared in John Louis O'Sullivan's
Democratic Review, and Julia hoped that Ticknor's publishing
house might be willing to bring out a small volume. According
to Longfellow, Ticknor had liked the poems,[42] but they were
never published and the originals have since disappeared.

The great literary event of the winter of 1842 in Boston and
New York was the triumphal tour of Charles Dickens. Julia saw
him first in Boston and wrote Louisa and Annie all about a party
"given to *Boz* [Dickens] *and me,* at least I was invited before he
came here, so think that I will only give him an equal share of the
honor. I danced a good deal, with some very agreeable partners,
and talked as usual with Sumner, Hillard, Longo, etc. I was quite
pleased that Boz recognized Fanny Appleton and myself, and
gave us a smile and a bow *en passant.* He could do no more, being
almost torn to pieces by the crowd wh[ich] throngs his
footsteps." Julia thought Dickens a capital fellow: "I like to look
at him, he has a bright and most sparkling countenance, and his
face is all wrinkled with the lines not of care, but of laughter. His

manners are very free and cordial. . . . He circulates as universally as small change, and understands the art of gratifying others without troubling himself —."[43]

In New York the entertainments provided for the famous novelist were numerous and lavish, and Julia was back from Boston in time to enjoy at least some of them. Philip Hone noted in his diary, "There is a danger of overdoing the matter and making our well-meant hospitalities oppressive to the recipient."[44] He was right. Dickens himself wrote of his stay in New York: "I can do nothing that I want to do, go nowhere that I want to go, and see nothing that I want to see. If I turn into the street I am followed by a multitude. If I stay at home the house becomes with callers like a fair. . . . I have no rest or peace."[45] On the evening of February 19, a dinner in Dickens's honor was given at the City Hotel. No ladies had been invited to the dinner, but a few, including Julia, Mrs. Dickens and Catherine Sedgwick, the novelist, had hidden themselves in a small room from which they could catch a glimpse of the proceedings. Overcome by curiosity they slowly moved further and further out from their hiding place until they were in full view of the assembled company.[46] Julia would not have been there if it hadn't been for Sam, and Sam was already showing his ability to charm and persuade people into doing almost anything he wished them to do.

That same winter Sam and his sisters gave a party to which two hundred people were invited. Julia wrote Mary Ward that everything had gone off "beautifully. The planed floor was smooth as glass — the music heavenly — the supper superb — we danced till two." But she missed Boston. "Boston is an oasis in the desert, a place where the larger proportion of people are loving, rational and happy. I long for its green pastures and still waters, its pure intellectual atmosphere and its sunlight of kindness and truth."[47] Later in life Julia would claim that if she had married a New Yorker she would have remained a "frequenter of fashionable society, a musical amateur and a *dilettante* in literature."[48] A letter she wrote Mary during the course of that gay winter of 1842 explains her feelings: "How utterly are one's best thoughts invaded by this going out in society. I feel it. I have striven to be myself, everywhere, to retain my own principles, and notions of things, and so I hope to get through the winter without any more serious evil than the loss of time, and the ruin of ball dresses. The former of these is serious enough, but I had wanted to see something of society, it seemed hardly fair that I should never give myself an opportunity of judging and being judged by it."[49]

Julia Ward had, in fact, enjoyed an extraordinary amount of freedom in the years after her father's death. She could go where she pleased and see whom she pleased. Neither Uncle John nor her brother Sam had approved of Samuel Ward's overprotective ways. But while Julia enjoyed her newfound freedom, she also found it bewildering. She had been so protected, not only from the enjoyable aspects of life but also from its responsibilities, that when these were suddenly thrust upon her she almost longed to have her restrictions back again. It was therefore not surprising that when Julia did fall in love, it was with someone whom she regarded with awe and respect as much as with love, a man nearly twenty years older than herself, a person in whom she could lose herself as a child does in its father.

3

The Chevalier

A great grieved heart, an iron will,
As Fearless blood as ever ran;
A form elate with nervous strength
And fibrous vigor, — all a man.
— Julia Ward Howe,
"The Rough Sketch"

Julia first met Samuel Gridley Howe during the summer of
1841. She was staying with Mary Ward in Dorchester, not far
from South Boston, where Dr. Howe was director of the Perkins
Institution and Massachusetts Asylum for the Blind, familiarly
known as the Perkins Institute. One lovely summer afternoon
Longfellow and Sumner came over from Cambridge to pay a call
on the girls, and proposed they should drive over together to the
institute, made so famous by Dr. Howe and his equally renowned
pupil, Laura Bridgman, the Helen Keller of the midnineteenth
century. The girls were delighted with the idea and all four set off
in a carriage hired expressly for the occasion. Julia was in high
spirits. As the carriage climbed up Broadway toward the institute, a large imposing building which had originally been a
seaside hotel built on a promontory overlooking the Atlantic, she
picked a flower with which to decorate Longfellow's hat.[1]

Dr. Howe was not in when they arrived but Julia and her
companions were shown up and down the marble corridors. They

saw blind children wherever they went and Julia, who had a distaste so common to healthy people for the deformed and defective, was surprised at how happy they seemed. In one of the classrooms they found Laura Bridgman, then a little girl of ten. She and another child were seated at desks talking to one another in sign language. The first deaf-blind person to be fully educated, Laura learned by having the letters of the sign language traced on her palm. Julia was struck by her pleasant expression and Laura, running her fingers over Julia's face, pronounced her pretty.

The visitors had given up hope of seeing Dr. Howe and were on the point of leaving, when Sumner glanced out a window and saw his friend approaching the institute on horseback across the broad meadow that bordered it. He motioned to Julia to come to the window, and following his gaze she "beheld a noble rider on a noble steed." Then, Julia later recalled, "the doctor dismounted, and presently came to make our acquaintance. One of our party proposed to give Laura some trinket which she wore, but Dr. Howe forbade this rather sternly. He made upon us an impression of unusual force and reserve."[2]

Julia, of course, had heard of Samuel Gridley Howe, who had been a popular hero since his return from Greece. He had fought in the Greek war of independence against the Turks, and his *History of the Greek Revolution* was one of the books Julia had read in her father's library at The Corner. A true Byronic hero, handsome, fearless and with inexhaustible amounts of energy, he was determined to reform the world.

Samuel Gridley Howe had been born in Boston on November 10, 1801.[3] His father had been a ropemaker by trade and a Jeffersonian Republican in his politics. Boston in the early nineteenth century had been overwhelmingly Federalist, scornful of anyone who did not share its views, and Sam Howe had learned early in life what it meant to be a nonconformist. His father sent him to Brown instead of to Federalist Harvard. At college he was not a particularly good student but managed well enough to get into medical school. There he worked more conscientiously. Meanwhile, the Greek revolution had aroused the sympathy of many in Europe and America who viewed the struggle against the Turks as a reenactment of the glories of the past, when the Hellenic hero valiantly fought the barbarian. Once Howe graduated from medical school, he spurned a future as an ordinary doctor, dispensing pills and collecting fees. Instead, he decided to follow the example of his favorite poet and hero, Lord Byron, and join the crusade against the Turks. He offered his services as a surgeon to the Greek army and spent the next two years fighting and giving medical aid to the revolutionaries.

In 1828 he returned home to raise money. With him on his return journey he carried Byron's helmet, having acquired it at an auction. His native city welcomed him as though he were Byron himself and Howe played the part of a hero well. He was slender, with a soldierly bearing, and his strong features were dominated by a pair of piercing blue eyes and jet-black hair. When he rode down Beacon Street on his black stallion, which was decked out with an embroidered crimson saddle cloth, it was said that the Boston maidens rushed to their parlor windows to look after him.[4] He had little trouble raising the money he wanted and before many months had passed he was back in Greece for another two years, this time helping in the reconstruction of the war-torn country.

Howe returned to Boston for good in 1831. His years in Greece had matured him but his success had also fostered in him a streak of arrogance and an intolerance of others' weaknesses. He had seen what it meant to be really desperate. He had also grown used to being in authority and giving orders to people twice his age. For several months after his return he remained in a state of indecision as to what the future course of his life would be. He could not bear the thought of pursuing a medical career; his idealism made him more ambitious than that. Fortunately, before he had time to become concerned for his future, the perfect opportunity presented itself. An old college friend informed him one day that the New England Asylum for the Blind was looking for a new director. Howe jumped at the opportunity, and having accepted the post was immediately off across the Atlantic for the third time in five years (no small feat in the days before steamers), this time to study methods of instructing the blind and to hire teachers.

While in Paris, Howe once more became involved in relief work. On this occasion the victims were the Poles, who had risen unsuccessfully in 1830, and upon his return from a mission to Prussia, where he had been distributing funds raised in Paris, he was imprisoned in Berlin for suspicious activities. He appealed to Kaiser Frederick Wilhelm III without success and might have spent years in prison had it not been for the presence in Berlin of Albert Brisbane, a well-known American social reformer, who speeded his release through diplomatic channels.

From Berlin, Sam Howe returned to America and was soon hard at work at the Asylum for the Blind, then located in the heart of Boston on Pearl Street. Immediately he began applying the new techniques he had learned in Paris. His teachers there had confirmed his own belief that the blind were in no way inferior to other persons, despite their handicap, a view that was not very widely held at the time. He considered them as capable of acquiring a common school education as those with unimpaired vision. "Deep in his heart," Julia recalled, "lay a sense of the dignity and ability of human nature. . . . The blind must not only be fed and housed and cared for; they must learn to make their lives useful to the community; they must be taught and trained to earn their own support."[5]

Money poured in; over sixty thousand dollars from various sources became available in the year 1833 alone. By 1839 the asylum had outgrown its house on Pearl Street and moved out to the Mount Washington Hotel in South Boston. Renamed the

Perkins Institution and Massachusetts Asylum for the Blind after Colonel Thomas H. Perkins, a wealthy Boston merchant who had donated the original building on Pearl Street, the school remained in these new quarters for the next seventy years.

One wing of the new institute was designated the Doctor's Wing, and here Howe settled himself with his unmarried sister, Jeanette, as his housekeeper. Jeanette, a large, handsome woman, adored her brother but never intruded herself on his affairs, preferring to stay silently and discreetly in the background as an endless stream of people passed through his rooms. Charles Sumner was a frequent visitor; so was George Hillard, the gifted lawyer and orator whom Julia had already met in New York and at several Beacon Street parties; and so too was Horace Mann. But besides these and other close friends there were Greeks and Poles seeking refuge in America. Samuel Howe had acquired something of a name among them, and it was natural that they should turn to him in seeking support for their causes. The Greek government, moreover, had recently bestowed upon him the title of Chevalier of the Greek Legion of Honor, a decoration that led Howe's friends to give him the nickname of Chev.

Chev's immediate circle of friends consisted largely of men preoccupied with questions of reform. Though his work with the blind took up most of his time, he was concerned with many other social reforms as well, and the man to whom he looked for guidance in such matters was his friend Horace Mann. Both shared the conviction that man has the power to transform the world. In their eyes humanity was infinitely perfectible and the way to achieve perfectibility was through education. Mann's chief interest was public education, and when he became secretary of the Massachusetts Board of Education in 1838, he was as dependent on Sam Howe for help and encouragement as the latter was on him. Mann admired his friend's driving energy and told him once, "I should rather have built up the Blind Asylum than to have written Hamlet, & when human vitality gets up into the coronal region every body will think so."[6] Howe for his part regarded Horace Mann as the embodiment of selflessness and nobility, and agreed that the establishment of normal schools and other educational reforms proposed by this friend were of the most vital significance. Howe worked hard for Mann, lecturing and writing as well as giving aid and advice on practical matters. Besides sharing a zeal for reform, both men were firm advocates of the then-popular pseudoscience of phrenology. Character traits and abilities, it was believed, could be discovered by examining and measuring the conformations of the skull, thereby enabling the subject to make the best use of his endowments. Phrenology was, of course, little better than a superstition, but it so exactly suited Samuel Howe's view of mankind that he stubbornly adhered to its principles throughout his life.

Not only the blind, but the insane, the persecuted, the imprisoned — all victims of mental, physical or social ills — became objects of concern for Howe. His attitude toward the slave was at first one of detachment. He abhorred the institution of slavery but was convinced, like many other northerners who were concerned with social welfare, that the slave owners would sooner or later abolish the system on their own. He spared little sympathy for the abolitionists, whom he regarded as impractical fanatics. During the winter of 1841–1842 Howe journeyed through the South and West and was able to see the effects of slavery at first hand. Appalled by what he found, he became convinced that the evils of the peculiar institution caused as much suffering among whites as blacks, if not more. "Let a man be dropped from a balloon upon the surface of the earth, & he could tell in three minutes whether he were in a Slave State or not: The very first sights, the very first sounds, the very first odours would attest the fact: the whites stand with their hands in their breeches pockets & the blacks are 'helping them do nothing.' "[7] On a plantation in Georgia, Howe had a conversation with an overseer who told him that slaves in the South were better off than free

Negroes and poor whites in the North. Howe agreed that this was undoubtedly true, "but in this he speaks his own condemnation, & the brutalizing effects of a system which can make a human being content in such utter degradation."[8] From this time on, Howe would become more and more committed to the freedom of the slaves.

Julia Ward may not have been aware of it on that bright summer day in 1841 when she first met Howe, but there were qualities about the man that were reminiscent of her own father. Both were ambitious and hardworking; both were philanthropists, although their philanthropy took very different forms. Samuel Ward's concerns had centered on the church and education; Sam Howe, who was not a regular attendant at any church, had his hand in a large number of activities, from education to prison reform. A stern, puritanical streak in both Ward and Howe often obscured their fundamentally warm and affectionate natures.

But whereas Ward was soft-spoken and even humble in the presence of others, Howe had a vital, outgoing personality. His restless, driving energy led him to pursue one cause after another and he hated to stay in one place for any length of time. Ward, on the other hand, hardly left New York and pursued his banking career with a quiet, dogged determination. Julia would soon discover one aspect of Howe's character her father had not shared, and that was his bullheadedness; once he decided to do a thing no amount of persuasion could stop him. Julia's brother Marion later referred to Sam Howe as "that confounded bit of New England granite."[9] He could not bear to be teased and contradicted; but the Wards were great teasers, Julia most of all.

Looking out the institute window on that warm June day, Julia saw only a handsome hero on a black stallion. Later, the two exchanged a few brief words, but they did not see one another again for a year. Julia returned to New York and was soon swept up in a gay round of balls and parties, culminating in all the excitement of Charles Dickens's visit the following winter. She did meet Howe in the winter of 1842 during the course of her visit to Boston and reported to her sisters that she had taken a dislike to him.[10] But a real affection between the two did develop several months later.

It all started at a farewell dinner for Dickens at the country house of James Gore King in Weehawken, New Jersey. The party was grand; it was a glorious June day; they had a majestic view of the Hudson River and consumed masses of strawberries. Philip Hone noted in his diary that he had seen Julia Ward walking about the lawns, but he did not mention that she was with a stranger, Dr. Howe from Boston.[11]

Howe was planning to leave for Boston as soon as the festivities were over; Julia did not expect to see him again. But that night there was a party at 32 Bond Street. Julia sang, the guests ate more strawberries, and into the midst of this gaiety walked Dr. Howe. He had missed the boat to Providence and a visit to Miss Ward's seemed as pleasant a way as any to pass the evening.

From that day on, Julia and Dr. Howe were seen together a good deal. A young New Yorker noted in her diary that she "walked down Broadway with all the fashion and met the pretty blue-stocking, Miss Julia Ward, with her admirer, Dr. Howe. . . . She had on a blue satin cloak and a white muslin dress. I looked to see if she had on blue stockings, but I think not. I suspect that her stockings were pink and she wore low slippers, as Grandmamma does. They say she dreams in Italian and quotes French verses. She sang very prettily at a party last evening, and accompanied herself on the piano. I noticed how white her hands were."[12]

Not since before his years in Greece had Chev been in love with anyone. His life had been too full of causes to allow room for romance. He had heard much of the three Ward sisters and the gay parties they gave, from his friends Hillard and Sumner, and now he found himself completely smitten by the eldest. As with everything else he pursued, once he determined that Julia was the wife for him, he would not give up until she was his. Julia was equally in love but unlike the determined Dr. Howe she had her reservations about such a marriage. Underneath her love lay the realization that she would lose much if she let herself be captured by this proud, domineering man. She yearned for the strength he would provide and admired his courage and idealism but she also knew her own pride and valued her newfound independence. The first would have to be stifled, the latter would disappear entirely if she married Sam Howe.

The courtship turned out to be a stormy one. Julia's independent spirit rose to the surface often enough between the party in June 1842 and the wedding day in April 1843 for Chev to be disturbed. He never considered giving her up but he did do his best to try and change her. It was not that he minded independent women. In fact he had been working very closely with Dorothea Dix in her efforts to better the terrible conditions in prisons and mental asylums. From Sam Howe's point of view, for an unmarried woman to be independent was one thing, but it was quite another for his own wife, or prospective wife. He was very aware of Julia's literary ambitions but made it clear that once they were married she must discard them. Julia herself was rightly concerned that her future husband should have so little sympathy for her interests, and she therefore had many moments of doubting the wisdom of giving up so many of her own dreams in order to remain obedient to her lover.

Her family and friends were of little help to her. She was obviously in love and they do not seem to have taken very seriously Chev's obstinacy with regard to the necessity of her sacrificing all for him. Mary Ward thoroughly approved of Sam Howe as a husband for her friend, and had encouraged the romance from the beginning. Several years earlier, when Julia had become briefly engaged to a clergyman (his name is now unknown), Mary had counseled her "to think of how much you will

require from one to whom your whole life and yourself are given"
and urged her to "be sure that he for whom you make this
sacrifice and to whom you give your whole heart is worthy of
possessing it. . . . Remember too that yours is no common
character and that it ought to be committed to the charge of no
common person, but to one who could feel that your destiny is a
noble one, and who would share it with you."[13] Mary had understood rightly that Julia had chosen the minister with her mind
and not with her heart. Now, Julia was so obviously in love with
Chev that Mary could only give her encouragement.

In February 1843, before they were officially engaged, Julia
went to Dorchester for a long visit, presumably to be near her
lover. During this period their romance reached a crisis. Chev
was becoming tired of pleading with Julia to accept him, and
employing the best possible tactic to insure her acquiescence, he
took off one day for New York without saying goodbye or even
letting her know where he was going. When Julia heard that he
had left for New York she immediately suspected that all was
over between them and that he was at that very moment in the
parlor at 32 Bond Street proposing to her sister Louisa. Actually,
Chev had no intention of marrying Louisa and before many days
had passed he was back in Boston. The engagement took place
without further hesitation on Julia's part.

Julia returned to New York early in March. No word was
said about her engagement but her brother Sam was immediately
aware of a change in his sister. "It was very funny to see the little
difficulty our truant warbler found in tuning her throat to a pitch
in concert with us. We were the same laughing and screaming set
of madcaps and the intensity of our pleasures was heightened by
her presence. But a gentle change had come over the spirit of the
'old bird's dream' — 'Care sits upon the brow of Cupid.' "[14]

A week later Sam wrote Chev that there were rumors of an
engagement. Julia's behavior seems to have sparked these
rumors, Sam observed, as she "has been refusing to go out,

declines balls — e.g. a most agreeable one at Mrs. Otis'." He pleaded with Chev to come to New York so Julia could go to Mrs. Astor's delightful music party the following Monday.[15]

Chev declined the invitation but he and Julia maintained a long correspondence during the few remaining weeks before the wedding, which was planned for April 23. Sam was delighted with his sister's engagement; he thought Chev a perfect husband for her but he was worried by his sister's melancholy expression when she read her fiancé's letters. Having persuaded Julia to marry him, Chev was now having doubts about whether or not she really loved him. Sam forthwith dispelled these doubts in a letter to Howe, written early in March. He had deduced correctly that a struggle was going on "between the Ideal and the Real":

> I assure you that a close scrutiny of it [her character] since her return has disclosed to me more essential changes in all features of *relation* than I ever conceived could be affected by the alchemy of any man's love. . . . Therefore I consider the doubts and fears expressed in your letter as unfounded and groundless. . . . The delicate ingredients of a woman's love are too subtle for the frigid analysis of reason. . . . you have been tormented by a phantom of your own imagination.[16]

What Sam Ward had yet to realize was that his future brother-in-law had far stricter and more inflexible ideas about a wife's proper ways of thinking and acting than Sam himself did. It was Sam, after all, who had encouraged Julia's scholarly and literary activities. His own mother had been a poet and he saw no reason why Chev should be so upset by this spirit of independence in his wife-to-be. His letter to Chev continued: "As for a woman's poetical aspirations, I should cherish them as I would the melody of her voice. . . . Our lives are filled up by action and I think it fortunate when intellectual occupation, strengthening the mind and refining the taste, fills up those lonely hours, so often consoled by scandal and romances, and render the woman a fitter companion for the man."[17] As Sam clearly understood, Julia's qualities and accomplishments that had first attracted Howe were the very ones he was demanding that she stifle or abandon, and Howe never seems to have recognized this contradiction. In his view, the ideal wife for him was a penniless, uneducated young woman who was willing to submit her body, mind and soul totally to his wishes. And, in fact, a man's insistence on a submissive wife was considered a reasonable demand in the 1840's. When a girl married she was expected to sacrifice the relative independence she had enjoyed. Legally, the American wife was completely at the mercy of her husband. He could grant her certain freedoms if he wished to, but he was perfectly within his rights to do as he pleased with her money and her person.

That Julia was an heiress with a considerable fortune of her own was a fact that Chev claimed to have discovered after their engagement, although he must surely have been aware during their courtship that she was scarcely suffering from want. At the time of the engagement Julia had some $3,000 a year, as well as considerable holdings in New York real estate.[18] Chev, who had always sworn that he would never marry a rich girl, demanded that she give all of this up completely once they were married.[19] He insisted he was not a fortune hunter and considered the $2,000 a year he made as director of the Perkins Institute, together with another $1,000 from investments, sufficient for their needs. Julia appears not to have objected to giving up her inheritance, feeling that money should not stand in the way of love. But her relatives, especially Sam and Uncle John, were horrified that Howe should propose such a thing. Uncle John, suspicious of anyone who pretended an unconcern for riches, went so far as to accuse Howe of marrying Julia for her money, and refused under any circumstances to allow her to give it up. Howe's next move was to try to secure control of Julia's property himself, thus confirming Uncle John's suspicions. But the Wards would not allow this either. Finally a compromise was reached: Julia was to receive $3,000 annually; the remainder of her property would be handled by her brother and uncle, with $10,000 available for purchasing a house.

Howe remained uncomfortable about this and so did Uncle John. Indeed, Uncle John had good reason to be worried about Howe's attitude toward his niece's money, for although Chev was no fortune hunter, cash had a way of disappearing once it was put in his hands. Later, when he did get control of Julia's property he invested it so unwisely that the greater part was lost. Julia, on the other hand, had inherited something of her father's business sense and would probably have handled her fortune very sensibly with a little sound advice. Later in life, when strapped for money and in charge of her own budget, she managed very well with what little she had. But as a young woman of twenty-four, she had had scant opportunity to prove her financial skill. Few people in 1843 would have considered giving a married woman the right to manage her own property, and besides, Julia's demonstrated inefficiency when it came to practical matters belied this hidden talent.

Despite all the troubles attending the courtship, Sam Howe insisted that he and Julia should be married as soon as possible. The date for the wedding was consequently set and Julia's sisters, Louisa and Annie, rushed about making preparations.

Sam Howe's friends, on the whole, seem to have approved of the match. They wrote enthusiastically to him and Julia, but some of the letters they wrote one another indicated that there were those among them who had doubts. Charles Sumner had the least reason to be happy about the marriage. Dependent as he was on his friend, he feared more than anyone else a loss of their intimacy once Chev and Julia were married. On her part, Julia was fond of teasing Chev about his and Sumner's affection for one another. Even after they were married she would laughingly suggest that Chev should have married Sumner instead of her. Howe would cheer his friend up by encouraging him to share the experience of falling in love.[20] For a time Sumner did flirt with Louisa Ward, but when he realized she was old enough to marry and that his advances might be taken seriously, he stopped his courting.

Longfellow was not very enthusiastic about the match despite his friendship with both Julia and Chev. In fact, he had always been rather shy of Julia. He found her very forthright, a thing unbecoming in a woman, and described her to a friend as "a fine, young, buxom damsel of force and beauty, who is full of talent, indeed carrying almost too many guns for any man who does not want to be firing salutes all the time."[21] Nevertheless, as he wrote Sam shortly before the wedding, "Everybody seems delighted with Julia's engagement. She is wise as well as witty. Howe is a grand fellow and deserves his good fortune. This everybody feels and acknowledges."[22]

Chev did not see his future bride until the end of March, as he spent the better part of that month in Maine doing work for the blind. The trip over bad roads at the end of winter was a hazardous one and on March 5 he wrote Sumner: "I am sure one of the fates means to marry Julia, for ever since my engagement I have been beset every day, and nearly killed. First I nearly died of joy; then I fell and almost broke my neck; then I was overset in Louisburg Square and nearly cracked my crown; last night I was overset, clean and twice during the several gyrations performed by the coach during twelve hours pitching over snow banks."[23] But the fates were cheated, and as soon as he returned from Maine, Chev immediately went down to New York to be with Julia.

Howe, like all people deeply in love, could not imagine that anyone could feel the way he did. Julia, too, was in a disembodied state and as the day of the wedding approached all mention of doubts ceased. Completely under the spell of this man who loved her with such passion, Julia resolved to give of herself completely. "His true devotion has won me from the world and from myself," she wrote her brother Sam. "I am the captive of his bow and spear."[24]

The day of the wedding dawned happily. All disagreements between Sam Howe and his in-laws were laid aside for the time being. The wedding took place in the parlor of Uncle John's house at 8 Bond Street and Julia came out of the clouds long enough to enjoy herself. Louisa and Annie had seen to it that she looked as pretty as possible; her dress was made of fine white muslin trimmed with lace. Only a veil of fine net covered her lovely red hair and she wore a diamond pin that Chev had given her, as well as her mother's diamond necklace. The groom attracted almost as much attention as the bride in his magnificent blue broadcloth coat, brocaded vest and fawn-colored trousers.

The reception was gay; Julia's parties always were. The bride could not resist playing a trick on Charles Sumner. While the guests were seated at the wedding supper, that serious young man was so deeply engrossed in conversation with the lady next to him that he failed to notice that Julia had managed to slip three silver spoons into his pocket. They were soon discovered and nearly everyone enjoyed the joke except perhaps Sumner himself.

As much in love with one another as Chev and Julia were, it is hard to find many ways in which they were compatible. Besides the great difference in their ages — he was nearly twenty years older than she — Julia would not be one to put aside her dreams of writing plays and novels forever, even though she had capitulated in good faith. For the time being she would willingly submit to Chev's desire that she be the traditional, subservient wife, but once the honeymoon was over, her interests and ambitions would reassert themselves. She would then discover that the freedom she had enjoyed before her marriage could not be so easily resurrected.

As one final gesture in favor of their sister's independence, Julia's brothers had insisted that she retain her maiden name and call herself Mrs. Julia Ward Howe — not Mrs. Samuel Gridley Howe.

4

Honeymoon in Europe

Where was the man in New England who could take pride and pleasure in a life with an ambitious, intellectually brilliant woman unless he was absolutely confident that he was her superior?
— Alice S. Rossi, *The Feminist Papers*

A week after the wedding the newly married pair were in Boston preparing to board the Cunard steamer *Britannia,* which was to sail for Liverpool the afternoon of May first. In those early days of steamship travel the Cunard line was the only one making the Atlantic crossing, and since the Cunarders sailed from Boston, Julia and Chev had had to make the trip up from New York to catch their ship.

The day, which had been rainy to begin with, was clear and sunny by the time the ship left the dock. The Howes were by no means without company on board. Annie Ward was to be their companion throughout their European travels, and the Horace Manns shared both the voyage across the ocean and the Wards' lodgings during their stay in London. Chev's friend had married Mary Peabody, one of the three Peabody sisters of Salem, that very morning. But it was no accident that the two couples found each other on the same ship: Howe and Mann had planned that they should travel together.[1]

No sooner had the *Britannia* sailed out beyond the islands in Boston Harbor than the sea became very rough. Mary Mann was the only woman at dinner the first evening.[2] Julia and Annie immediately took to their narrow bunks, where they remained until the ship passed Halifax. Julia was much comforted by Chev's solicitude. "I cannot tell you how good my husband is, how kind how devoted," she wrote her sister Louisa. "He is all made of pure gold. While I was ill, I slept continually and whenever I awoke, I found him sitting at my side, looking at me."[3]

Before many days had passed, Chev managed to get both girls up on deck, and in the fresh sea air they quickly revived. Julia was once more her old, jolly self. "When the ship rolled and I felt myself going, I generally made for the stoutest man in sight and pitched into him, the result being various apologies on both sides and great merriment on the part of the spectators . . . little of the old mischief left, you see."[4]

The last evening on shipboard featured the usual captain's dinner complete with champagne and toasts to Queen Victoria. Julia was so amused by the little ceremony that she decided to hold a "mock celebration" in the ladies' cabin the following morning. A good many of the women on board attended, and the high point of the entertainment was a song composed by Julia in praise of Mrs. Bean, the stewardess.

> *God save our Mrs. Bean,*
> *Best woman ever seen,*
> *God save Mrs. Bean.*
> *God bless her gown and cap,*
> *Pour guineas in her lap,*
> *Keep her from all mishap,*
> *God save Mrs. Bean.*[5]

Mrs. Bean, the center of all this attention, was rather taken aback by the unexpected homage rendered to her. When the assembled company called out, "Speech! Speech!" she curtsied and replied, "Good ladies make good stewardesses." The ladies then drank the health of the ship's cow since she had provided the milk and cream for the voyage. A Scottish lady objected to this: "I don't want to drink her health at a'. I think she is the poorest *coo* I ever heard of."[6] Perhaps the cow suffered from the rolling and pitching of the ship as much as the passengers did.

Upon landing in England the Howes and Manns went straight to London, where they found comfortable rooms in Upper Baker Street. Well provided with letters of introduction, both from the Wards' banking connections and Chev's friends, many of whom had also been handsomely entertained by the English, the Howes were plied with invitations of all sorts. The bitterness engendered by the American Revolution and the War of 1812 had since died away and the young Americans were now regarded by their onetime rulers as amusing curiosities. Howe's fame as the great educator of the blind had preceded him, making him much in demand. Edward Everett, then minister to Britain from the United States, said of the Howes' visit, "None of our countrymen, since I have been here, have excited greater interest, — received more attention, — or left a better impression than the Howes."[7]

Julia and Chev had arrived in London at the height of the "season," that period of the year from late winter into early summer when the English aristocracy left the country to settle in the fashionable districts of London for five or six months of continuous social activity. It amused these high-born folk to patronize an occasional clever individual of the lower classes or visiting Americans like the Howes. Invitations poured into the rooms in Baker Street for breakfast, supper and theater parties as well as weekends in the country. At first Julia and Annie had to go out alone. Chev had hurt himself shortly before sailing by putting his foot through a wash basin. The wound failed to heal and when they arrived in London he was forced to see a surgeon, who kept him confined to their lodgings for several weeks.[8] It sometimes took all of Julia's ingenuity to give herself and Annie a good time. One evening they went to a party given by the Sydney Smiths. Smith, a well-known London wit and a protégé of the Whig aristocrats, had befriended Julia soon after their arrival and urged the two young women to come to a reception he was giving. They consented and at the appointed time arrived at the Smith house. "Mrs. 'owe, and Miss Vord," Julia heard the servant announce in a loud voice as they entered a room full of people they had never seen before. The Smiths were apparently too busy playing host to show much attention to their young American friends. Julia was bored and Annie frightened but finally they "got hold of some good people . . . made friends, drank execrable tea, finished the evening by a crack with Sir Sidney himself and came off victorious, that is to say alive. Sir S. very like old Mrs. Prime, three chins and such corposity!"[9] Sometimes the effort to survive these social ordeals became too much even for Julia. "Annie and I are little people here," she wrote Louisa in early June when Chev was up and around again. "We are too young? to be noticed . . . we are very demure, and have learned humility. Chev receives a great deal of attention, ladies press forward to look at him, roll up their eyes, and exclaim 'Oh! he is such a wonner!' I do not like that the pretty women should pay him so many compliments . . . It will turn his little head! He is now almost well, and so handsome! the wrinkles are almost gone."[10]

Poor Julia! She was now under the shadow of her handsome and famous husband, but she was still too much in love with him to mind very greatly having to stand in the background. If she regretted anything it was the setting aside of her literary aspirations. Even in these early months of her marriage she realized that a piece of her had gone. Early in June she wrote a poem describing her feelings:

> *I feel my varied powers all depart*
> *With scarce a hope they may be born anew*

And nought is left, save one poor loving heart,
Of what I was — and that may perish too.

She was perhaps already discovering that Chev was not really very interested in what she thought or did, and despite his kindness and affection for her he appeared to have little need for either the spiritual or intellectual companionship she so very much desired to give him.

> *Come nearer to me, let our spirits meet,*
> *Let us be of one light, one truth possessed;*
> *Tis true our blended life on earth is sweet,*
> *But can our souls within one heaven rest?*[11]

As far as Chev himself was concerned everything about being married was delightful. His letters home are full of praise for Julia's virtues and he told Longfellow that he found her a pure, noble and gifted creature, "gushing over with tenderness and love."[12]

But Sam Howe had other things besides love to occupy his mind. Incapable of putting work entirely aside, he spent a good deal of time visiting English prisons, workhouses and insane asylums. Julia accompanied him on a visit to Pentonville, a model prison he was particularly interested in since it employed the system of solitary confinement he very much favored. Charles Dickens, who was a great admirer of Chev's and who had written a glowing account of the Perkins Institute in his *American Notes*,[13] took the Howes to visit the old prison of Bridewell, which Julia to her surprise found to be a "clean, spacious, well arranged building."[14] (Later in life she remembered only the horror of the treadmill and Dickens's remark at the sight of it: "My God! if a woman thinks her son may come to this, I don't blame her if she strangles him in infancy.")[15] Dickens took them to the Marylebone workhouse as well, and Julia was once more surprised by what she saw and declared that it was not at all the sort of place Dickens had described in *Oliver Twist*. "It is comfortable and clean — the children are well instructed, taught trades and exercised in gymnastics." The great charity school in Norwood she found "extensive and well managed but not so clean as the workhouse."[16]

There were places where Julia and Annie were not allowed to go, and these showed Chev a darker side of London life. One night in early June he received a note from Dickens:

MY DEAR HOWE, — Drive to-night to St. Giles's Church. Be there at half-past 11 — and wait. One of Tracey's people will put his head into the coach after a Venetian and mysterious fashion, and breathe your name. Follow that man. Trust him to the death.

So no more at present from

THE MASK[17]

Such excursions into the slums of London convinced Chev of the superiority of his native Boston, where there was less of a gap between rich and poor. He wrote Sumner that he had not been so "dazzled" by the glories of the British capital that he could ever forget "the foulest slough through which humanity ever wallowed."[18]

Sam Howe and Horace Mann were eager to meet Thomas Carlyle, that penetrating critic of English society and government, whose ideas had helped to stimulate the transcendentalist movement in New England. Having been invited to the Carlyles' for tea one afternoon, they drove out to Chelsea accompanied by Mary Mann, Julia and Annie. Mrs. Carlyle, who was not feeling well that day, did not appear and Julia was asked to pour the tea. Since her host drank unlimited cupfuls she was kept quite busy while Carlyle himself indulged in a steady monologue. Julia was fascinated by the shaggy, unkempt genius whose eyes were so "full of fire" and thought he sounded just like his writing.[19]

In July, with the London season at an end, the Howes made a short visit to Ireland. Julia found Dublin dirty but interesting; Chev was appalled by the sight of so many starving people. Hordes of wretches flocked around them as soon as they stepped off the boat and followed them everywhere. Julia wrote Louisa that there were so many beggars "you cannot get into the carriage without being surrounded by ragged women, holding out their dirty hands and clamouring for ha'pence."[20] Chev had a horror of almsgiving but even he weakened occasionally and reached into his pocket. In 1843 the Irish potato famine was already killing thousands yearly and forcing others to flee the country. But Chev appears to have been unaware that the true cause of the poverty he saw all around him lay in the nature of the social and economic controls that England and the Anglo-Irish landed aristocracy had imposed, and he blamed Daniel O'Connell, the noted Irish political leader, for not seeing to it that the destitute were placed in "well-regulated" workhouses. Surely, he argued, the beggars would be better off there; he was convinced that outright charity was no solution to Ireland's problems and that those who resorted to beggary only did so because they preferred it to the workhouse.[21]

Both Howes were glad when they finally returned to England. There they had one important visit to make before they left for the Continent: George Ticknor had given them a letter of introduction to William Wordsworth. Although the old gentleman was usually very cordial to his guests, the Howes found their reception a cool one. Julia later recalled:

> The widowed daughter of our host had lost heavily by the failure of certain American securities. These losses formed the sole topic of conversation not only between Wordsworth and Dr. Howe, but also between the ladies of the family, my sister, and myself. The tea to which we had been bidden was simply a cup of tea, served without a table. We bore the harassing conversation as long as we could. The only remark of

Wordsworth's which I brought away was this: "The misfortune of Ireland is that it was only a partially conquered country." When we took leave the poet expressed his willingness to serve us during our stay in the neighborhood. We left it, however, the following morning, without seeing him or his again.[22]

Julia's letter to Louisa telling of their visit showed that the rudeness may not have been all on the Wordsworths' part. When the ladies had finished "whining" about their losses, Julia described herself as remarking, "Why did you not keep your money at home? It was safe enough in England — you know there was a risk in investing it so far from you — if we should speculate in yours, we should no doubt be ruined also." This remark apparently startled the Wordsworths into silence and the Howes took this opportunity to make their departure. As to her impression of the great poet himself, Julia described him to Louisa as a "crabbed old sinner, who gave us a very indifferent muffin."[23]

Despite the worries Julia expressed in her poems she found the months in London as exciting as any she had ever known. The English on the whole seemed rather cold people and she complained to Sam about the "inconceivable amount of twaddle which was talked among the higher classes," but she had derived great pleasure from numerous evenings at the theater, and frequent offers of a box at Covent Garden or at Her Majesty's Theater were never turned down. The "crowning ecstasy of all" was the ballet. She and Annie had been deeply moved by a particularly graceful Italian dancer named Cerito and Julia had agreed with her sister that "it seems to make us better to see anything so beautiful."[24]

Shortly after their visit to the Lake District, the Howes left England for the Continent. They traveled through the Swiss and Austrian Alps, first to Vienna where they spent two weeks, and then south to Milan where they stayed for a month. Chev by this time was getting a bit restless. He had been away from the real business of life long enough, and besides, this traveling with two female companions was not the same as being on one's own. Such pleasures as making friends with the local populace, a thing he had always enjoyed doing, now seemed almost impossible. He wrote his friend Sumner: "The family man walks with his wife on one arm and his sister on the other, so that he cannot run against a passenger purposely, beg his pardon and make then an introduction to further acquaintance; he sits at table, flanked on each side by a formidable barrier of wadded silk, which cuts him off from his neighbors; . . . wherever he goes he is as much cut off from the crowd that he wanders among as if he had a police officer on either hand to keep him silent."

But Chev admitted there were compensations. One was "the infinite pleasure [derived] from the constant presence of a beloved companion, who clings closer to you from the strangeness of everything about her; . . . a being whose constant presence, like the light and heat of the sun, makes constant and pleasant the day, even in the darkness and storm; a companion who throws around everything you do the charm and agreeable association for future reminiscence."[25] Howe had another reason to be happy: Julia was expecting their first child in March.

By October they were in Rome, where they planned to spend the winter. The Eternal City was very popular with Americans in the 1840's. About a thousand came there every year and they found something in the strangeness of the Latin, Catholic culture that they missed at home. Julia never forgot her first sight of the dome of Saint Peter's as they approached the city across the Campagna. Once inside Rome itself she was immediately struck by its "medieval" aspect. "A great gloom and silence" hung over it and the past appeared to well up in front of her eyes, so remote the city seemed from the modern Europe they had been seeing.[26] The vast and neglected ruins increased the aura of romance, and it seemed natural to visit the Colosseum by moonlight. The contrasts of life within the city amazed Americans used to their own relatively clean middle-class towns where few were either very rich or very poor. Here in Rome the poor were everywhere, especially in the winter months when they poured in from the countryside and hung about the churches and the doors of the great palaces. The streets of the city were narrow and dark and smelled horribly. Yet many Americans could not help feeling deeply attracted to this city smothered in its past.[27] Julia certainly did. All the history she knew had been learned from reading the books in her father's and brother Sam's libraries, and now here it was in reality.

Chev, however, was depressed and bored in Rome. Less entranced than his wife by the glitter of jewels worn by lavishly dressed countesses in cold, marble palaces, Sam Howe found Rome decadent. His romanticism did not embrace musty relics as Julia's did. Besides, he was becoming even more restless and impatient with continued leisure. "Life without labor is nothing," he wrote Sumner, "nothing; not even love can load the wings of time with those delightful recollections which come from a consciousness of usefulness in its widest sense."[28] Everything about Rome annoyed or repelled him. Of the educational system he wrote: "There is not a school in Rome which must not be considered as a beacon to warn rather than a light to guide the inquirer."[29] As for Roman charitable institutions, they seemed actually to encourage begging and were concerned mainly, as were the schools and churches, in maintaining the status quo. Chev placed the burden of responsibility for the stagnant condition of Roman social and religious institutions squarely on the shoulders of the Pope and the Roman Catholic Church.[30]

Julia also found the number of poor she saw about her depressing and she too tended to make the Roman Church the scapegoat for the city's evils. She wrote Uncle John back in Bond Street that "the city seems to contain scarce anything but artists, priests and beggars. I have seen the Pope three times, he looked like an old woman dressed up very finely. . . . They take, I think, the fattest priests to make the Cardinals and the fattest Cardinal to make the Pope."[31] Julia's scorn for what she considered to be the decayed pomp of the Roman hierarchy confirmed her growing conviction that true religion should be unencumbered by such ceremonial trappings. Writing to the most religiously liberal of her relatives, Dr. John Francis, she told him that she now sympathized with his "wishes for a simpler, purer and more righteous religion than that even which prevails in our country." She felt that religion should not make men "ascetic and visionary, but earnest, truthful, just and charitable. That which I have seen in Rome, ay, and even in England, leads me to believe that men have, so far, strangely mistaken the spirit in their zeal for the letter of Christianity. Theology in general seems to me a substitution of human ingenuity for divine wisdom."[32]

It is quite possible that Julia's thoughts on religion and particularly on the kind of Catholicism she saw in Rome were being influenced by a new friend. Here for the first time she met the great transcendentalist preacher Theodore Parker, in Rome for a rest cure after a hard winter of lecturing and writing and coping with criticism from fellow clergymen and friends in Boston who found his ideas heretical. Sam Howe and Theodore Parker had much in common: both shared the same zeal for social reform and the same hatred for suffering and injustice. But Parker also shared many of Julia's interests. His learning was famous in New England. Familiar with more than forty languages, he had translated some of Longfellow's poetry into Sanskrit. It is not hard to imagine that he and Julia found much to talk about, and she must have quickly discovered that this shy, warmhearted man had views very different from those of her husband on the proper place for women. Like many men of that time Parker idealized and romanticized women, placing them on a moral pedestal, but he also understood that society, by confining women to home and motherhood, was fundamentally holding them in contempt.[33] Was it perhaps with Parker in mind that Julia wrote a poem in April 1844 entitled "Parting from a New Friend"?

Thou hast brought back to me my golden youth,
The early days I passed with such as thou;
I know the look that dwells in thy blue eyes
I know the thought that sits upon thy brow.

Again I hear the sounds of other days,
The laugh, the jest, the pleasant melody,
The voice of sympathy and gentle praise,
The breath of kindred souls comes back to me.[34]

Julia and Chev had gone their separate ways during most of that winter in Rome. Chev went to Paris to have his teeth fixed and then came back to start a kindergarten for the blind. Meanwhile Julia pursued her music and her studies and wrote poetry despite her husband's disapproval. As the spring approached, her thoughts turned more and more to the birth of her child. These thoughts were by no means pleasant ones. Her recollection of her own mother's death was all too vivid in her mind. She was consumed by depression and acute fear — convinced that she would not survive the baby's birth.[35] Chev was no help. He regarded his wife as a healthy young creature with nothing to worry about. Fortunately, Julia had Annie to turn to for sympathy and support.

One day, several weeks after the Howes and Annie had settled into their lodgings in Rome, the door to the apartment opened without warning and there stood a young woman whom Julia and Annie did not at first recognize. When after a few seconds of bewilderment they realized that this was Louisa and couldn't be anyone else there were shrieks of delight and much hugging and kissing.[36] Julia saw at once that her sister was not looking very well, and in fact Uncle John had sent his niece to Rome with the hope that the change of air would restore her spirits. Louisa was indeed low in mind as well as in body. She had just broken a brief engagement to John Ward, the brother of Julia's friend Mary. Worse than this had been her recent treatment by the William B. Astors, her brother Sam's in-laws. Louisa had been staying at Rokeby, the Astors' house in the Hudson Valley, when word came that Sam had not only remarried, to a reputedly "fast woman" from New Orleans named Medora Grimes, but had moved with his new bride into 32 Bond Street. The Astors considered the house theirs even though it had been given to Sam and Emily by Sam's father.[37] Sam would keep the house despite the Astors' protestations, but now, with no warning, Louisa was asked to leave Rokeby. When she arrived back at her Uncle John's house in Bond Street her relatives agreed that something had to be done to distract the unhappy girl. As it happened, the American consul in Rome that year was the Wards' cousin, George Washington Greene. On his way back to Rome after several months in the United States, Greene kindly offered to let Louisa accompany him so that she could join her two sisters. By Christmas the three Ward girls were reunited and Chev now had Three Graces instead of two.

With their cousin to take them about, the Howes and Wards found themselves invited to all the great Roman houses. Chev thought these stiffly formal gatherings a terrible bore, except when his young wife was asked to sing. As for Julia, she admitted that the parties were sometimes dreary but she could not resist the glamour of a Roman ball, particularly one attended by Princess Torlonia, her fair hair encircled by a tiara of diamonds. The princess was as beautiful as the duchess of Sutherland, whom Julia had seen in London.[38]

There were also small parties with members of the English colony, who lived their own lives, largely cut off from the Italian social world. Howe described one such evening to Sumner:

There was music and singing, and after several English ladies had tried their hands at Italian music and gained the usual marks of applause . . . with a few forced tappings of kid gloves, Julia was led to the piano-forte, and there was soon a marked difference in the kind of attention paid to the singer; the low whisperings about the piano, the more audible voices in the far corners, soon ceased entirely, and everyone became a listener. She sang most beautifully, far better indeed than she usually does; and then she reaped the most hearty and un- qualified music of praise, which you may well imagine was to my ears sweet music itself.[39]

The birth of the Howes' first baby apparently passed smoothly enough in spite of Julia's depression and fear. Julia Romana was born on March 12, 1844, and Chev wrote ecstati- cally to Sumner of the joys of fatherhood. He couldn't imagine why Julia had made so much fuss over such an elementary matter as giving birth to a child. Julia, now that she was a mother, was more appealing to him than ever. "How beautiful — how won- derful is nature! Only a year ago Julia was a New York belle — apparently an artificial — probably some thought a beautiful one." Now, he exulted, she lives only for her husband and child. "To see her watching with eager, anxious eyes every movement of her offspring, to witness her entire self-forgetfulness and the total absorption of her nature in this new object of love, is to have a fresh revelation of the strength and beauty of woman's character, and new proof of their superiority even in what most ennobles humanity — love for others.[40] Comparing his wife to one of Raphael's madonnas, he told Uncle John Francis, "You have seen Julia as she developed the various parts of her strong and en- thusiastic nature, and you have watched with admiration the ever-increasing strength and beauty of her character; but all that you have seen approaches not what she now displays when, a perfect woman, she performs the duties of a loving mother."[41]

Judging by Julia's poems written at the time — only a few

have survived — her absorption was not as complete as he thought.[42]

The baby was christened by Theodore Parker and soon after that Howe took off for Greece, leaving Julia with Louisa and Annie to look after her. Of the two, Annie was the more faithful. Louisa had met and fallen in love with an American sculptor named Thomas Crawford. This young man — he was thirty-two — turned out to be none other than the carver of the marble mantels in the parlors of The Corner. Now he employed scores of young men and was at the zenith of his fame as one of America's most successful sculptors.[43] As impulsive as he was talented, Crawford, having fallen in love with Louisa Ward, wished to marry her right away in Rome, and instead of writing to Uncle John and asking properly for her hand he simply announced that they were to be married. Uncle John was outraged by Crawford's impudence and immediately wrote back forbidding the union entirely.[44]

Soon after this, Chev returned from Greece, and the party of Howes and Wards, with Crawford following close behind, set off on the long journey back to America. Julia was fast becoming used to her husband's peculiar ways. He never seemed to do anything the way other people did, and his idea of the best way to go from Italy to France was by steamer. The idea of taking a ship was perhaps not so strange, but the particular one he chose was hardly suitable for transporting three young women and a small baby, for there were no sleeping accommodations. Every night the little steamer anchored in some port or other and Chev would rush on shore and acquire enough mattresses for everyone; these always had to be returned by daybreak before the ship weighed anchor. If this was Chev's idea of an adventure it was hardly Julia's, especially with a small baby to care for.[45]

After traveling through France and spending a number of weeks in Paris, where Louisa almost eloped with Thomas Crawford, the Howes went back to England for a brief stay before sailing home. It was midsummer when they reached London. Their friends had all departed for the country and left invitations for them to come down for weekends. Julia recalled with pleasure a visit to Atherstone, the home of Charles Nolte Bracebridge, whom she later described as "one of the best specimens of an English country gentleman of the old school."[46]

During their stay at Atherstone, Julia and Chev heard much talk of a young neighbor of the Bracebridges. Florence Nightingale, then twenty-four, was considered to be a young woman of unusual intelligence and ambition. As it happened Florence herself had also heard that the eminent American philanthropist, Samuel Gridley Howe, was staying with her neighbors. She was most anxious to meet him and persuaded her parents to invite the Howes over to Elbee, the Nightingales' Elizabethan manor house, for the night. The invitation was accepted and Julia found herself much impressed with Florence, who was "tall and graceful of figure, her countenance mobile and expressive, her conversation most interesting."[47] Chev, too, was impressed. Before the household retired for the night, Florence drew Chev aside and asked him if he would speak with her privately before the family gathered for breakfast the following morning. He happily consented and when they were alone she opened the conversation by coming immediately to the point.

"Dr. Howe, if I should determine to study nursing, and to devote my life to that profession, do you think it would be a dreadful thing?"

"By no means," the doctor replied. "I think that it would be a very good thing."[48]

Years later, when Julia herself was determined to embark on a public career, she rebuked her husband for having encouraged a young woman the same age as herself to be a professional while he had not allowed his own wife even to publish a book of poems. Chev's reply was that "if he had been engaged to Florence Nightingale, and had loved her ever so dearly, he would have given her up as soon as she commenced her career as a public woman."[49]

In the verses Julia wrote that winter in Rome she does not appear to blame Chev for his views of the proper functions of a wife and mother. She appeared rather to blame herself for loving and marrying Chev in the first place:

> *Hope died as I was led*
> *Unto my marriage bed;*
> *Nay, do not weep, 'twas I*
> *Not thou, that slew my happiest destiny.*[50]

Once in England, knowing that her wedding trip was almost over and that the time was fast approaching when she must return to Boston and begin the real business of being a housewife, she seems to have determined to somehow make the best of things:

> *When once I know my sphere*
> *Life shall no more be drear*
> *I will be all thou wilt*
> *To cross thy least desire shall be guilt. . . .*
>
> *Then, husband smile on me,*
> *Smile, and smile tenderly;*
> *Pure angel that thou art,*
> *Build up again the ruins of my heart!*[51]

Early Years in South Boston

Marriage, like death, is a debt we owe to nature.
— Julia Ward Howe, 1846

The autumn of 1844 saw the Howes back from Europe and settled in the Doctor's Wing of the Perkins Institute. Boston would now be Julia's adopted city, and although she had looked forward to living there, as Chev's wife she would now regard it from a very different point of view. "I had formerly seen Boston as a petted visitor from another city would be apt to see it. I had found it altogether hospitable and rather eager to entertain a novelty. . . . I was now to make acquaintance with quite another city, — with the Boston of the teachers, of the reformers, of the cranks, and also — of the apostles."[1]

At first Julia saw little of the city at all. The institute was two miles from Boston proper, and since the Howes had no carriage the only way Julia could get into town was by an omnibus, which crossed the South Boston bridge every hour. With one baby to care for and another on the way by midwinter, Julia rarely made the journey and so spent the greater part of her first year confined to her new home, and that was certainly not the cozy, comfortable place a young bride dreams of.

The Doctor's Wing of the Perkins Institute was reached by

following one of the many long marble corridors that radiated out from the central hall of the building. Like the rest of the old Mount Washington Hotel the Howes' apartment was cold and drafty and smelled of drains. Julia's brother Sam was horrified by the conditions under which his sister was expected to live,[2] and certainly for a young woman straight from the luxury of Bond Street, this cold and lofty building must have seemed a dreary place. Julia had not even the satisfaction of running her own house: the Doctor's Wing was still presided over by Chev's sister, Jeanette, who adored her brother and resented the presence of this "society girl" from New York. Jeanette Howe was also a tireless and efficient housekeeper, and Julia, ignorant of the domestic arts and untidy by nature, was spreading her finery and Julia Romana's things all over the apartment, to the despair of her sister-in-law. Jeanette provided little companionship, being naturally rather taciturn, and Julia was therefore forced to pass the time dandling her baby on her knee, an occupation that quickly palled, although she adored the child and sometimes thought that baby Julia was the only person in the world who really loved her.[3]

Chev was rarely at home. After a year of idleness he had been only too happy to plunge back into the world of philanthropy and reform, and within a few weeks of his return, Horace Mann succeeded in getting him elected to the Boston School Committee. For a year Howe labored ceaselessly to discover weaknesses in the educational system. Julia hardly ever saw him. When he was not out examining the pupils of various schools in an effort to discover how little they were being taught, he was working at the institute or conferring with Mann about School Committee matters. By the time his term was up in October 1845, Chev was in a state of collapse and Julia herself almost ill from sheer loneliness.

In July she wrote her sister Louisa a long letter on the subject of marriage. Louisa was now married herself to Thomas Crawford, having finally secured permission from Uncle John, and the newly wedded pair had once more crossed the ocean and were living in Rome. Julia apologized for the rather cold and selfish letters she had written her sister, and explained: "But to tell you the truth, Weavie, I never could be good when I was not happy, and this year has not, as you know, been a happy one." She then went on to counsel wifely resignation: "We are fulfilling the destiny of women, we are learning to live for others more than for ourselves, and in following thus the guiding of Providence, we have acted more wisely than we would have done in marking out any eccentric course of our own and adhering to it."[4]

Once Chev had recovered from the exhaustion of serving on the School Committee he became more attentive and Julia consequently happier. The Howes' second child, Florence (named after Florence Nightingale), was born in the late summer of 1845 and Julia informed Louisa shortly afterward that the baby was "the image of our dear father." She was also happy to say that Chev was "very good and kind; he is a darling when he is not sick and driven to death."[5] The following summer the Howes moved out of the institute into a house of their own five minutes' walk away. Julia was, of course, delighted to be free of marble corridors and mistress at last in her own house. Mercifully, Jeanette Howe stayed behind to care for the Doctor's Wing and to keep it open for Chev's use. The day the Howes moved in, "the sight of the old house, quaint and comfortable," standing in a sunny garden protected from the raw ocean winds, made Julia cry out, "This is Green Peace!"[6]

The name stayed and she grew very fond of the old place, though never as fond of it as Chev was. Over the years, he did much to improve both buildings and grounds. The original cottage, which dated from early colonial times, was small and squat. The ceilings were so low that a man of normal height standing at the bottom of the staircase could reach up and touch the floor above. Gradually Chev added on to the house, but to begin with the downstairs consisted of three rooms built around a big, square, central chimney. At first a living room and then a whole new wing were added; the house became full of odd staircases and little passageways. A sixteenth-century cabinet from Avignon, a prie-dieu of oak and ebony, and a second cabinet from Rome helped to furnish the parlor. But the greatest treasure of all was Byron's helmet. The Howe children remembered it as "a superb affair of blue and steel and gold with a floating blue plume."[7] The ocean lay behind the cottage but the view was blocked and the garden protected by a steep bank, which was later terraced and planted with cedar trees. On summer days, when the sun lay hot on the garden, the cedars gave forth their own warm fragrance.

By the time the Howes moved into Green Peace in the spring of 1846, Chev had done a good deal to make the old farmhouse more comfortable, adding on a new square parlor and turning the old one into a "snug library." In the last days of May, Julia wrote Louisa describing the house and confessing that her spirits had "risen wonderfully" since she had left the institute. "My little corner is so green and pretty, so quiet and hidden from all. I have not those dreadful stairs to go up and down, all the rooms are so near together." Chev's health was better that spring and she told her sister that her heart no longer ached "with the thought that I have given up all else on earth to make one man happy, and have yet utterly failed to accomplish it."[8] Green Peace would always be Chev's favorite spot, but he was by nature a restless man and needed frequent changes of scene. Sometimes he would pick the whole family up and move them back to the Doctor's Wing for several months, to Julia's great distress. But he always came back happily to Green Peace. There in the big living room he loved to romp with his children and sometimes on cold winter days, when the cannel coal fire was roaring in the big fireplace, Chev would muffle himself in a great fur coat and lumber into the room, growling like a bear, and when the children were old enough he and Julia would take turns reading aloud.

But for all the charm and comfort of Green Peace compared to the institute, Julia was as lonely and cut off from the outside world as ever. In a letter addressed to an unknown person and preserved in one of her many scrapbooks, she described her life in South Boston during those first years of her marriage:

> I live in a place in which I have few social relations, and all too recent to be intimate. I have no family around me, my children are babies and my husband has scarcely half an hour in twenty-four to give me. So, as I think much in my way, and nobody takes the least interest in what I think, I am forced to make myself an imaginary public, and to tell it the secrets of my poor little ridiculous brain. While I am employed with fictions my husband is dealing with facts, but as we both seek truth which lies beyond either, we do not get so very far apart as you would think. At least I know all that is in *his* mind, if he does not occupy himself much with mine.[9]

For all the loneliness of these first years of her marriage, there were distractions and bright moments when she appeared almost contented with her lot. From the beginning she enjoyed her daily walks with Julia Romana. As she wrote Sam, the baby was already at nine months beginning to resemble her, for "like mine, the breadth of her face exceeds its length."[10] In March 1845, Annie came to spend ten days with her sister and the following summer the newly married Crawfords joined Annie for another visit before sailing for Europe. Mary Ward occasionally came to call from Dorchester, which was nearby, but the friendship between the two young women had become strained after Louisa had broken off her engagement to Mary's brother John. In those days an engagement was almost as binding a contract as marriage, and the Boston Wards felt, perhaps rightly, that John had been badly treated. Mary and her sister Martha called on Julia at the institute soon after the Howes returned from Europe. "Martha was very constrained," Julia informed her sisters, "but tried to be kind. Mary was more like her old self than I expected — the interview was, however, a painful one. It was kind of them to call — I think Mary will love me again, as I will ever love her."[11]

As was the custom both on Bond Street and Beacon Street, Julia let it be known that she would receive callers every Friday afternoon between twelve and two. Her first At Home could hardly be called a great success. "I dressed myself quite nicely, opened the two parlors, and remained from twelve to two o'clock in readiness to receive visitors — none came but the Everetts, nor do I expect ever to see many people at my receptions."[12] The fact was that few Bostonians in those days had private carriages, and therefore only Julia's and Chev's closest friends were willing to make the effort to cross the South Boston bridge to pay a call on the Howes. Julia did go to an occasional evening party during her first winter in South Boston.

It may perhaps seem surprising that she was not asked out more frequently, considering the charming impression she had made on the Ticknors during her visit in the winter of 1842. But as Mrs. Howe, Julia was no longer a novelty and Boston showed less eagerness to accept her now that she was claiming the right of citizenship. Sam Howe had never belonged to the inner circle of Beacon Street society or the "Boston of the Forty" as Julia later called it.[13] His family had always been made up of nonconformists, and although Chev was admired for his work with the blind, when he began tampering with such matters as their school system he lost favor with conservative Bostonians. Not that Chev particularly minded what people like the Ticknors thought of him. He was no socialite and had no intentions that his wife should be one either. Furthermore, he was too occupied with his various causes to have much time to spare for evening parties.

One of the livelier hostesses on Beacon Hill, however, was Mrs. Harrison Gray Otis, the widowed daughter-in-law of the onetime mayor of Boston. Julia had been to her house a number of times before her marriage and Mother Otis, as she was familiarly known, did give entertaining parties. Determined to infuse Boston social life with a bit of vitality, she opened her house every Saturday afternoon and Thursday evening to all sorts of people, from poets and sculptors to dukes and China merchants — the same sort of hodgepodge Uncle John Francis had gathered together to enliven the gloomy parlors of The Corner.[14] Someday Julia herself would give similar parties, but for the moment she enjoyed Mother Otis's At Homes so much that even when Chev was philanthropically engaged and could not take her she ventured to go on her own. After one such evening Julia called for Chev at the Horace Manns' but found the two men so engrossed in a report that they decided to make a night of it, and Julia was obliged to return home alone. She told Annie that Chev came in at one in the morning "quite intoxicated with benevolence."[15]

Chev must have been somewhat aware of his wife's lonely existence; he did agree that they should give little weekly dinner parties. But these posed certain problems for Julia. During their two years at the institute Jeanette always managed to absent herself on such occasions and left Julia to do the planning and the cooking, neither of which she was trained for or suited to. "I often did not know where to look for various articles which were requisite and necessary," she later recalled. "I remember one dinner for which I had relied upon a form of ice as the principal feature of the dessert. . . . The ice, which had been ordered from town, did not appear. I did my best to conceal my chagrin, but was scarcely consoled when the missing refreshment was found, the next morning, in a snowbank near our door, where the messenger had deposited it without word or comment."[16] With this discovery Julia nearly wept with frustration.

The guests at these first dinner parties were usually the members of the Five of Clubs, Chev's most intimate circle. They included Longfellow, Sumner, George Hillard and Cornelius Felton, all of whom Julia had known before her marriage. But with no other women present, the talk would be solely of reform and philanthropy, and Julia would feel left out — particularly galling when the occasion was the only social event of her week. When Chev did allow the wives to come, Julia presumably enjoyed herself.

If Julia was beginning to find Boston a rather cold and unfriendly place, she was not alone. Compared to New Yorkers, Bostonians had never been famous for their hospitality. Charles Dickens, who had been thoroughly entertained during his stay there in 1842, and who had so admired Boston's appearance and its sense of community responsibility, was nevertheless rather put off by several invitations to share a family pew in church on a given Sunday instead of the roast beef dinner, which he certainly would have preferred. Another visitor from abroad, who had entertained a certain Bostonian in her own country, was repaid for her hospitality by an invitation to call on her Boston friend *after* tea on Sunday.[17]

If Bostonians were not famous for their balls or champagne suppers, neither was their theater much to boast about. In the early 1840's theatricals in the city had been at a very low ebb, and proper Bostonians shared old Samuel Ward's disapproval of such entertainment. Even Fanny Essler's extraordinary dancing, which had enthralled Boston audiences in 1840 and netted her $15,000, did not prevent the theater in which she had performed from closing three years later.[18] By the time the Howes had settled in South Boston things had begun to improve. Bostonians did not seem to think attending dramatic performances in a museum was sinful, so a certain Moses Kimball began producing plays in his Museum and Gallery of Fine Arts. These were such a success that theater in Boston began to revive once more and it was at the Howard Atheneum, once a Millerite temple, that Julia saw the first opera to be performed in the city. Chev procured for her one of the best boxes in the house, and for a whole week in

March 1847, Julia went to a performance nearly every night. "This is a great indulgence," she wrote Louisa, "as it is rather expensive."[19]

Money problems were in fact one of the dark shadows of Julia's early married life. It will be recalled that shortly before their marriage Julia and Chev had been presented with an antenuptial agreement that set up a trust to be managed by Sam and Uncle John, and out of which Julia was to be paid $3,000 a year, a sum equivalent to Chev's own income. Despite being dazed by love, Chev had followed Sumner's advice and protested the arrangement, claiming his right to control his wife's money himself. In the end a compromise was reached: besides the $3,000 a year Julia was to receive an additional $10,000, when needed, for a house.

Chev apparently paid little heed to the exact provisions of the agreement, for he deluded himself into thinking that when he and Julia had a child the trust would end and the money would be his to control. Once Julia Romana was born he felt no compunctions about overdrawing his bank account at Baring Brothers in London by some three hundred dollars. Upon returning home he wrote Sam asking for an advance on Julia's income. Sam wrote back that there was no money for such an advance; the annual $3,000, which Julia received as an allowance, was her only income and stocks would have had to be sold for Chev to receive the money he requested. Meanwhile, Chev received word from Sumner that he had been mistaken in assuming that once he had a child the trust would end. Despite these clarifications, Chev was furious with Sam for denying him access to Julia's money in such a preemptive manner. He retaliated by announcing that he would never again touch any of her money. Certainly he would no longer accept periodic doles from his brother-in-law.

Assured by Sumner that there was no way of breaking the trust, Chev convinced Julia that she should sign a power of attorney, placing her yearly allowance in his hands. He then proceeded to return any money that came to Julia from Prime Ward & King; from now on he and she would live solely on his income. Chev did not tell Julia he was returning her allowance, but Sam saw to it that his sister found out.[20] To ease the situation, Julia tried to persuade Sam to resign his trusteeship, but she made no complaint to Chev, even though she did feel the pinch. She wrote Louisa just before Julia Romana's first birthday that she did not have enough money to buy the child a present.[21] Eventually, Chev agreed to accept the income from the trust, but every year Julia signed the money to him and he decided how it should be spent. She did not acquire control over her own money again until after his death in 1876, and by then there was little left.

In the fall of 1846, after the move to Green Peace, Julia went down to Bordentown, New Jersey, to pay a visit to her sister Annie, then newly married to Adolphe Mailliard. She wrote Chev that Annie's mode of living was even more retired than her own at Green Peace; yet Annie seemed to be accommodating herself to it happily.[22] That winter Chev decided to indulge his wife by spending the winter in town. It bothered him that she did so much complaining to her family, especially to her sisters. So he rented some rooms in Winthrop House near Boston Common and Julia proceeded to enjoy herself thoroughly. She wrote ecstatically to Louisa that she had had "a devil of a winter, full of pleasure, of excitement, le tourbillon des passions! you understand."[23] To Annie her tone was more serious:

> It has been strange to me to return to life and to feel that I have any sympathy with human beings, after the long interval of quiet and indifference which succeeded my marriage. I have been singing and writing poetry, so you may know that I have been happy, alas, am I not a selfish creature to prize these enjoyments as I do. God forgive me if I do wrong in following with ardor the strongest instincts of my nature. . . . I have been giving a succession of little musical parties, on Saturday evenings, and I assure you they have been quite success-

ful. . . . Chev is very desirous of having a house in town and is
far more pleased with my success than I am.[24]

Early in the winter Julia had scarlet fever, which left her
thin and pale, but the months in town restored her spirits. When
the Howes returned to Green Peace in the spring, Julia was
unusually calm and happy, but she still tired easily and Chev
continued to indulge her with the gift of a carriage, a pair of
horses and a season ticket to the opera. Uncle John sent her $350
to buy herself a grand piano, so she resumed her playing and
singing, and Chev built her a little summerhouse in the apple
orchard where she could retire peacefully with her books.[25] He
spoke to her more and seemed more interested in what she was
thinking and doing. She assured Louisa that her mind was clearer
than it had ever been since her marriage. "I am able to think, to
study and to pray, things which I cannot accomplish when my
brain is oppressed." Chev was, for the time being at least, "the
most indulgent of husbands," but she feared that "Uncle John
was right about me, when he said that I ought not to marry —
every one else, instead of helping me on in my vocation tried to
turn me aside from it, and I was fool enough to believe that the
advice of others was better than the instinct of my own heart, so
you see, I have spoiled a good student, to make a most indifferent
wife. The longer I live, the more do I feel my utter childlike
helplessness about all practical affairs."[26]

Why had Chev suddenly become so attentive? Part of the
explanation was surely Julia's illness. Perhaps, too, he felt guilty
for his neglect of her during the arduous months of his term on
the School Committee and during the period of complete physical
collapse that followed. Moreover, the fact that Julia had not been
pregnant for almost two years made her more cheerful and con-
siderate of his feelings. Throughout their married life there
would be these moments when they seemed the happiest of
couples. Julia relied on Chev, not only for comfort and affection,

but also for friendship and understanding. Chev depended on Julia more than he realized. When she left him for short periods to visit Annie in Bordentown or her uncles in New York he always missed her keenly and was delighted when she came home. But he easily became impatient with Julia's dependence on him, little realizing that she had no one else. A letter, written about this time, explains Julia's views of the difficulties of their relationship. Chev was constantly worried that Julia was keeping things from him and yet so often when she tried to tell him something on her mind he appeared not to be interested. One day she simply sat down and wrote him a letter:

> From you dear husband, I would have no secrets — if I have not told you everything and shown you everything, it is not because I have not the disposition, but because you have made me feel that, in spite of all your kindness, you could not take much interest in my spiritual experience, such as it has been. . . . These three years of married life have wiped out, as with a sponge, all living memory of the past — I have gone with you into a new world, and am become in many things a new creature, and, I think, a better and happier one. I firmly resolved when I married you, to admit no thought, to cultivate no taste, in which you could not sympathize — you *must know* that my heart has been very loyal. It was long before I realized that you neither desired, nor appreciated this renunciation on my part. . . . I will not expect too much from you. I will enjoy the moments of sunshine which we can enjoy together . . . to comfort me in those long, cold wintry days, when I feel you do not love me.[27]

Julia's short happy year ended in September 1847, when she discovered she was once more pregnant. At first she cried and raved about it. Again, the fear of death in childbirth haunted her, and again she fell into a black depression. Chev was little comfort to her in these times. He considered her anxieties mere foolishness and would react to them by neglecting her more than ever. She came to dread each pregnancy as much for the strain it put on their relationship as for the fears in her own mind. It was shortly before the birth of one of her children that she wrote Annie: "When the unwelcome little unborn shall have seen the light my brain will be lightened, and I shall have a clearer mind. The time wears on — thank God that even this weary nine months shall come to an end, and leave me in possession of my own body and my own soul."[28]

Julia's unhappiness over her third pregnancy was soon overshadowed by more troubles over her trust money. Difficulties had been mounting between the partners of Prime Ward & King. Sam Ward, always anxious to make as much money as possible as fast as possible, had been speculating with the firm's capital, thereby so outraging his father's old partner, James Gore King, that the latter resigned his partnership in December 1846. Renamed Prime Ward & Company, the newly aligned firm appeared to prosper for a time, but the crash of September 1847 revealed the unsoundness of Sam's banking methods and Prime Ward & Company went bankrupt. Sam immediately resigned his trusteeship of Julia's estate, and Chev hurried to New York to claim control over her fortune. Being mainly invested in real estate, it had hardly been affected by the crash. Julia owned property all over the city: uptown on Fifty-eighth and Sixtieth streets, downtown on Exchange Place, Beaver and Pearl streets and Maiden Lane, plus a big stretch of land west of Eighth Avenue. Besides all this she shared other properties jointly with her brothers and sisters. The remainder of this considerable fortune was in stocks, bonds, securities and mortgages. Unwilling to believe that New York would develop as far north as the sixties, Chev sold all of Julia's New York properties and invested the proceeds in South Boston real estate, which eventually proved to be a total loss.[29]

Later that fall came news of the death of Marion Ward,

Julia's younger brother. For some years he had been Prime Ward & Company's representative in New Orleans and had shown great promise as a banker. His death was a blow to all the Wards, but especially to Sam, who had looked to him for advice and support. Julia went to New York as soon as she could get away and found her Uncle John "in great agony and depression of mind . . . poverty is little to him, but bankruptcy looks hideous and frightful."[30] Sam was in an even greater state of distress. His second wife Medora, the beautiful but spoiled southerner from New Orleans, could not bear the prospect of poverty and so had left him to go home to her mother. Sam's only income now was the rent he received from the Bond Street house.

Julia's studies became her only comfort during the long winter of 1848. There was little gaiety that season, even though the Howes rented a house on Beacon Hill. Julia complained to Annie that she had been to only three parties and that Tom Appleton, Longfellow's brother-in-law, was "the only cheering vision that enlivens the gloomy streets — he flits about throwing fireballs of wit to charm one's frozen fancy."[31] All the other Bostonians had apparently retreated behind the closed doors of their brick mansions with the excuse that they were recovering from the financial panic of the autumn before.

Julia, however, could not suppress her natural gregariousness and that winter she organized the first of the innumerable women's clubs she was destined to found during the course of her long lifetime. She told Annie about it. "We are getting up a club of ladies, called the Crochet Party, which is to meet once a fortnight for crochet and fun."[32] At the same time Julia kept at her studies. Devoting most of her time to learning Latin and Hebrew, she was also developing a lifelong interest in philosophy through reading Swedenborg. She continued to write poetry, and in 1849 seven of her pieces appeared in Rufus Griswold's *Female Poets of America,* which also contained one poem by her mother.

The great comfort Julia continued to find in religion is

constantly reflected in her poetry and in her letters to her sisters. "While your life is the true expression of your faith, whom can you fear?"[33] she wrote Annie in an effort to persuade her sister not to be frightened by Uncle John's efforts to keep her a good Calvinist. Julia now thought of herself as a liberal Christian. Having rejected the exclusive doctrine that "made Christianity and special forms of it the only way of spiritual redemption," she now accepted the belief that not only Christians but all human beings, no matter what their religion, were capable of redemption. Christianity was but one of God's plans for bringing all of humanity to a state of ultimate perfection.[34]

By the winter of 1846 Julia was a regular attendant at Theodore Parker's rather unorthodox services held weekly in the old Melodeon. People poured into this great ugly building on Washington Street from all over the city of Boston. No less than seven thousand persons considered themselves members of Parker's parish and most of them were humble men and women. Some had never belonged to any church before; others had left more orthodox parishes to join this radical minister who had the courage to criticize the rich.[35] It was Parker's preaching that drew the enormous crowds. As Julia told Horace Mann, "To give up Parker's ministry for any other would be like going to the synagogue when Paul was preaching near at hand."[36]

When Julia was newly married she wrote down a classification of her enjoyments:

> I had rather hear Theodore Parker than go to the theater.
> I had rather go to the theater than to a party.
> I had rather go to a party than stay at home.[37]

Julia wrote this when she was newly married, and later as an elderly lady she explained the attraction of these sermons. Parker seemed "to hold in solution, as it were, the agonies and aspirations of human society. His preaching, like that of Henry Ward

Beecher, moved now to tears now to laughter. Yet one left his presence with a heart solemnized and uplifted."[38]

Intoxicated as Julia was by Parker's sermons she was never quite able to accept his denial of the divinity of Christ. Not until the Civil War did she officially join a Unitarian church and reluctantly accept the fact that Christ was merely a great teacher with no higher claim to preeminence in wisdom, goodness and power than many other great men.

As the Howe children became old enough to attend church, Chev felt strongly that the irregularities of Parker's services were unsuitable for them. The atmosphere of the old Melodeon was indeed very informal. There was a constant coming and going, and people even read their newspapers while waiting for the sermon to begin. Chev himself apparently went to church rarely, preferring, as he once said, to pray with "his hands and his feet."[39] But he told Julia sometime in the late 1840's or early '50's that "the children are now of an age at which they should receive impressions of reverence, they should, therefore, see nothing at the Sunday service which would militate against that feeling."[40] Julia reluctantly complied and took herself and the children to Williams Hall to attend the services conducted by James Freeman Clarke. Clarke was a Christian transcendentalist and more of an institutionalist than Parker, with whom nonetheless he sympathized enough to offer him a place to preach when Parker was first removed from his parish in West Roxbury. Although Clarke would in time become a very close friend of Julia's, she minded horribly having to miss Parker's sermons, and some Sundays, when the weather was inclement and the children stayed at home she would sneak back to the Melodeon to hear him. If Chev disapproved of Julia's taking the children to hear Parker preach, Beacon Street apparently disapproved of her going there at all. Julia later remembered that one of her friends inquired of another in her presence, "What is Julia Howe trying to

בֿא

find at Parker's meeting?" "Atheism" was the reply, to which Julia retorted, "Not atheism, but a theism."[41]

In fact, Parker was one of the few close friends Julia had in Boston. He was as busy a man as Chev but somehow he and Julia managed to find time to discuss the books Julia was reading and the poems she was writing, matters Chev took no interest in. The Howes were frequent visitors at the Parkers' house in Exeter Place. There every Sunday evening a varied group of visitors assembled. Some were old friends — Sumner, Elizabeth Peabody, the Horace Manns — but there were new people for Julia to meet also: for one, Ednah Cheney, the crusader for women's rights, and for another, Thomas Wentworth Higginson, the Unitarian minister and reformer who like Julia would live on into the new world of the twentieth century. Some of those who came to the Parkers' Sunday evenings were people whom Julia would just as happily have avoided. Her image of William Lloyd Garrison, the abolitionist, for example, was that of a cranky fanatic. She dreaded meeting him as she had dreaded her first sight of Emerson. But one evening in Exeter Place she found herself singing side by side with Garrison and was amazed at herself for having regarded this gentle and unassuming person with such distaste.[42]

Slowly Julia was being won over by this totally new society into which her marriage had plunged her, and Beacon Street was looking askance at the charming Miss Ward now that she was the wife of a reformer. Beacon Street didn't like reformers. It didn't like to be criticized and asked to change its ways. Julia was beginning to discover that proper Bostonians were dull and cold and she rather enjoyed horrifying them with her sharp wit and radical ideas, both of which were considered unsuitable for a young matron of good family. By the 1850's she was coming to look on Beacon Street society as part of "cold roast Boston."

6

Passion Flowers

To make one half the human race consume its energies in the functions of housekeeper, wife and mother is a monstrous waste of the most precious material God ever made.
— Theodore Parker, 1853

By the time the 1840's were drawing to a close Julia had given birth to three children and was expecting a fourth. The third child, a boy, had arrived on March 2, 1848. Named Henry Marion after his mother's two brothers he was a placid, gentle baby and a joy to both his parents. Chev, delighted that he at last had a son, entered the child's birth in the family Bible, writing after his name, "Dieu Donné!"[1] By the late spring of 1849, after a little over a year's respite, Julia was pregnant once again. She wrote Annie that she felt so dull and cross that neither music nor poetry had any place in her life at the moment. She described herself as being "intent mainly upon holding on to the ropes, and upon getting through the present without too much consciousness of it."[2] Laura Elizabeth Howe was born at the end of February 1850, and within six weeks of her birth she was traveling with her mother to Bordentown to be introduced to her Aunt Annie.

Annie's husband, Adolphe Mailliard, was a Bonaparte.[3] His father had been the natural son of Napoleon's elder brother,

Joseph Bonaparte, who had been king of Naples and then of Spain. Adolphe had come to the United States with his cousin, Prince Joseph, to consult his old friend Sam Ward about the investments held by the late King Joseph in the United States. It was at her brother Sam's that Annie had met the handsome, chivalrous Frenchman. Annie herself was shy and timid but she spoke French beautifully and was a good listener, two accomplishments that endeared her to Adolphe immediately. They had married in June 1846, and were now living near Point Breeze, King Joseph's old palace in Bordentown. Having been handed Annie's inheritance by her Ward uncles without any fuss, Adolphe proceeded to sell a good part of it to buy a house for his wife. Spring Villa had been a boardinghouse for young ladies, but Adolphe transformed it into an elegant mansion surrounded by acres of garden. He was a man who liked to live well.

From Annie's point of view Spring Villa had the great advantage of being big enough to accommodate a large number of her relatives. Every spring Julia looked forward to the month or so she spent there, and this year their brother Sam and Louisa and her family would be there as well. Not only did Julia enjoy the contrast between Spring Villa and her own relatively cramped house in Boston, but she relished the quiet moments when she could be alone with Annie and pour out all her troubles into Annie's willing ear. Julia always came home to Green Peace comforted by her visit.

Chev accompanied Julia as far as Bordentown. He then went on to Washington, leaving his wife unrestricted in her enjoyment of a happy family reunion. Chev had no particular desire to linger with his in-laws. He regarded Sam as a ne'er-do-well and could hardly bear to be in the same room with him. He apparently got along reasonably well with Adolphe Mailliard, although the two had little in common. But Thomas Crawford and Chev had, in recent years, developed a mutual antipathy. The two were alike in many ways. Each had a will of his own and a temper that flared easily. Crawford resented Howe's determination to rule other people's lives and felt, perhaps quite rightly, that he was too hard on Julia.[4]

But despite the unfriendly relations between Chev and his in-laws, the reunion was a happy one for the three Ward sisters. They had not been together since the summer of 1846 and there was much to talk about. Brother Sam made frequent trips to Bordentown from New York while his sisters were together. Armed with presents for mothers and children he regaled them all with an endless stream of jokes and stories, songs and laughter. As the three sisters sat around the fire each evening they began to make plans for a trip to Europe. Louisa and her husband had just acquired an old palace in Rome and she longed to have her sisters come and stay. For Julia the thought of returning to Europe after six years of isolation in Boston was very tempting and she broached the idea to Chev on her return. Chev, who had been bored and restless in Rome, was not very anxious to go back but he perhaps understood that Julia needed the change and agreed to a compromise: he would accompany her to England and part of the way across the continent; then he would return to Boston while she went on to Italy.

Julia reached Rome with the two youngest children, Harry and Laura, in September 1850. The two eldest, Julia and Flossy, had been left with friends of the Howes in Boston to await their father's return. Once in Rome, Julia decided that rather than move into the Villa Negroni with the Crawfords, she would rent an apartment of her own. She found a very pleasant one with a large enough parlor to hold a grand piano. A donkey brought her sufficient firewood to last through the short Roman winter.[5] For the most part her days passed peacefully and quietly, but compared to South Boston, a winter in Rome offered endless little pleasures. Wishing to continue her study of Hebrew, she was happy to find "a learned rabbi from the Ghetto" who was willing to give her lessons.[6] He would appear at her apartment attired in the black robe required of all Jews in Rome, and if he came in the afternoon he would sometimes slip away early in order to be behind the ghetto walls by six.[7]

When Julia was not studying or caring for her two babies (Harry was then two and Laura less than a year old) she found many pleasant distractions to fill her days. She discovered that she had congenial neighbors, among them the artist Edward Freeman and his wife. "Our little colony was very harmonious," she later recalled, and she particularly enjoyed the company of Mrs. Freeman, with whom she would go on long walks around the city.[8] Annie Mailliard had also come to Rome to stay at the Villa Negroni with the Crawfords, and thus the three sisters found themselves once more united. On warm winter afternoons they would take a drive together on the Campagna; in the evening there were occasional balls or a box at the opera.

By the time Julia arrived in Rome, the abortive republican revolution of 1848–1849 had come and gone. Faith in the unifying powers of the papacy under the initial liberalism of Pius IX had quickly faded when the pope failed to lend his support to the revolutionary cause, and he was forced to flee to Naples. For a few short months Rome was a democratic republic, but in July 1849 French troops brought about the downfall of the new government, and the pope came back. The republican dream was all but dead. It was natural that Julia, married to a hero of the Greek revolution, should be sympathetic to the cause of Italian independence. She knew all about what had taken place in Rome during the last two years, for Thomas Crawford had played an active part as a member of the civic guard of the Republic.[9] But to Julia's eyes things appeared much the same as they had been six years before. The Italians she met seemed unwilling to talk of what had happened. Only occasionally, in the privacy of a tête-à-tête, would she get glimpses of how they felt about the failure of the republican revolution. When she asked an Italian acquaintance why Pope Pius had so suddenly forsaken his earlier liberal policy, she was told that he was merely "a puppet moved from without,"[10] and she found others who expressed their resentment at the power of the French behind the Papacy.

When alone among British and American friends, Julia defended the cause of Italian independence. The arguments were often lively, and after one such discussion the host or hostess, perhaps wishing to divert the talk to a subject less controversial, asked Julia to entertain the party with some music. Many years later she described the incident. "Seating myself at the piano, I made it ring out the Marseillaise with a will. But I was myself too much disconcerted by the recent failure to find in my thoughts any promise of better things. My friends said, "The Italians are not fit for self-government." I may ask fifty years later, 'Who is?' "[11]

At Christmastime the Crawfords gave a large party complete with Christmas tree, a novelty then unheard of in Rome, and Julia was asked to play for the dancing. At the party she met an old acquaintance, Horace Binney Wallace of Philadelphia. A brilliant young lawyer who wrote morbid and violent stories under the pseudonym William Landor, Wallace was outwardly charming and had impeccable manners. But his rather cool exterior concealed a tortured mind obsessed with thoughts of death and fears of insanity.[12] To people he knew and liked he was extremely cordial and open, and he was particularly fond of encouraging young authors. So it was not surprising that he took an immediate interest in the intense and obviously gifted Julia. For her part, she was immediately drawn to him. The fact that they were both redheaded seemed to be another bond. Every morning he would walk over from his rooms on the Via Felice, stopping on the way to buy Julia a nosegay of violets, and together they would wander all over the city. There were expeditions to the Pantheon, the Tarpeian Rock and Horatius' bridge, and all the while the two would discuss poetry and philosophy.[13] Wallace was a great admirer of Auguste Comte, and did his best to convert Julia to Comte's particular brand of positivism. At the same time he was invaluable to her as a critic of her own verses. Not since her girlhood in New York had Julia had so much sympathy and encouragement as well as much-needed criticism, and she would look back on her friendship with Wallace as having above all given her the self-confidence to work toward the eventual publication of a volume of her poetry.

Yet though she was coming to love the city, Julia realized that she could not stay in Rome forever. The inevitable return to America had to be faced. In her *Reminiscences,* written some fifty years later, she recalled her anguish at having to leave after having been caught up in the "subtle fascination of Roman life."[14] Fanny Longfellow, who had known her for years and who had heard something about the gay life Julia was leading in Rome, was concerned about her readjustment to life in South Boston. "I hear she was much admired," Fanny wrote a cousin shortly after Julia's return to America, "and her soirées much courted. With her many resources of languages, music, and clever conversation, I can imagine how attractive she must have made them, where people really *love* society, which they cannot be said to do in America — for its own sake. How dull she will probably find it in South Boston, for she is not to be satisfied with the society of husband and children, and a social nature like hers really requires more not to consume itself."[15]

More important, perhaps, than the simple contrast between Rome and South Boston was Julia's dread of returning to life with Chev. It was not that she did not love him, but there were times when her fear of him was greater than her love. She dreaded his moods, particularly the long stretches when he turned cold and remote and hardly seemed to notice her. She dreaded as well his criticisms of her sloppy housekeeping and his disapproval of her literary aspirations.

But return home she must and in early June of 1851 she set off across the Alps to begin her journey to Boston. In London she spent a number of pleasant hours with a man she had met two years earlier in America, and whom she had described to Annie as "the most agreeable John Bull I have seen this many a day."[16] Edward Twistleton was a learned London barrister who shared Julia's interests in poetry and philosophy and did much to encourage her literary efforts. Like Wallace he gave her the kind of encouragement she needed, and she felt her stay would be far too short. "I should like to find out how Joshua contrived to make the sun stand still," she had written him from Rome. "So should my two days in London be each a week long, and include Panoramas, libraries, Anthems in Westminster Abbey, an evening at the French plays, and a quiet cup of tea at my ancient lodgings in Gower Street, seasoned with endless philosophic dissertations."[17]

The voyage home across the Atlantic lasted a month, long enough for Julia to prepare herself for the difficult time she knew lay ahead. Much of what she was thinking she put into verse. Later the poems would be published in a small volume called *Passion Flowers*. In some of these verses there are glimpses of the quiet pleasures she had enjoyed during her winter of independence:

> *I knew a day of glad surprise in Rome*
> *Free to the childish joy of wandering,*
> *Without a 'wherefore' or 'to what good end?'*
> *By querulous voice propounded, or a thought*
> *Of punctual duty, waiting at the door*
> *Of home, with weapon duly poised to slay*
> *Delight ere it across the threshold bound. . . .*
>
> *The winter, like a college boy's vacation,*
> *Seemed endless to anticipate, and lay*
> *Stretched in a boundless glittering before me. . . .*
> *I felt my life so calm and deep*
> *Such rapture, settling to such peace.*

Yet alternating with this feeling of having been refreshed was a dread of what lay ahead and a knowledge that her brief months of independence were over:

> *The gate is closed — the air without is drear.*
> *Look back! the dome! gorgeous in the sunset still —*
> *I see it — soul is concentrate in sight —*
> *The dome is gone — gone seems the heaven with it.*
> *Night hides my sorrow from me. Oh my Rome,*
> *As I have loved thee, rest God's love with thee!*[18]

While Julia had been in Rome, Chev had hardly had time to miss her. Every hour of his day was taken up with one cause or another. Among these, the antislavery movement had now become the most important. Back in 1846 the kidnapping of a fugitive slave named Joe had brought Howe solidly into the abolitionist camp. Joe had tried to escape from his ship, which was anchored in Boston Harbor, but he was caught onshore and was returned to his master. Sam Howe's reaction to the "kidnapping" was immediate. Outraged, he and other antislavery members of the Whig party called a protest meeting on the night of September 24. Faneuil Hall was packed with angry Bostonians. Charles Sumner, Theodore Parker and Wendell Phillips all spoke, but Howe gave the major address. He admitted that he had now lost all faith in the ability or desire of the South to rid itself of slavery. The time had come, he said, to take action and prevent similar outrages. It was decided that night that a vigilance committee should be appointed to prevent any further capture of slaves. Howe was elected chairman, and from that moment was counted among the leaders of the antislavery wing of the Whig party.[19]

Howe was particularly disturbed by the passage of the Fugitive Slave Act, a harsh measure that authorized federal commissioners to arrest alleged fugitives and return them to their masters after a summary hearing. Part of the Compromise of 1850, the law had been passed while Chev was still in Europe, and its first effects were being felt in Boston in the days just after his return. On an evening in late October, Theodore Parker, returning from a trip to Plymouth, found Howe waiting impatiently in his parlor. The Vigilance Committee must meet at once; there were slave catchers in town tracking down two fugitives, Ellen and William Craft. The committee met promptly, decided to find the Crafts a safe hiding place, and then to scare the kidnappers out of town. The committee marched sixty strong to the hotel where the slave hunters were staying, forced the landlord to call his guests down to the lobby, and told the frightened group to get out of town before evening. By midafternoon the slave catchers were on the New York train, glad to be out of Boston and away from the angry crowds and the jeers of "Slave hunters, slave hunters, there go the slave hunters!"[20]

It was a year after the rescue of the Crafts that Julia returned to Boston. She wrote her sister Annie as soon as she had a moment to sit at her desk:

> After a very dusty and dirty journey, I arrived at Green Peace at six o'clock, on Saturday evening — two children whom I should not have recognized for mine ran out to meet me, and after some little show of shyness hugged me heartily. . . . Chev was and is, very kind, and seems to wish to make me happy. At first I was quite overpowered at the newness of my position, after so different a life, but I already begin to feel at home, and think that I shall be able to satisfy myself here."[21]

Julia and Flossy were indeed glad to see their mother. They would never really understand why she had left them for so long. The months their father had been gone had seemed dreary enough, as the couple they lived with, a Dr. Jarvis and his wife, ran a school for "idiot children" in their own house.[22] Once Chev returned home the girls came happily back to Green Peace, but they saw little enough of him even then. Julia told Annie that she was worried by her daughters' rough manners. They whined, lacked discipline, and were generally suffering from neglect.[23] Now that she was home she would have to see to it that they received more attention.

Life seemed very quiet at Green Peace, and for a few months Julia was happy, enjoying the companionship of her children and the challenge of her studies. It began to seem as though she had never been away. Chev, who had a penchant for firing the housemaid, the nursemaid or even the cook whenever Julia left home, had this time taken the trouble to provide her with a housekeeper, so that, for a time at least, she was "delivered from all the useless contentions with servants."[24] A brief visit from Edward Twistleton, soon after her return, meant several happy evenings passed in his company, but by early November a sad note was creeping into Julia's letters to her sisters. Chev, as usual, was hardly ever at home. He was either at the institute or occupied with Free Soil activities, and when he did appear he was cranky and critical now that he was used to having Julia back again. Besides abolition, Chev was championing the cause of temperance, and Julia, perhaps forgetting her own strictures against wine at The Corner, complained to Annie that she was no longer allowed to serve any wine at dinner parties. She might as well give up the idea of having people entirely since "it is better not to entertain at all, than to entertain badly."[25]

If Chev was once more his old demanding self perhaps Julia was failing in her resolutions to make every effort to be an obedient wife and conscientious mother. Her year abroad had intensified her need for independence and her desire to realize her talents. Having been encouraged by such friends as Wallace and Twistleton to pursue her studies and literary efforts she was determined to continue both. Back home she knew she had the support of Theodore Parker, who had written her in Rome urging her to "do something in the way of literature" and not fritter her time away by indulging too much in society. "You have not only talent in literature but *genius*," he assured her, and "it need not interfere with housekeeping — a disagreeable thing no doubt but rather necessary to the healthful development of woman in America."[26] Settled once more into the monotonous and lonely routine of life at Green Peace, Julia found her only sources of comfort in writing, books and religion. She wrote Annie on November 25 that Chev was so silent and reserved "I take refuge in my books and do not molest him with my overflowing sympathies . . . I find society most uninteresting after that of Rome — my books are now the only things for me."[27]

To add to Julia's misery that fall, in November the Howe children's beloved nurse died of consumption. Lizzie had been a great comfort to Julia during the long empty days. She had kept the children happy, amusing them with jokes and stories, and in the afternoon when Julia would sometimes seat herself at the piano and sing, Lizzie would sit by her, mending the children's clothes and listening, enraptured, to the sound of her mistress's voice. Lizzie was always happy and cheerful, and her presence alone was a comfort as she

> *Flitted like sunshine, in and out*
> *Among my little ones and me.*[28]

The monotony of Julia's life was broken in the spring of 1852, when Boston gave a rousing reception to Louis Kossuth, the exiled leader of the Hungarian revolution of 1848. The Howes arranged a big dinner for the Kossuths and Longfellow noted that the hero was rather silent at table, "like a man fatigued."[29] But Julia was very impressed with him. She heard three of the speeches he gave in the course of his stay in Boston and wrote Annie that "he is deeper, greater, and better than I had even supposed him to be."[30]

The summer after the Kossuths' visit the Howes went to Newport for the months of July and August. The old Ward cottage had long since been sold, so Julia and Chev shared a rented house with the Longfellows. Boston was beginning to "discover" Newport as a quiet, unostentatious place in which to spend a summer by the sea. Besides the Howes and Longfellows there were the George William Curtises, George Bancroft and his wife, as well as Tom Appleton and Charles Sumner. Fanny Longfellow remarked that Julia Howe was a great addition to their circle and described her as being "so full of spirits and every variety of talent, her wit rouses us all out of the languor this climate induces, and her singing (greatly improved in Italy) is a perpetual delight."[31] According to Henry Longfellow, Julia's social graces gave the Newport house so much the atmosphere of a European salon that it came to be referred to as the "Hôtel de Rambouillet."[32] Julia for her part was delighted to be back in Newport's balmy climate. Unlike Fanny Longfellow she found the air refreshing rather than languorous. "It agrees with me perfectly." she once wrote Annie. Even Chev seemed to enjoy himself. He must have realized how much a summer in Newport had restored his wife's spirits, for late in August he bought a summer place called Lawton's Valley in nearby Portsmouth.

The Longfellows and Howes left Newport early in September and Julia returned to Green Peace and the routine of her studies and occasional housekeeping. For all her dread of returning to South Boston, there were things she was happy to get back to. She still listened with admiration to the sermons of Theodore Parker, and she was at the Melodeon on that Sunday late in November 1852, a few days after the death of Daniel Webster, when Parker seized on the occasion to give one of his greatest sermons. He spoke for over an hour, and respectable Boston was shocked that a minister would use the pulpit to attack a public figure who had been one of New England's idols, and desecrate a place of worship with political oratory. Into his sermon Parker poured all his idealism, all his love of freedom, all his hatred of slavery. Parker loved Webster, but he deplored what he called Webster's stooping low to supplicate the South:

> Do men now mourn for him, the great man eloquent? I put on sackcloth long ago. . . . I mourned when he spoke the speech of the 7th of March. I mourned when the Fugitive Slave Bill passed Congress, and the same cannons which have just fired minute-guns for him fired also one hundred rounds of joy at the forging of a new fetter for the fugitive's foot. . . . O Webster! Webster! would God that I had died for thee![33]

Julia came home for dinner late that day and begged the family to forgive her. "Let no one find fault," she implored them. "I have just heard the greatest thing I shall ever hear!"[34]

Parker was one of the few people in Boston Julia could talk to. His influence on her during the last decade of his life was very great indeed. Their admiration was mutual, and just as Julia's most intimate friends were likely to be men, Parker preferred the company of women. Margaret Fuller had been too strong-minded for him but Julia Howe was poetic and feminine. He appreciated the subtlety of her mind and enjoyed talking to her about philosophy.[35] It would be Parker's influence as much as anyone's that would eventually guide Julia's literary ambitions in a socially useful direction. He encouraged her to teach as well as study, and when shortly before his death in 1859, she spoke to him of her desire to preach, he found this entirely natural. As she recalled later on, he considered it in accordance with

> the spirit of the age, which, he said, "called for the living presence and the living utterance." I did not act at once, or even very soon, upon this prompting; the difficulties to overcome were many. My husband was himself averse to public appearances. Women speakers were few in those days, and

113

were frowned upon by general society. He would have been doubly sensitive to such undesirable publicity on my account.[36]

Nevertheless, during the winter of 1852–1853 Julia had an opportunity to appear in print with Chev's full consent. For a few months he took over the management of the *Commonwealth,* a Free Soil journal of which he was already a trustee. Julia helped him with the editorial work and every week wrote several critical or literary pieces.[37] Chev had both their desks moved into the large dining room at Green Peace, and every morning he would write an article or two before going to the institute. Julia found more time to work on her contributions but she quickly discovered that writing under pressure was hard work. It was good experience even so, and Chev seemed to appreciate her efforts.[38] The *Commonwealth* was not the success the Howes had hoped it would be, however, and late in the spring lack of funds forced them to give up the enterprise.

That winter they did not rent a house in town but spent the long cold months isolated in South Boston. Julia brooded over the "frozen ocean of Boston life" and as early as December 3 wrote Annie that "the season has, so far, been much less comfortable (mentally) than usual, great fault is found with everything I do, and very little account is made of my comfort and pleasure. I cannot remember any period, even in my worst days, in which my nerves have been so completely worn down. I enjoy one thing, the morning undisturbed in my room."[39] Since returning from Rome she had dropped the reading of Swedenborg in favor of Comte, having been encouraged by Horace Binney Wallace to broaden her philosophical studies. The long morning hours of hard intellectual labor seemed to have an extraordinarily soothing effect on her, and when she felt an attack of depression coming over her she would cram herself with "Philosophic positive" and succeed in quieting the "nervous agitation entirely."[40] Having finished her seven or eight pages of philosophy she would turn to writing poetry, for she was still determined to bring out a small volume of verse, and as soon as possible.

She had hoped for considerable help and advice from Wallace, but in February 1853 she received the terrible news that he had killed himself in Paris. Wallace had been suffering from severe "nervous complaints" and presumably took his life out of fear that he was going mad. Julia had only just written him a long letter in which she spoke of looking forward to his approaching visit to New York:

> I miss you so much, and life is so short, and friendship so precious — ah me! . . . I have been laborious ever since we last exchanged letters, have nearly finished the second volume of Comte, read much of Dante, and have completed two long, headache-compelling poems. . . . Horace, these poems lose half their worth to me, for want of your criticism. I depend much upon it — your severity of taste has already helped me to write far better than I could have written without it. . . . Far greater is my need of you as a friend. I have been leading a very lonely and unsympathetic life ever since I came from Newport. I need to be practically reminded that Love is the Religion of Life, and who can bring us back to its standard, if it be not one who is dear to us.

She pleaded with him to write her from Paris. "I am too lonely, too helpless, too orphaned to be deserted by you, my brother."[41]

Before the letter was mailed news reached Julia of Wallace's death, leaving her more broken-hearted than she had been since she had lost her brother Henry. "We were very sympathetic to each other," she wrote Louisa. "He helped me to my best thoughts."[42] Steeped in misery and self-pity Julia, surely for the only time in her life, sought comfort from someone she did not know, but whose works had come to mean much to her. She proceeded to write a long letter to Auguste Comte, the man whom Wallace had most admired, and indeed the letter might have been written to Horace. To Comte, she poured out all the miseries of her soul, hoping that he would be as sympathetic as his disciple had been. She described herself to him as a woman with a very emotional temperament: "Je souffre et suis heureuse à l'excès." She complained that she had no woman friends and had trouble getting along with her children. She spoke of the dreariness of life in America after Rome and of the difficulty she had readjusting to life in South Boston. Her studies, she told him, had provided the only consolation and she credited Comte himself, whom she had recently been reading, with having made her sad little life happy. Would he help her to direct her studies and cultivate her talents?[43]

There is no record that Comte ever answered Julia's letter or that she ever wrote him another. The day after she mailed hers she wrote to Annie about it and begged her to tell no one. "I am so wretched today that you alone can comfort me."[44]

Sam was the only member of Julia's family to whom she could have turned but she saw little of him in these years. Her brother's fortunes had taken yet another plunge since her return from Europe. Having lost nearly everything in the crash of 1847 he had gone to San Francisco and in less than a year was once more a rich man. True to form, his prosperity was short-lived. After a few months in New York, the new fortune disappeared as fast as it had come and Sam found himself once more in California, this time in the hills prospecting for gold. For the next eight years his finances rose and fell, but mostly fell, as he moved restlessly about the world. Apart from two reunions in Lawton's Valley, the Howes' new summer place in Portsmouth, and occasional letters there was little opportunity for Sam to give his sister the kind of support she needed.

Nor did Julia have any close women friends who could give her the stimulus and encouragement she so yearned for. She still saw Mary Ward (now Mrs. Dorr) but the two were no longer close. Julia had to rely on the few sympathetic men she knew and they were fairly inaccessible. Twistleton was in London. Parker was as busy as Chev and she saw him only occasionally; in Rome she had seen Wallace nearly every day. She could write to Twistleton, however, and she did, hoping that he would help her find a publisher for her poems in England. But her letters often failed to reach him and in the end it was through her own efforts that a small volume of her verses was printed.

With the coming of spring, Julia's spirits rose. There was the annual trip to Bordentown to visit Annie. In May she and Chev nearly always gave a party for the children, and it was invariably a great success. Laura and Maud, the youngest of the Howe girls, later recalled that the parties at Green Peace were such "as no other children ever had."[45] At four o'clock on the appointed afternoon omnibus loads of children and adults would arrive at Green Peace. There would be donkey rides, a bowling alley, and best of all a play: "Blue Beard" or "The Rose and the Ring" or perhaps a skit written by Julia for the occasion. The Longfellows were usually among the guests and always enjoyed themselves thoroughly. "Howe has so much sympathy with children that he manages such matters admirably well," Longfellow noted in his diary after one such affair.[46] Julia's part in planning these amusements seems to have escaped him.

In July 1853, Julia moved down to Portsmouth, Rhode Island, with the children to spend the first of many summers at Lawton's Valley, the little place Chev had bought the year before. Dismayed at first by the dilapidated condition of the house and its remoteness from the town of Newport, Julia had tried to persuade Chev to sell it. It was so like her husband to choose a house so far from the center of things and so small that she could not see how they were all going to fit in it. But Chev, unlike his wife, saw that the place had possibilities and quickly went to work enlarging the house and transforming the underbrush surrounding it into a garden. Several hundred yards below the old cottage was a valley or ravine, "rock-walled, with trees clinging wherever they could; at one side a swift little stream, brown and bright, breaking in foam over ledges."[47] Chev turned the open space by the ravine into a lawn and planted it with Norway spruces. Close by, under a towering ash tree, an inviting group of chairs and tables had been placed. Here Julia loved to sit quietly reading or enjoying the company of friends, who often drove the five miles out from Newport to pay a call on fine afternoons. Julia quickly grew to love Lawton's Valley and enjoy the simplicity of life there, where so much time was spent out of doors.

Julia occupied a good part of that summer in working on the poems she hoped to publish, and on her return to Boston in October, one of the first things she did was to take her manuscript into the Old Corner Bookstore, the office of the famous Boston publishers Ticknor, Reed & Fields. She was extremely nervous about the outcome of this venture, but James T. Fields liked the poems very much and agreed to their immediate publication. By the middle of November Julia was deep in proofs and very much enjoying her frequent meetings with Fields, a charming man, much respected among New England authors for his business tact, sympathy and humor.[48] Later Julia and Fields would not get along so well, but for this first book of poems the relationship between author and publisher was smooth and easy. Fields assured her that the poems would sell well but she hardly dared believe him. "I feel much excited, quite unsettled, sometimes a little frantic," she told Annie, "If I succeed, I feel that I shall be humbled by my happiness, devoutly thankful to God."[49]

Chev knew nothing of the poems and Julia did not dare tell him of their imminent publication, knowing how angry he would surely be. Fields had wanted her to publish them under her own name but she dared not do that and they came out anonymously. On December 29 she wrote Annie an ecstatic letter:

> My book came out, darling, on Friday last. You have it, I
> hope, ere this time. The title simply, *Passion Flowers*, was

invented by Sherb* and approved by Longfellow. Its success became certain at once. Hundreds of copies have already been sold and everyone likes it. Fields foretells a second edition — it is sure to pay for itself. It has done more for me, in point of consideration here, than a fortune of a hundred thousand dollars. Parker quoted seven of my verses in his Xmas sermon, and this I considered as the greatest of honours. I sat there and heard them, glowing all over. One bitter drop poisoned all this. Chev took it *very* hard. He is now consoled by its success and behaves very well indeed. The authorship is, of course, no secret now, and you had best talk openly of it all of you, as it may help the sale of the book in N.Y.[50]

The book was indeed a success and Julia eventually made two hundred dollars from the sales, enough to furnish the little house in Lawton's Valley. Tributes poured in from friends. Emerson wrote from Concord that the book had given him much pleasure, "because, I fancy, that among all your friends few had so earnest a desire to know your thought. . . . And the book as I read in it meets this curiosity of mine by its poems of character and confiding, private lyrics, whose air and words [are] all your own."[51]

It is interesting to note that in his letter to Julia, Emerson refrained from commenting at all on her poetic powers, preferring rather to emphasize the insight the verses gave into her inmost thoughts and feelings. The fact is that except for a few intense poems which touch on then-forbidden subjects, there is little true poetry in *Passion Flowers*. The book's popularity can surely be explained in much the terms Emerson used to praise it. The depth of feeling, even of passion, the poems revealed constituted a rather daring outburst for a lady of genteel upbringing and aroused people's curiosity. A review in the New York *Tribune* praised the poet's sad sincerity: "Nothing but the profound ex-

*A German scholar and close friend of the Howes.

perience of a rarely endowed nature could give such an air of
reality to such impassioned wails of suffering."⁵²

Here and there a lighter note crept into the verse. "Mind
Versus Mill-Stream" portrays a miller trying to tame a rushing
brook. He twice builds a dam but twice the stream breaks
through and destroys his work. At the end there is a moral:

> *If you would marry happily*
> *On the shady side of life*
> *Choose out some quietly-disposed*
> *And placid tempered wife,*
>
> *To share the length of sober days,*
> *And dimly slumberous nights,*
> *But well beware those fitful souls*
> *Fate wings for wilder flights,*
>
> *For men will woo the tempest*
> *And wed it to their cost,*
> *Then swear they took it for summer dew*
> *And ah! their peace is lost!*⁵³

In some people's minds the poem was a satire, its real message being that Howe was having difficulty keeping his wife
under control. Rumors of this reached Chev and upset him to
such a degree that he actually became ill. He had never been able
to take Julia's teasing and here she was doing it in print. The first
glow of literary success faded overnight as Chev's pride in his wife
changed to anger and bitterness; the next few months were the
most difficult Julia had ever known. She was so miserable that she
could not even write Annie until the worst was over:

> Things are better now, but we have been very unhappy.
> The Book, you see, was a blow to him, and some foolish and
> impertinent people have hinted that the Miller was meant for

himself — this has made him almost crazy. He had fancied, moreover, that everyone despised and neglected him, and indeed it is true that I have left him too much to himself. I will not expound upon the topic of our miseries — he has been in a very dangerous state, I think, very near insanity, and if I have done best for him and my children by staying here, you, my darling Annie, will neither regret nor complain of it. . . . We have had the devil's own time of it, and as I tell you, I hardly know myself, after all that I have endured. You must not blame poor Chev, however, he could not help it.[54]

Julia realized that she was the cause of Chev's unhappiness and she did her best at first to be a dutiful and affectionate wife even to the extent of allowing herself to become pregnant again. She wrote Louisa in July that she dreaded her approaching confinement. The future seemed to show her not a single gleam of light, but she was determined to make one last attempt at reconciliation or agree reluctantly to a final separation. The latter she claimed was a "favorite project" of Chev's:

He would bring it up even in our quieter hours, when there was nothing whatever to suggest it. . . . Before God, dear Louisa, I thought it my real duty to give up everything that was dear and sacred to me, rather than be forced to leave two of my children and those two the dearest, Julia and Harry. In this view I made the greatest sacrifice I can ever be called upon to make. God must accept it and the bitter sufferings of these subsequent months, as some expiation for the errors of my life.[55]

Another letter to Annie, undated but probably written about the same time as the one to Louisa, mentions Julia's suspicions that Chev has taken a mistress. "Chev is as cold and indifferent to me as a man can well be. I sometimes suspect him of having relations with another woman, and regret more bitterly the sacrifice which entailed upon me these months of fatigue and suffering." This pregnancy had been no easier than the previous one and Julia described to Annie one of the many attacks of hysteria she suffered as a result of her struggle against tears. "I was perfectly mad and rushed from room to room like a wild creature." Chev, who happened to be at home when the fit came over her, was apparently thoroughly frightened by her behavior but when the crisis subsided his indifference returned.[56] He even went so far as to insist that the whole family move back to the institute for a year, and it was here that Maud was born on November 9, 1854.

For a time Julia refrained from publishing any more poetry. But when the worst of the crisis was over her inner drive to write got the better of her. *Passion Flowers* was only the beginning. In 1857 her second book of verse, *Words for the Hour,* came out, followed by a play, *The World's Own,* and then by *A Trip to Cuba,* a published diary of the Howes' voyage to that island in 1859. Unquestionably the decade of the 1850's established Julia as an author of considerable promise. It also solidified her determination to follow her own bent even if this meant arousing the wrath of her husband. She succeeded in receiving enough encouragement from friends and critics to pursue her ambitions. The support of men like Parker and Longfellow, of Wallace and Twistleton, gave her the courage to defy Chev's wishes. By 1854 Julia Ward Howe was no longer simply the wife of a great hero and reformer but a woman with a reputation of her own. With the sixties and the coming of the Civil War the focus of Julia's ambitions would slowly change and her talents would become directed to ends that seemed at the time to be more socially useful. But the fifties gave her a taste of independence she was determined not to lose and convinced her that her desire to share her thoughts with others through the printed word was not only good but necessary.

Prelude to War

All the great charters of humanity have been written in blood.

— Theodore Parker, 1859

On January 30, 1854, a month after *Passion Flowers* was published, Senator Stephen Douglas of Illinois, the best orator in the Old Northwest (now the northern Midwest) stood up in Congress to introduce what at first appeared to be a routine bill organizing the Great Plains as the Territory of Nebraska. Included in the bill was the concept of "popular sovereignty," which in effect opened all the unsettled territory in the West to the possibility of slavery. Douglas was convinced that popular sovereignty would be greeted with approval by southerners in both houses — they had always opposed the provisions of the Missouri Compromise barring slavery from all land north of latitude 36° 30′ — but he failed to anticipate the furor his proposal would arouse in the North. In Boston where conservative or "cotton" Whigs had resisted the introduction of the slavery issue, factional rivalry cooled as both Whigs and Democrats rallied to oppose passage of the act. Sam Howe organized a protest meeting in Faneuil Hall on February 16, but then refused to attend because he found the proposed resolutions too mild and conciliatory in tone.[1] More to his liking was a new organization, the New

123

England Emigrant Aid Society, which met for the first time in March for the purpose of creating a corporation to assist those New Englanders wishing to emigrate to the new territories. On June 6 Howe was appointed to a committee formed to raise subscriptions in Boston, and in July the first band of settlers set off for Kansas.

During the debate on the Kansas-Nebraska Bill, William Seward, senator from New York, predicted the violent outcome of the measure: "We will engage in competition for the virgin soil of Kansas, and God give the victory to the side that is stronger in numbers as it is in right."[2] The first indication of trouble came in November 1854, when a large number of Missourians crossed the border into Kansas and helped that territory elect a proslavery delegate to Congress. By the spring of 1856 Kansas had two governments, one proslavery, one antislavery, both illegal. When the New England Emigrant Aid Society prepared to send its annual band of settlers to Kansas that summer, it sent them fully armed.

"New England spunk seems to be pretty well up," Julia wrote both her sisters on May 29.[3] The last ten days had seen disaster follow upon disaster. On the nineteenth, Charles Sumner, now considered the most eloquent antislavery spokesman in the Senate, had stood up and launched his long and famous denunciation of the "Crime Against Kansas." The Senate chamber was crowded when he got up to speak. Every senator was present, the galleries were packed, and all the doors were blocked with people craning their necks to see and hear. A reporter from the New York *Evening Post* observed, "No such scene has been witnessed in that body since the days of Webster."[4] Sumner spoke for three hours that afternoon and finished the speech the following day. Every word of it had been carefully memorized. Attacking the administration's policy in Kansas, he demanded that the territory be immediately admitted as a free state. Sumner's language was harsh and full of invective as he lashed out at Douglas and Senators Mason of Virginia and Butler of South Carolina. Pacing up and down at the rear of the chamber, Douglas was overheard muttering, "That damn fool will get himself killed by some other damned fool."[5] Two days later his prophecy came close to realization when Congressman Preston Brooks, a nephew of Senator Butler's, beat Sumner to insensibility as he was seated alone at his Senate desk.

The Howes were grief-stricken at the news of the attack on Sumner. They had known that their friend was planning an important speech on the Kansas question because he had written Theodore Parker to that effect some days earlier. Brooks's violence further convinced Sam Howe that no reconciliation was possible between North and South, and he came to the conclusion that the North would do well to have a separate government. Yet he comforted Sumner with the assurance that "out of the evil will come good — great good, & you have not bled in vain."[6]

The news from Kansas was very bad in those last days of May 1856. Civil war broke out there and continued for the rest of the summer. On the twenty-first, the free state community of Lawrence was sacked by the "Border Ruffians" from Missouri. Three nights later the antislavery fanatic John Brown, convinced that it was the will of God that he should attempt to crush slavery single-handed, stole into the proslavery settlement of Pottawatomie (Kansas), where together with six companions he slaughtered five unarmed settlers asleep in their cabins.

Back in Boston, Howe and other abolitionists reacted to the trouble in Kansas by staging a series of protest meetings. Howe addressed a huge gathering at Faneuil Hall on the night of June 3: something must be done to aid the Kansas settlers still further. Thereupon a committee was organized to raise funds for sending arms to Kansas, and Howe was elected chairman. His abilities as a fund raiser dated back to the days of the Greek revolution and now his skill combined with the urgency of the cause enabled him to raise ten thousand dollars in one month.

Prelude to War
 אא

Early in July, having left Julia and the children in Newport, Howe set off for Kansas himself, to supervise the distribution of arms to the settlers. Julia, although surely worried for his safety, did not mind spending the summer alone with the children. On the contrary, it was a relief not to have Chev about, critical and complaining as he often was. Lawton's Valley allowed her a freedom to do as she wished and see whom she pleased, which was not possible at Green Peace. It was at Lawton's Valley that she did most of her writing. At the top of the attic stairs of the old farmhouse was a window facing north. A little table two feet square was placed on the narrow platform under the window; "the stairs were shut off from the rest of the house by a stout door." And here Julia sat on hot summer mornings with the wasps flying about her, composing her poetry and her plays, and studying her philosophy.[7]

The summer Chev went to Kansas she wrote *The World's Own,* a melodrama that shocked proper Bostonians and New Yorkers when it was produced in both cities the following year. Julia had committed the unforgivable sin of allowing her heroine, Leonora, a passionate village maiden, to be seduced without suffering any ill consequences. Sam Ward, in New York when the play opened there in late March, tried to assure his sister of its success when he wrote her on the thirtieth: "Leonora draws the best houses. There was hardly any standing room on Friday night. . . . Whatever you do here you are assured of creating a sensation." He told her to counter her critics with the argument that "you stand up for woman's rights and had in view how abominable our sex can be and how ill-used yours."[8] Despite Sam's reassurance, *The World's Own* was not a success and Fanny Longfellow's rather prudish reaction to the play was probably more typical than Sam's. "Julia Howe's play has been abused by all the papers here and in New York," she wrote in her journal on April 18, "except in one or two cases, but she is serenely indifferent and thinks it was a success. . . . It is strange so clever a

126

woman should have chosen so hackneyed a story and so wretched a heroine, and should not see there is tragedy enough in life to inspire a drama without descending to vice. It is cleverly written, and the close has a good deal of vigor, but it should never have been published. The poor doctor must feel it painfully as a thing he cannot give his daughters to read."[9]

There is no surviving record of how Chev felt about *The World's Own,* but Fanny was correct in describing Julia's unconcern for the opinions of her critics. She easily convinced herself that such abuse was proof positive of the play's real literary merit, "for so treated they, the critics, the poets that went before me: Byron, Keats, even holy Wordsworth — and the world is little wiser since then." She even went so far as to claim that "the most competent critics" regarded it as a success ("I may name Ripley, Whipple, Longfellow, Emerson, Sanborn, Curtis, and others")[10] when it is likely that those so named had merely written or spoken kind words about the play in order not to offend this rather touchy poet. For if Julia ignored her newspaper critics, she reacted strongly to criticism from her friends, and under such circumstances one of the less attractive sides of her character came to the surface. When the *Atlantic Monthly* first appeared in 1857, Julia began bombarding its editor, James Russell Lowell, with requests amounting to demands that he publish her poetry. When he did print her poems she was pleased and during the magazine's early years a good number of her verses appeared on its pages, but once when Lowell had the audacity to ignore some poems she had sent him she fired a broadside in the most vituperative language she had at her command:

Friend, I rush into your presence with all the madness of a disordered mind — it is your fault, yours. What care I, ha, ha, if you don't like my verses? Who said you could understand them? I didn't. Yet you print worse ones, your own, very likely — Oh! you do. I swear it by the forearm of Fanny Kemble, the temper of Margaret Fuller, the hair and hands of

127

E[lizabeth] L. Peabody, and whatever else is frightful and feminine. . . . Holmes, any trash of his passes, Longfellow also has the right key, and gets in when he pleases. But! it must be because I am a woman! You lose verses too, by your own confession. What you have done with mine, fancy labors to invent. The kindlings being low, or paper wanted to singe the chickens, "Mrs. Howe's last" you say with a hideous look of intelligence and deliver my darling to the flames. And I once wished to make your acquaintance! fatal curiosity, punished, of course, in the usual way. Anathema on the Monthly and all its poets.[11]

Julia apparently had a right to be upset. Lowell did have a reputation among his authors for rather sloppy business methods. He often mislaid manuscripts for months at a time; sometimes they vanished entirely, at which point he would blame the author for not keeping a copy or resort to total silence. Julia finally had to persuade Dr. Oliver Wendell Holmes, a mutual friend, to intercede with Lowell on her behalf. But Julia herself could be difficult. James C. Fields, who brought out her first two books of poems and succeeded Lowell as the editor of the *Atlantic Monthly,* was driven nearly to distraction by her criticisms of his editorial policies and demands for better fees.[12] Like many authors, Julia sometimes had an exaggerated view of the worth of her writing. *The World's Own* has many serious weaknesses, both dramatic and literary, and *Words for the Hour,* her second book of poems, lacks even the occasional interest of *Passion Flowers,* the intensity of emotion that had so struck the critics. The verses in *Words for the Hour* are more concerned with public issues and events. One poem, for example, is a hymn of praise to Sumner, written after his beating in the Senate chamber:

> *SUMNER, the task thou hast chosen was thine for*
> *its fitness,*
> *Never was Paschal victim more stainlessly offered,*
> *Never on milder brow gleamed crown of martyr.*[13]

Julia had not always been an ardent abolitionist. In the early 1850's, when Chev was involved with the Free Soilers, she had shared little of his sympathy with their aims. Her family had brought her up to distrust the antislavery movement and had shared the southern view that "the result of any pronounced opposition to slavery would be the signal for a general uprising of the slaves, and for a widespread massacre of their former owners." These views were also shared by a number of her friends in Boston. As she later recalled, "The general dislike of Abolitionists was extreme."[14] But by the mid-1850's Julia had become a thorough convert to the cause and her children were now chided in school for being antislavery.[15]

Although Julia now considered herself an abolitionist, she often voiced disapproval of the methods its adherents used and their lack of charity toward those with whom they disagreed. Chev felt much as she did, and as far back as 1854 had chided his friend Parker for being too intolerant of the way an antislavery meeting was run: "What do you mean by abusing folks for not having red-hot Garrisonian abolition lectures, when they expressly stated that they are going to have an 'independent' course, and one representing all shades of opinion? . . . The great and glorious mission which you are performing, so stoutly and so fearlessly, with so much more than Channing's strength, — oh — how much more beautiful it would be if performed with more of his meek gentleness."[16]

Five years later Julia criticized Wendell Phillips, the abolitionist orator, for his rough language: "A vocabulary of filth helps no cause, however holy. May I say that Mr. Phillips and his friends have too long ignored the old legends of good feeling and good manners and have brought into vogue a vulgar and arrogant style of abuse which has neither the fairness of criticism nor the dignity of censure."[17] But neither Chev nor Julia, for all their disapproval of abolitionist intolerance, had a word of criticism for Sumner's tactics toward those of proslavery persuasion. Intolerance toward fellow abolitionists they considered un-Christian, but prejudice against the proponents of slave power was charity itself.

The fighting in Kansas had pretty well died down by the autumn of 1856. A new governor for the territory, John W. Geary, arrived in September. An honest, capable man, he turned the settlers' attention away from the issue of slavery to that of land. Real estate values boomed and even Howe, excited by the prospect of owning a bit of Kansas, bought some property there. In the spring of 1857 he went out west again, this time taking Julia and Flossy with him. Julia described the exhausting journey in a letter to Annie: "Heaven knows what I have not been through with, since I saw you — dust, dirt, dyspepsia — hotels, railroads, prairies, Western steamboats, Western people — more prairies, tobacco juice. Captains of boats — pilots of ditto — long days of jolting in the cars, with stoppages of ten minutes for dinner." When they reached Saint Louis, Flossy became quite sick from drinking bad water. Chev, too restless to wait around for his daughter to recover, went on up the Missouri to Leavenworth and left Julia and Flossy to make their own way back to Boston. The best part of the whole trip had been a visit to the Manns, who were then in Ohio at Antioch College, where Horace was president. "They almost ate us up, so glad were they to see us," Julia told Annie.[18]

One of Chev's purposes in traveling to Kansas that spring was to see John Brown, whom he had met some months earlier in Boston, and give him the money he and others had raised to help further Brown's antislavery activities in the territory. Despite Brown's role in the massacre at Pottawatomie, Chev was convinced that he was an honorable man, intent on devoting "his life to the redemption of the colored race from slavery, even as Christ had willingly offered his life for the salvation of mankind."[19] As late as 1899, when Julia wrote her memoirs, she was still convinced that Brown "had had much to do with the successful contest which kept slavery out of the territory of Kansas."[20] The effectiveness of Brown's activities, including the raid on Pottawatomie, had been grossly exaggerated in the eastern newspapers. Obscured was the fact that Brown's exploits were unplanned and often dangerous to the cause of Free Soil.[21] But if Brown was not a major factor in the Kansas civil war, he came to symbolize in the minds of antislavery men the struggle of Free Soil against slavery, and it was Brown the Hero who appealed to Howe as well as to men like Emerson and Thoreau. For them Brown was above the law; the atrocities at Pottawatomie were glossed over and romanticized; he was working for the Lord against the evils of slavery and the means he used to achieve this end appeared to many as irrelevant.

Brown had come to Boston in January 1857 and it was probably then that Julia first met him. Chev had described Brown to her before and now he reminded her, "Do you remember that man of whom I spoke to you, — the one who wished to be a saviour for the human race?" Julia replied that she did indeed remember. "That man," Howe continued, "will call here this afternoon. You will receive him." At the expected time Julia heard the bell ring, "and, on answering it, beheld a middle-aged, middle-sized man, with hair and beard of amber color, streaked with gray. He looked a Puritan of the Puritans, forceful, concentrated, and self-contained. We had a brief interview, of which I only remember my great gratification at meeting one of whom I had heard so good an account."[22]

The men who met with Brown that January day in 1857 were members of a loyal group of supporters known as the Secret Six. The six included Howe and Parker; George L. Stearns, a businessman from Medford; Thomas Wentworth Higginson, minister of the Unitarian Free Church in Worcester; Gerrit Smith, a wealthy New York landowner; and finally a young schoolteacher only two years out of Harvard, Franklin Sanborn. Gerrit Smith was the only one of the six not present but the other five were completely won over by the bearded patriarch who appeared to them as a character out of the Old Testament. Howe, normally a good judge of men, found him both noble and admirable, and was as eager as any to support Brown with guns, money and ammunition for the purpose of defensive action in Kansas and raids into Missouri.[23] John Brown was willing enough to accept material support from the Secret Six, but he kept his own counsel on how it would be used until one day in February 1958, when he revealed to Gerrit Smith a plan to take offensive action somewhere in slaveholding country, for the purpose of fomenting a slave uprising. Both Sanborn and Smith tried in vain to dissuade him from his plan, and later when Howe heard of it he admitted the hopelessness of the undertaking but thought the old fellow still had enough of a chance to make the enterprise feasible.[24]

When Julia Howe took up her Boston *Transcript* one evening in mid-October 1859, she read that an unidentified group of men had raided the arsenal at Harpers Ferry, Virginia. Later, when Chev came in she told him what she had read. "Brown has got to work," he concluded as he glanced at the report. Julia herself had guessed as much. Chev assured her that Brown's plan was not as impossible as it appeared, there being a widespread belief at the time that only the slightest encouragement was needed to touch off a general slave rebellion.[25] Years later, however, Julia recalled that she had had her doubts and had privately thought the whole scheme "wild and chimerical. Of its details I knew nothing, and never learned more. None of us could exactly approve an act so revolutionary in its character, yet the greathearted attempt enlisted our sympathies very strongly."[26]

For two days John Brown and his little company held the federal armory at Harpers Ferry. By the time Colonel Robert E. Lee arrived with a contingent of marines, only four of Brown's men remained alive and unwounded. Eight days after his capture Brown's trial opened in the courthouse of Charles Town, Virginia. Within a week it was over and Brown was convicted of murder, treason and criminal conspiracy. From the time of his capture the old Puritan was calm and dignified; he refused to be declared insane and accepted full responsibility for the raid.

December 2, the day of Brown's execution, was one of general mourning throughout New England. A few Bostonians continued to think of the antislavery hero as a "pig-headed old fool,"[27] but for the most part Brown's death aroused great emotional sympathy all over the North. At the Church of the Disciples a special service was held that day and James Freeman Clarke gave a sermon entitled "It Is Enough for the Disciple That He Be as His Master."[28] Julia had been correct when she had predicted some weeks earlier that "his death will be holy and glorious — and the gallows cannot dishonor him."[29]

If Brown's courage and integrity during the time of his imprisonment and execution added to his glory, the behavior of his supporters added little to their reputations. They panicked at the news that papers had been found in John Brown's possession which implicated Howe and the rest of the Secret Six in the conspiracy to bring about a slave uprising. Unlike Brown, who throughout the period of his trial and imprisonment assumed a dignity that belied his reputed insanity, Howe all but lost his wits at the thought that he might be apprehended and sent to prison himself. Perhaps the horrors of those months in a Berlin jail back in 1832 still haunted him. In any case his behavior exhibited little of the courage and heroism expected of a "chevalier." After sending a letter to the Boston *Advertiser,* in which he disclaimed all knowledge of the raid (he had not, in fact, known exactly when or where it would take place), he quickly set out for Canada, ostensibly for the purpose of promoting the education of the Canadian blind. Later he admitted that his flight had been the result of bad judgment, and upon his return, shortly after Brown's execution, he consented to appear before an investigating committee in Washington. At the hearing he admitted giving Brown guns and money but denied any knowledge of the raid on Harpers Ferry.[30]

Howe was not the only one of the Secret Six to behave in a less than courageous fashion over the whole affair. In Concord, Franklin Sanborn stoutly refused arrest, while in Peterboro, New York, Gerrit Smith went temporarily mad and had to be committed to an asylum. Stearns was persuaded by Howe to accompany him to Canada. Both Parker's and Higginson's behavior were more dignified, although the latter did refuse to obey a summons.[31]

From Julia, meanwhile, there was no hint of criticism of her husband's conduct or of anyone else's. She believed Chev innocent of any implication in the raid itself, and knowing how anxious and fatigued he had become over the whole business, she perhaps understood and forgave his panicked reaction as at least human though not admirable.

By now, in the late 1850's, relations between Julia and Chev had eased considerably. They continued to quarrel and Chev occasionally broached the subject of separation, but the "living death" Julia had described as having lasted for such a long time had passed. "I now have a clearer perception of things," she wrote Annie, "and am better reconciled with the spiritual world than I have been for a long time."[32] In another letter to Annie she described a quarrel with Chev and in conclusion admitted, "This is all naughty — I'se reforming Annie dear, only somehow I want to begin with Chev, and not with myself."[33] In the spring of 1859, she was pregnant for the sixth and last time. That February the Howes had left Boston to spend several months in Cuba. Chev had needed a change that winter before Harpers Ferry. The years of worry over the Kansas question and over slavery in general, combined with his regular work at the institute, had taken their toll. Now fifty-eight, Sam Howe did not have the stamina he had once had, and he and Julia were easily persuaded to accompany Theodore Parker on a trip to the Caribbean.

Parker too, worn out from overwork, was very ill with tuberculosis and had been persuaded by his doctors and relatives that although death was nearly certain, an ocean voyage would do him good. The journey south was a sad one. Parker knew he would probably never return to his native New England and that this was the last time he would see Julia and Chev. The sea was rough for most of the trip and all of them spent a large portion of the voyage in their cabins. Considerably weakened by seasickness, Parker's condition had hardly improved when they reached Havana. He then left the Howes and boarded a steamer for Vera Cruz. From there he sailed to Europe and died in Florence in the late spring. Julia never forgot her last sight of him: "his serious face, crowned with gray locks and a soft gray hat, as he looked over the side of the vessel and waved us a last farewell."[34]

It was surely obvious to the Howes, during the course of their stay in Cuba, that the island was a thriving center of the illegal slave trade. A British authority estimated that in the year 1859 alone, approximately thirty thousand slaves were transported to Cuba from Africa, largely by vessels from American ports, flying the American flag.[35] Numerous southerners, including Jefferson Davis, talked of the possibility of the United States' annexing Cuba and legally reviving the African slave trade.[36] But Julia Howe mentioned nothing about the slave trade in *A Trip to Cuba,* which came out in serial form in the *Atlantic Monthly* in 1859 and then was published in book form in 1860. Essentially a travelogue of the type then popular in America, with descriptions of people and places, it provided a vicarious holiday for those back home.

If Julia failed to mention the slave trade she could not avoid inserting her views on the institution of slavery itself. This was the first time she had seen large numbers of blacks, and she observed them closely. In May she wrote in a letter to Parker, which probably never reached him: "I shall stick to my resolution of writing always what I think no matter whom it offends. No-

135

thing is more vicious than to make observations conform to theory. Observation must be genuine, clear, immediate, and theory must make the best of it afterwards."[37]

Julia was not impressed with what she saw of the slaves in Cuba, and what she wrote on this occasion is proof that abolitionist sentiments did not necessarily include a belief in racial equality. She compared the Cuban Negro with the few blacks she had known in Boston. "The negro of the North is an ideal negro; it is the negro refined by white culture, elevated by white blood, instructed even by white iniquity; — the negro among negroes is a coarse, grinning, flat-footed, thick-skulled creature, ugly as Caliban, lazy as the laziest of brutes, chiefly ambitious to be of no use to any in the world. . . . He must go to school to the white race and his discipline must be long and laborious."[38] Julia wondered whether compulsory labor was not "better than none," and although she was opposed to the institution of slavery she did not consider the Cubans or the southerners of her own country capable of doing away with it on their own. "From the North the impulse must come. . . . The enslaved race . . . gradually conquering the finer arts of its masters, will rise up to meet the hand of deliverance, having in due course of time reached the spiritual level at which enslavement becomes impossible."[39]

Julia knew these words would be considered heresy by some of her New England friends and acquaintances. William Lloyd Garrison, for one, was appalled by her description of the blacks as naturally indolent and fit only for compulsory labor if not for slavery. He attacked her in a scathing article in the *Liberator* entitled "The Refuge of Oppression."[40] Most northerners, however, agreed with Julia's view of blacks as racially inferior to whites. Even Chev, who may well have disagreed with his wife's ideas on compulsory labor, regarded the black race as intrinsically weaker than the white.[41]

Near the end of their stay in Cuba the Howes made the

acquaintance of one of the largest slaveholders in the South, Wade Hampton II and his wife. Julia took a great liking to Mrs. Hampton and the two couples traveled back north together, the Howes stopping off for a stay at the great plantation of Millwood near Columbia, South Carolina, which young Wade had recently inherited from his father. In good southern fashion the Howes, who had originally planned to stay at Millwood for two days, remained for two weeks. Julia was undoubtedly delighted to taste something of the society out of which her own grandmother Cutler had come.

But the Howes would gladly have avoided the endless talk of strained relations between North and South. Wade Hampton assured them that the South meant to fight for the cause of slavery. Howe found this hard to believe. "They cannot be in earnest about meaning to fight," he assured Julia in the privacy of their own room. "It would be too insane, too fatal to their own interests."[42] It is hard to understand why Chev should have found it so difficult to comprehend the thought of the South's contemplating war. Surely every move that he and his fellow abolitionists had made for the last decade was rendering the possibility of conflict more and more inevitable.

8

Battle Hymn

*Let the lines be drawn distinctly; &, with freedom
and right on one side & slavery and wrong on the
other, he is an infidel and an Atheist who can doubt
the final result.*

*Oh, God! for a tithe of your power, that I too might
take part in this glorious struggle.*

— Samuel Gridley Howe, December 1860

The last of Julia and Chev's children was born on Christmas morning 1859. Named Samuel Gridley after his father, this little boy lived less than four years, but during his short life he was a great comfort to his parents. They were delighted to have a son after so many girls, especially one with such a sunny and easy disposition. His presence did much to cheer them both up during that last year before the outbreak of the war.

By the early months of 1860 Chev was convinced that bloodshed between North and South was inevitable, but not desirable. When, after Lincoln's election in November, one southern state after another left the Union, Howe was inclined to let them go and avoid strife if possible. "I do think we are making a fetish out of this political union," he had written Sumner the previous April.[1] As abolitionists both men were very suspicious of the fact that those northerners, including a majority of the Republican party, who favored coercion to bring an end to secession, had little interest in abolishing slavery. They were only concerned, it seemed, with preserving the Union and asserting the authority of the national government. All through that long secession winter the discussion of slavery became so bitter that Howe had to escort Wendell Phillips home from an abolitionist meeting on January 21, to avoid his being attacked by the mob which had gathered outside the Music Hall in Boston. At the meeting Phillips had spoken out strongly in favor of moral coercion over force as the best way to change the hearts of the slaveholders. But in New England, even at this late date, antislavery motives for making war were supported by only a minority of the people. As Howe and other abolitionists had noted, most northerners saw the approaching conflict as a crusade to save the Union. Not until later would many come to accept it as a war against slavery as well.

The acquiescence which Howe and other antislavery men evinced toward secession was a long cry from pacifism. No sooner did word come of the attack on Fort Sumter, and of Lincoln's call for troops, than the abolitionists rallied with one voice to support armed intervention. Howe even rebuked Lincoln for permitting the surrender of the fort instead of retaliating with military force.[2]

While Howe was condemning Lincoln as a compromiser, his brother-in-law Sam Ward, then living in Washington, was convinced that extremists like Howe were the ones responsible for the crisis facing the nation. Sam was a Democrat and a friend of former President Buchanan, and during the last year of Buchanan's administration Sam had moved into a little house on F Street, which soon became famous for dinner parties at which Republicans and Democrats met on equal terms. Sam's political interests were eclectic and would remain so for the rest of his life. Furthermore, he refused to take sides on the question of slavery, thereby upsetting his sister Julia profoundly. In October 1860, a few weeks before the national election, Sam had warned his sister:

"We shall have trouble with the South if Lincoln carries New York. Nor do I blame them, for with all their violence and vaporings they have vested rights, and if they submit to the irrepressible conflict, after all their declarations, they will stultify their records and become ridiculous."[3]

This was not the only accurate prediction Sam Ward would make in the course of the next few years. While Confederate guns were firing on Fort Sumter on April 13, 1861, Sam arrived on a peacemaking expedition of his own. He had stopped first in Richmond and then proceeded on to Charleston. His known political neutrality combined with his great tact and charm made him welcome among the influential families of both cities, and in Charleston these included relatives of Grandma Cutler's as well as friends from his Round Hill School days. He hoped that by talking matters over with people whose judgment he trusted he could help them find a solution to the crisis that threatened the Union. What Sam saw and heard during his visit in Charleston he also relayed back to his friend William Seward, Lincoln's secretary of state. Sam was convinced that Seward was laboring under severe misconceptions regarding attitudes in the South. His own observations and conversations with Confederates assured him that the war was not going to be the short one that many northerners, including his brother-in-law Sam Howe, predicted it would be. He also found that little or no Union sentiment existed in the South. He was convinced, he wrote Seward, that "the people *here* will *never* come back."[4]

At the time Sam was acting as a combined peacemaker and informant for Secretary Seward, Howe told John Andrew, the recently elected governor of Massachusetts, that he would be more than willing to serve the northern cause in any capacity except espionage work.[5] Scarcely two years had passed since Chev and Julia's stay on a South Carolina plantation, yet now it was more than either of them could do to even look at a southerner. When Julia was returning from her annual spring visit to Annie in Bordentown in 1861, she noticed a woman seated next to her on the boat from New York "who had a southerly aspect" and at whom she glared "like a tigress."[6] The lines of battle were drawn and Julia was girded for the fight. Any thought of letting the South quietly go its own way had long since vanished.

The great crusade was on, the holy war begun. Old John Brown, the Moses of the North, was still the leader of the northern cause. Even though his bones lay "a-mouldering in the grave," his "soul" was "marching on." The skirmishes that had been fought in the last ten years to rescue fugitive slaves and bleeding Kansas, Brown's raid at Harpers Ferry, and finally his capture and execution had prepared all but the most extreme pacifists for war. Even the peaceloving Emerson was calling it "the battle for Humanity."[7] In 1859 John Brown's martyrdom had rallied to his support those conservative northerners, who as confirmed nationalists, were concerned lest southern sectionalism destroy the organic balance of the Union. For them John Brown was a hero not because he was an abolitionist — they hated the abolitionists — but because to them he represented the old Puritan virtues and had been an instrument in the hands of the Lord for restoring order to the land. Now in 1861 as it became obvious that the North was not fighting to free the slave but to preserve the Union, even the abolitionists who had earlier preached the new American creed of humanitarianism and democracy were beginning to look upon the war as a crusade to save the nation as a whole from sin and corruption and not simply to bring an end to slavery.[8]

Within weeks after the firing on Fort Sumter, Governor John Andrew heeded Chev's request to serve. On May 6, Howe headed south to inspect the hygienic condition of the Massachusetts troops stations in Washington. While there, he and several others requested that a sanitary commission be organized under the auspices of the federal government, to inspect the troops for signs of cleanliness and health, and care for the wounded. The request was soon granted and the commission was given headquarters in Washington. Chev was appointed a member, and his duties necessarily took him to the capital frequently. Julia went with him in the fall of 1861.

Governor Andrew, his wife and James Freeman Clarke accompanied the Howes on their journey to Washington. As their train left Baltimore and approached the capital, Julia noted that here and there alongside the track were "small groups of armed men seated on the ground near a fire."[9] Chev explained that these were pickets posted at intervals to guard the railroad. The sight of these men brought the reality of war close to Julia for the first time and she began to think of all the women of her acquaintance whose husbands, sons, or brothers were fighting for the Union cause. Saddened by the thought that Chev was too old to fight and her sons too young, while her only living brother was — in her eyes — as good as a traitor, she began to wonder what she could do. "I could not leave my nursery to follow the march of our armies, neither had I the practical deftness which the preparing and packing of sanitary stores demanded. Something seemed to say to me, 'You would be glad to serve, but you cannot help anyone; you have nothing to give and there is nothing for you to do.' "[10]

On the immediate outskirts of Washington the travelers noted great numbers of troops — soldiers on foot, others on horseback — milling around among the brown tents pitched in a wide circle around the city. Here was Julia's first sight of the Grand Army of the Potomac, protecting the capital from attack by the Confederates, who were stationed only a few miles away, across the river in Virginia.

The Howes went immediately from the train to their rooms in Willard's Hotel, the most famous hostelry in all of Washington. A great rambling building full of noise, bustle and cigar smoke, Willard's bore little resemblance to the small, cozy inns Julia had patronized in Europe. Politicians gathered downstairs every morning at eight when Congress was in session; hotel guests, legislators and bureaucrats mingled in the crowded public rooms and devoured enormous meals four times a day, and all the time the din of voices was loud and unceasing.

Outside the hotel lay the city of Washington itself, a strange sprawling town, hardly more than a village, with its wide, unpaved, rutted avenues, its scattered, unfinished federal buildings, its domeless Capitol. How bleak the town must have appeared to Julia, its strange austerity augmented by the sight of mounted soldiers galloping ceaselessly up and down the streets, a constant reminder of the war that threatened the security of Washington and of the Union as well.[11]

After the disastrous defeat at the First Battle of Bull Run in the previous July, General George B. McClellan, the hero of a small Union victory in western Virginia in the early months of the war, had been appointed commander of the Union forces around Washington. This popular young officer, short of stature but commanding in appearance, set about training and organizing the Grand Army of the Potomac. By the autumn of 1861 a real army was taking shape under his able direction, and the North was beginning to wonder when the training would stop and the action begin.

All during the cool autumn days hundreds of sightseers poured out of the capital to watch the Union commander review his troops at Munson's Hill, Virginia. On November 18 the Howes were invited to attend a grand review and drove out accompanied by the Andrews' and James Freeman Clarke. While they were engaged in watching the maneuvers the Confederate forces suddenly attacked and the sightseers were forced to turn back to Washington. The drive home was long and tedious as carriages and troops filled the road. To help pass the time the Howes and their companions began singing familiar army songs, including "John Brown's Body lies a-mouldering in the grave." The soldiers particularly liked this one and joined their voices to the chorus, at which point Clarke turned to Julia and suggested that she write "some good words for that stirring tune." She replied that she had often wished to do this, "but had not as yet found in my mind any leading toward it."

She went to bed that night as usual and slept soundly. "I awoke in the gray of the morning twilight; and as I lay waiting for the dawn, the long lines of the desired poem began to twine themselves in my mind. Having thought out all the stanzas, I said to myself, 'I must get up and write these verses down, lest I fall asleep again and forget them.' So, with a sudden effort, I sprang out of bed, and found in the dimness an old stump of a pen which I remembered to have used the day before. I scrawled the verses almost without looking at the paper. . . . Having completed my writing I returned to bed and fell asleep, saying to myself, 'I like this better than most things I have written.' "[12]

In this way the "Battle Hymn" was composed and the very method of its writing acquired an importance almost equal to the poem itself. So easily the words had come to Mrs. Howe! Had God himself inspired her as he had apparently inspired Harriet Beecher Stowe to write *Uncle Tom's Cabin?* Was he not himself on the side of the Union forces?

> *Mine eyes have seen the glory of the coming of the*
> *Lord;*
> *He is trampling out the vintage where the grapes of*
> *wrath are stored;*
> *He hath loosed the fateful lightning of His terrible*
> *swift sword:*
> *His truth is marching on.*[13]

She recalled the sight from her train window of the groups of soldiers as they sat around their campfires on the outskirts of Washington, waiting to defend the Union cause:

Battle Hymn

אא

I have seen Him in the watch-fires of a hundred circling
    camps;
They have builded Him an altar in the evening dews
    and damps;
I can read His righteous sentence by the dim and flaring
    lamps.
    His day is marching on.

Line after line rolled out as she scribbled in the half-light. Julia often wrote her poems this way, rising in the middle of the night, leaving the lamp unlit lest it wake the baby that invariably slept by her side. By morning she would have forgotten the words like a vanished dream, but always they were there on some scrap of paper waiting to be deciphered and recopied. Nor is it amazing that Julia was able to write the "Battle Hymn" with such ease. Much of her inspiration came from the Bible and she knew certain parts of the Old Testament by heart. So it was, for example, with the apocalyptic poem on the vengeance of God in chapter 63 of Isaiah: "I have trodden the winepress alone; and of the people there was none with me; for I will tread them in mine anger, and trample them in my fury." The words of the Old Testament prophet had inspired Julia as they had inspired others before her.[14]

I have read a fiery gospel, writ in burnished rows
    of steel:
"As ye deal with my contemners, so with you my grace
    shall deal;
Let the Hero, born of woman crush the serpent with
    his heel,
    Since God is marching on."

In this picture, so vividly painted of a vengeful God destroying his enemies, Julia was saying what lay on many northern minds. In her words there is but little trace of the kind, merciful God of whom William Ellery Channing had spoken in Boston nearly twenty years before.

> *He has sounded forth the trumpet that shall never*
> *call retreat;*
> *He is sifting out the hearts of men before his judgment*
> *seat:*
> *Oh! be swift my soul, to answer Him! be jubilant,*
> *my feet!*
> *Our God is marching on.*

The religious nationalism of the "Battle Hymn" asserts God's justice rather than his mercy. Julia, like so many liberal Christians, had reverted to the stern evangelical creed of her childhood.

> *In the beauty of the lilies Christ was born across the*
> *sea,*
> *With a glory in his bosom that transfigures you and me;*
> *As he died to make men holy, let us die to make men free,*
> *While God is marching on.*

But it is not the gentle, reasonable Christ who is pronouncing the righteous sentence on the evil supporters of slavery; he is across the sea in Jerusalem. The God who is "sounding out the trumpet that shall never call retreat" carries a sword and marches with the North as he crushes the serpent, symbol of the South, with his heel.[15]

Julia submitted her new poem to the *Atlantic Monthly* in early December after her return from Washington. Various poems, an essay on George Sand and the whole of her *Trip to Cuba* had by then appeared in the magazine and she perhaps not unnaturally considered herself one of the firm's authors. "Fields! Do you want this, and do you like it, and have you any room for it in

January number?" inquired Julia rather flippantly in her note accompanying the manuscript. "I am sad and spleeny, and begin to have fears that I may not be after all, the greatest woman alive."[16]

The poem came out in February 1862 and Julia received five dollars for it. She later recalled that the "Battle Hymn" was "somewhat praised on its appearance, but the vicissitudes of the war so engrossed public attention that small heed was taken of literary matters."[17] Even so, the poem was read by a great many people, and not long after its publication regiments all over the North were singing it. In her old age Julia discovered that the first public singing of the hymn probably occurred at a Washington's Birthday celebration in Framingham in 1862.[18] President Lincoln first heard it in Washington sometime after the Battle of Gettysburg and amid the applause that followed was heard to call out, "Sing it again!"[19] Seven years later Ralph Waldo Emerson noted in his diary: "I honor the author of the Battle Hymn. . . . She was born in the city of New York. I could well wish she were a native of Massachusetts. We have no such poetess in New England."[20]

Never before had she directed such passionate personal feeling toward a cause of such consuming public interest, and she never would again. Indeed, no other wartime document reflects so accurately northern attitudes in that first year of the Civil War. The lines that rolled out so easily from Julia's mind onto that scrap of paper in Willard's Hotel were inspired by a thorough familiarity with the temper of the northern mind, and combined in a few verses, unmatched for their religious and nationalistic fervor, the public enthusiasm for the war as an instrument for the nation's salvation from sin and corruption.

Family Life in
the Sixties

Her greatest gift, as she well knew, was in conver-
sation. Her rare eloquence did not much avail her at
her desk, and though all that she wrote had the value
of thought and of study, it was in living speech alone
that her genius made itself entirely felt and ap-
preciated.
— Julia Ward Howe, *Margaret Fuller*

When the "Battle Hymn of the Republic" first appeared, the Howes were spending the winter at 13 Chestnut Street on Beacon Hill in Boston. Chev had taken a three-year lease on the tall brick Bulfinch house, and the whole family quickly developed a strong attachment for the beautifully proportioned dwelling with its sunny, high-ceilinged rooms and wide, gracefully curving staircase. These three winters of the war were unusually busy ones. Chev's days were filled with work for a number of war-related causes and his children remembered endless meetings held around the big dining-room table where, as one of them later recalled, "matters of vital concern" were continually being discussed.[1] Chev was asked in the winter of 1862 to be one of the vice-presidents of the newly formed Emancipation League. In the following year, after President Lincoln had issued his Emancipation Proclamation, Chev helped to organize the Freedman's Inquiry Commission to investigate the condition of the freed slaves. Besides these added activities, he continued to work for the Sanitary Commission; nor did he neglect the blind and insane. In 1863 he was made chairman of the Massachusetts Board of State Charities.

Julia's days were also filled. Caring for her six children took a considerable amount of time and so did war work. She and the older girls scraped lint and joined a ladies' sewing circle that met in the afternoons and evenings to make clothes for the Union soldiers. Never very clever with her needle, Julia did this work propelled only by a sense of duty, but she threw herself with enthusiasm into editing the *Boatswain's Whistle,* a daily newspaper for the National Sailors' Fair held in Boston in late 1864. This was one of many large wartime fairs organized by the Sanitary Commission to raise money and promote patriotism. Julia was the editor and counted among her advisors John Greenleaf Whittier, Edward Everett, Oliver Wendell Holmes and James Russell Lowell. The paper included poems, book reviews, and articles on such diverse matters as sea life and Roman archaeology. Emerson and James Freeman Clarke were among the contributors, but Julia herself did most of the writing, including an amusing short story in Dickensian style, entitled "Journal of a Fancy Fair," which described the efforts of a young official, or fair marshal, to win the affections of a pretty girl selling at the Baptist table.[2]

Although the *Boatswain's Whistle* occupied nearly every waking moment of Julia's time for a month or so, as soon as the fair ended she was at work studying and writing on more serious subjects. "My Ethics are now the joke of my family," she wrote Louisa, "and Flossy, or any child, wishing a second helping will say, "Is it ethical, Mamma?"[3] Even in the privacy of her room, Julia could not cut herself off completely from the inevitable distractions provided by a family of six children. When one of the girls was practicing the piano and played a wrong note, Julia would, likely as not, slip out of her room and call over the balcony to the floor below: "B *flat*, dear, not B natural."[4]

By the winter of 1861 the five older children were all in school, leaving little Sammy, then two, to accompany his mother on her daily walks. Julia Romana, the oldest, was then a shy, pretty girl of seventeen, with dark hair, clear gray eyes and a pink-and-white complexion. The most serious of the Howe children, she admired her father above all other human beings and from the time she was tiny she had followed him everywhere. Now that she was nearly grown up she tended to side with him on family matters, often to her mother's intense irritation. Julia, in fact, found her two oldest daughters difficult. Perhaps she resented their preference for Chev. Flossy, then sixteen, later explained their particular bond with him: it had originated when their mother was in Italy. "The absence in Europe for more than a year, of my mother and the two younger children, Harry and Laura, brought Julia and myself under his care when we were respectively five and six years old. We thus early formed the habit of close companionship with him, to which, as the elder, we had special claim."[5] Flossy, a stubborn child, was also very critical of her mother in these years before her father's death. But she was also a practical and sensible girl, a good seamstress, and adept at handling the family accounts.

Young Harry was the mischief-maker in the family. He apparently inherited this quality from his father, who had been a renowned practical joker while an undergraduate at Brown. One of Harry's sisters later recalled that it was "not safe to put him in the closet for misbehaviour; for he cut off the pockets of the dresses hanging there, and snipped the fringe off his teacher's best shawl."[6] Harry would grow up to be a dedicated and distinguished scientist, but until he graduated from Harvard in 1869, his parents were always fearful that he would disgrace himself. Actually, in college he was only put on probation once, although it was assumed by the authorities that if any mischief occurred,

Harry Howe was behind it.[7] Harry was closest to his sister Laura, who in turn was perhaps the closest of all the children to Julia and the most sympathetic to her. Known familiarly as "the Comforter," she was a happy, easy child, and although bright and clever, according to Flossy, she was too amiable to be critical of her mother as her older sisters were.[8]

Julia enjoyed her children — they provided her with much-needed companionship — but at the same time she often found them trying. Occasionally a despairing note would creep into her letters to her sisters, in which she complained of the difficulties of managing "the six children, their trouble-giving Papa, and the four servants. . . . My girls don't give me any assistance, and they do give a good deal of trouble, Julia being very helpless, and Flossy tolerably headstrong — they give great pleasure however."[9] Julia Romana had inherited her mother's aversion to domestic tasks. She much preferred to accompany her father to the Perkins Institute, where she eventually became a teacher, or to shut herself in her room to study or write. She was often tormented with what was known in the family as the "Howe shyness." Longfellow called her a "veiled lily," noting as others did that she was wont to sit quietly in a corner of the room while others carried on a conversation; occasionally the talk would become so interesting that she would forget herself and join in.[10]

Julia Romana's shyness was surely in part a reaction to her mother's extraordinary sociability. Even during the war years there was much entertaining at 13 Chestnut Street. Julia could scarcely resist the temptation to give one party after another as long as she had the good fortune to be spending the winter in town. There were musical parties, charade parties, literary parties, and "Owl" parties where the talk was "transcendental — philosophic."[11] Flossy remembered one such evening when Emerson and Holmes were among the guests. Holmes, always a great talker, had on that particular occasion dominated the conversation rather more than usual. When it came time to leave he remarked casually to Julia, "Well, I have told you a great deal about myself today." Whereupon one of the other guests interjected firmly that "others could have told of their experiences too, Doctor, if you had given them a chance."[12] It was in Chestnut Street in the early sixties that one of Julia's early clubs was formed — the Ladies Social Club of Boston, familiarly known as the Brain Club. Artists and writers were invited to the meetings to entertain the members with lectures, charades, music and recitations.[13] Flossy once said of her mother that "to entertain her friends was as essential to her happiness as to read and study," and Chev claimed that if Julia "were alone on a desert island, with one old negro, she would manage to have a party."[14]

During the war, summers were spent as usual at Lawton's Valley. The Howes, like most Bostonians, did not leave for the holidays until after the Fourth of July. Then, amid considerable confusion and accompanied by numerous boxes, trunks, barrels and Julia's grand piano, they would board the train for Fall River. From there they were obliged to ride the last twelve miles in an ancient vehicle, half hack, half stage, whose driver, according to Laura, was more concerned about the welfare of his ancient horses than that of his passengers. But the pleasure of finally arriving in the Valley, "to tumble out of the stuffy prison-coach, and race through the orchard and out to the barn, and up the hill behind the house . . . was worth all the miseries of the journey."[15]

Chev had continued to work on the house and grounds during the ten years he and Julia had owned the place. On the weekends when he came down from Boston, he occupied himself by cutting down trees, planting shrubs and curbing the stream, which had once turned the old mill wheel. On the carpet of grass next to the stream picnics and tea parties were held, as well as games of croquet. The girls went swimming in the millpond "in dresses of mattress-ticking, striped blue and white, close around throat, wrist and ankle." They were very proud of these rather awkward "swimsuits," which they admitted became frightfully heavy when wet.[16]

The Valley's "healing balm of quiet" did much to restore Julia after a hard winter's work.[17] But there was plenty of sociability too, whenever she wanted it. In the early years of the war Newport was still a haven for southerners willing to risk the journey into enemy territory to escape the heat and fevers of the Carolina swamps, but Julia found their behavior in 1861 very irritating. The women had a way of pulling aside their wide skirts whenever they passed a Union flag and they understandably behaved in a generally scornful manner toward northerners. It was said that when the prayer for the President was read in the Episcopal Church in Newport, the "Secesh" would mark their dissent by refusing to kneel.[18] Julia decided to teach these southerners a lesson. It was customary at many Howe picnics to include theatricals of some sort. On one occasion during the summer of 1861 Julia decided that a pantomime with one of her northern friends impersonating America would be just the thing. Mrs. Hall, the lady so chosen, had, as it happened, a son fighting in the Union army. Julia, her daughters and various other northern ladies then proceeded to crown Mrs. "America" with flowers and salute her with patriotic songs.[19] Whether or not they succeeded in making their point to the southern women present, for a number of other, obvious reasons few ventured to make the journey north the following summer.

Other signs of the war were evident in Newport. Shortly after hostilities opened, the Naval Academy was moved there from Annapolis. The presence of the young cadets provided many excuses for gay parties, among them the weekly dances held on board the old frigate *Constitution,* which was anchored in Newport Harbor. A military camp and hospital were set up only three miles from the Howes' cottage. The soldiers took to washing their clothes in the stream below the house, thereby disrupting a number of the Howe family picnics.

The war inevitably produced sad moments as well as happy ones. Julia never forgot an "afternoon on which I drove into town with my son . . . and found the main street lined with carriages, and the carriages filled with white-faced people, intent on I knew not what. Meeting a friend, I asked, 'Why are these people here? What are they waiting for, and why do they look as they do?' 'They are waiting for the mail,' was the reply. 'Don't you know that we have had a dreadful reverse?' "[20] The "dreadful reverse" was the Second Battle of Bull Run.

Even during the war Julia loved nothing better than to fill the old farmhouse to overflowing. Often the Mailliards and their children would come up from Bordentown to spend a few weeks. Flossy remembered being frequently awakened in the middle of the night and made to give up her bed to a relative who had arrived unexpectedly. Nor was it unknown for Harry to sleep on the top of the grand piano.[21] Uncle Sam Ward, whose dual role as northern spy and southern sympathizer continued during the war years, nearly always arrived unexpectedly. When Washington sweltered in the summer heat, he loved to come and spend a few weeks in the cool and quiet of Newport with Julia and her children. Because Chev rarely came to Lawton's Valley during the war years, brother and sister were free to enjoy one another's company. Julia, too, disapproved of much that her brother did, but she was too intimate with him and too conscious of the basic goodness of his character, to allow his actions to influence her affection for him.

Besides, her children adored their uncle. He was the visitor they awaited most eagerly, but they never knew when he would appear. Once Laura remembered waking at dawn to the sound of someone singing under her window. Slipping out of bed she peered behind the curtains and saw her beloved uncle standing on the doorstep with a basket of peaches beside him. He never came empty-handed, and his nieces and nephews claimed that "he would have shared his last crust with any of us, and the crust

Julia Ward when she was four years old. Collection of Eleanor Saunders

Henry, Sam and Julia Ward about 1825. Miniature on ivory by Anne Hall. Courtesy of the Redwood Library and Athenaeum, Newport, Rhode Island

Samuel Gridley Howe in the uniform of the Greek revolution, 1830. Courtesy of the John Hay Library, Brown University

The author of Passion Flowers *painted in Rome on her wedding journey during the winter of 1843–1844. Portrait courtesy of Mrs. Betty Wiggins*

Green Peace. Collection of Julia Ward Stickley

Julia Ward Howe taken at the time she wrote "The Battle Hymn of the Republic," 1861. Photograph courtesy of Julia Ward Stickley

Lawton's Valley. Photograph courtesy of Julia Ward Stickley

Julia Ward Howe at the age of eighty-nine. Collection of Julia Ward Stickley

would have been prepared in some marvelous way that made a tidbit of it."[22] Once inside the house and seated at the breakfast table, he would talk tirelessly. The younger children one after another would climb up on his lap and play with his great sapphire ring and wait to see what he would produce out of his pockets. During these years the old millhouse was fitted up as bachelor quarters for Sam. He and his second wife Medora had been reunited during the brief months of his prosperity in 1848 and she had been in and out of his life since then. But in the late 1850's, tired of living with his precarious fortunes, Medora had taken their two boys and left him to go abroad. Sam never saw either of his two sons again: both died in Europe and their mother did not long survive them. His only descendant was Maddie, the child of his first marriage. But she had been brought up by her Astor relatives to disapprove of her father. Thus Sam Ward was in many ways a very lonely man, and the person on whom he chiefly relied for comfort in these years was his sister Julia.

Newport in the 1860's was still a relatively quiet unpretentious resort. Ever since the '50's the number of Bostonians and New Yorkers who spent their summers there increased yearly. One summer Sam wrote Longfellow that nineteen members of his family were on hand.[23] Various Ward cousins, including Greenes and Rays, were scattered all over Rhode Island. The Ward McAllisters, Julia and Sam's Cutler cousins, still summered in Newport and so did the family of Cousin Samuel Ward Francis, Aunt Eliza's son. Maud, the youngest of the Howe girls, remembered that a great many of her mother's "Owls" followed her to Newport. As a child she found these literary and scientific folk very boring because they spent their time in the Valley sitting under the big ash tree drinking tea and talking philosophy. Occasionally they would behave sensibly in the children's eyes and consent to act in a charade or join in some signing.[24] In fact, Lawton's Valley became a kind of melting pot for all varieties of

Newporters. Here reform, poetry and fashion came together when Julia conducted her "salon" in the Green Parlor. Hardly the epitome of fashion, Julia, now in her middle forties, was already a rather dumpy figure. Her bright red hair was the last reminder of her past beauty. But she enjoyed, as she always had, mixing all sorts of people together.

By mid-October the Howes were back in Boston and ready for a winter of hard work. In January of 1863 Julia began keeping a diary for the first time since her marriage. To begin with she merely jotted down the record of various expenses. Then suddenly on Wednesday, May 13, the entry is fuller: "Walked out with dearest Sammy — his gaiters and scarf forgotten." That afternoon she sent the little boy, then three and a half, out for a drive, but noted that "he did not seem quite bright." By the following morning Sammy was very ill with diphtheria. Chev was away, and on Friday Julia telegraphed him to return as quickly as possible. Two days later the child was dead.[25]

Both parents were heartbroken at the loss of their youngest child and second son. For Chev it was an all but mortal blow. Julia, younger and more resilient than her husband, recovered eventually, but at first she too was numb with sorrow. The day after the funeral she sat for a time in the room where Sammy had died. She felt "almost strangled with grief." As she had many years before, after the death of her father and her brother Henry, Julia turned to religion and consoled herself by reading the Book of Common Prayer.[26]

It was only natural that she should also seek relief from sorrow through her pen, and several weeks after Sammy's death she sat down and wrote him a letter recounting the circumstances of his illness and death and including her memories of the few short years of his life. In the course of the letter she explained:

> It gives me dreadful pain to recall these things, and write them down, my dearest. I don't do it to make myself miserable, but

in order that I may have some lasting record of how you lived and died. You left little by which you might be remembered, save the love of kindred and friendly hearts, but in my heart, dear, your precious image is deeply sculptured. All my life will be full of grief for you, dearest boy, and I think that I shall hardly live so long as I should have lived, if I had you to make me happy. Perhaps it seems very foolish that I should write all this, and talk to you in it as if you could know what I wrote. But, my little darling, it comforts me to think that your sweet soul lives, and that you know something about me. Christ said: this day thou shall be with me in Paradise, and he knew that this was no vain promise. So, believing the dear Christ, I am led along to have faith in immortal life, of which, dear, I know nothing myself.[27]

A change of scene was imperative for the bereaved family, and on the twenty-first, Chev, Julia and Maud left the house on Chestnut Street to spend nearly a month in New York. "All hands improved by the journey," Julia stoically noted in her diary upon their arrival. The agony had lessened somewhat, "but the sorrow will ever remain."[28] She had already begun the slow, painful process of recovery, but Chev spent nearly all of that month confined to his bed, apparently felled by grief. His health was never the same again; to the recurring attacks of malaria from which he had suffered ever since his years in Greece were now added symptoms of neuralgia, rheumatism and heart trouble.

Shortly after returning from New York, Julia and the children left for Newport. Here she passed a quiet summer seeing few people and working hard at her studies. As Laura later noted: "Religion and philosophy went hand in hand with her."[29] She began that summer by reading Spinoza, then Fichte — whom she found very difficult — followed by Hegel and Schelling. But simple study was not enough for her and by the end of the summer she had composed half a dozen papers on ethical subjects. On September 24 she noted in her diary: "At 11:53 A.M.

157

finished Essay on Religion, for the power to produce which I thank God. I believe that I have in this built up a greater coherence between things natural and things divine than I have seen or heard made out by anyone else. I therefore rejoice over my work and thank God, hoping it may be of service to others as it has certainly been to me."[30]

The years immediately following Sammy's death appear to have been critical ones for Julia's own religious philosophy. Not only did she write a number of papers on religious subjects, but she also made the decision to become an official member of the Unitarian Church. Apparently the experience of extreme grief combined with a rigorous study of European philosophy had succeeded in clarifying and strengthening her religious convictions. By 1865 she could rightly claim to be a liberal Christian in the best nineteenth-century meaning of the term,[31] and "The Ideal Church," a paper she published that year in the *Christian Examiner,* gives a clear statement of her religious views. Emphasizing her belief in man's freedom and his innate capacity for goodness, Julia rejected what she saw as the traditional bondage of religious dogma, which she and other liberals claimed had been dividing rather than uniting Christians. "The spirit of the liberal Christian Church," she asserted, "lies not so much in what we believe as in the manner in which we believe it." It is not by dogma that we are led to the divine but rather by "the infallibility of moral instinct." Man must learn to govern himself by reason and not by passion, and to teach "this intimate and initial form of self-government, upon which all others rest, is the business of the Church." An essentially progressive theory, liberal Christianity must seek to work for a collective goal which would be "far higher and more stable" than any individual goal. Even man's imperfections were "an element of good and of pleasure," and "the interchange of thought" and "refutation of error" — by which she meant the false sense of values she saw in society — were both essential elements in the progress toward the ideal.[32]

In these years Julia began to feel that she had a particular part to play in the advancement of liberal Christianity, especially with regard to the "interchange of thought" and the "refutation of error." Some years earlier she had spoken to Theodore Parker about her wish to speak in public and he had encouraged her. Her plan was to give a series of parlor readings on ethical subjects in the Chestnut Street house, to which a select group of friends would be invited to listen and comment. "It was borne in upon me," she wrote many years later, "that I had much to say to my day and generation which could not and should not be communicated in rhyme."[33]

Back in Boston in October 1863 Julia spoke to Chev of her plan. She hoped that he would not only approve but also consent to her charging a small fee to those attending the readings. He apparently did not object to the readings themselves, but he was adamant that she should receive no compensation. That, he insisted, would put them in the same class with public lectures and he disapproved of his wife's leading any kind of public life. Julia, however, already had some idea of what it was like to speak to a large audience and the prospect held enormous appeal for her. At the Emancipation Day celebration in Boston on January 1, 1863, she had read her "Battle Hymn" to the great throng gathered in the Music Hall to applaud President Lincoln's freeing of the slaves. Her recital was by no means the high point of the festivities, for it was here that Emerson read his "Boston Hymn," written especially for the occasion. George L. Stearns, the old admirer of John Brown's, recalled that Mrs. Howe recited her verses in "a weird penetrating voice, which affected the whole company."[34] For the remainder of Julia's life people would continue to be amazed by the carrying power of her seemingly soft voice. It would become one of the keys to her popularity as a public speaker.

The following winter she preached her first sermon at the Parker Fraternity, having been encouraged to do so by her pastor,

James Freeman Clarke. On January 17, 1864, Clarke announced from the pulpit of the Church of the Disciples that "an essay on the Soul and Body would be read by a friend at the Wednesday evening meeting." The friend was Julia Ward Howe and the essay one of her lectures: "Duality of Character." For the occasion she wore a white cap instead of her usual thick bonnet and was pleased to discover a good audience, although she was upset that Chev was not among them.[35] Essentially progressive in its message, Julia's paper discussed the twofold aspect of man's character — its higher and lower natures. Urging her listeners to recognize this duality within themselves she claimed that such recognition, combined with a constant effort on the part of each individual to maintain the rule of the higher over the lower self, would assure the progress of civilization.[36]

All of this suggests that Julia's religious and ethical views, however important they may have been to her and to the progressive spirit she would later bring to her reform work, were for the most part undistinguished. They are both serious and highly literate, the product of much thought and reading, but essentially they are a mere restatement of the tenets of contemporary liberal Christianity.

For the time being Julia went along with Chev's opposition to her speaking in public and took no payment for the course of six lectures she delivered in the big double parlor in the house on Chestnut Street. According to the entries in her diary, the readings of "Equality," "The Dynamic Idea of God" and "Duality of Character" were well received, the audiences both large and attentive.

At the same time, she was continuing to publish in a number of periodicals. Besides an occasional letter on Newport society for the New York *Tribune* she submitted numerous poems to the *Atlantic Monthly*. The *Christian Examiner* published several of her philosophical essays, including "The Ideal Church," and at the end of 1865 her third volume of poems, *Later Lyrics,* came

160

out. The last was not very well received by the critics, but a few of the poems were generally admired. One of them, entitled "The Flag," though certainly not great poetry, became quite popular and may be worth quoting since it exemplifies the kind of fierce patriotism engendered by the Civil War:

> *There's a flag hangs over my threshold*
> *whose folds are more dear to me*
> *Than the blood that thrills in my bosom*
> *its earnest of liberty;*
> *And dear are the stars it harbors in its*
> *sunny field of blue*
> *As the hope of a further heaven, that*
> *lights all our dim lives through.* [37]

The word slavery, even the theme of freeing men from bondage, is rarely mentioned in *Later Lyrics*. The emphasis here is on fighting for the Union. The war had in fact changed Julia's outlook, much as it had changed the outlook of those around her. This emphasis on nationalism and the need for its active promotion were convincing many hitherto self-absorbed northern intellectuals that they must repudiate the solitary, individualistic, scholarly life in favor of becoming influential and politically active citizens. [38] Julia followed this pattern. The lukewarm reception that had greeted her last book of poems, combined with this new spirit of activism she saw all around her, convinced her that she must leave the privacy of her study and say what she had to say, not indirectly through the pages of a book, but directly with her own voice. She was beginning to discover that her real talent lay not in writing but in speaking, where the magnetism of her personality combined with her extraordinary voice, gave her words a power they lacked in cold print.

As Julia's ambition to mount the lecture platform grew with the evident success of her parlor readings and the occasional recital of her poems to large audiences, Chev became more and more obdurate in his disapproval. Late in the winter of 1864, her series of readings in the Chestnut Street house was completed. Because they were well received, Julia decided that she would like to give the same course for a similar audience in Washington. Even though she obtained little support from family and friends for this plan, she noted in her diary that she was going "in obedience to a deep and strong impulse."[39] The lectures in Washington apparently went well. Not surprisingly it was a local Unitarian minister, William Henry Channing, who gave her the greatest support.

In contrast, Charles Sumner was strongly outspoken in his disapproval and this pained Julia greatly. He not only refused her invitation to attend the readings but also made it quite clear that he considered her unqualified to speak on such abstruse matters.[40] She tried in vain to explain her reasons in a letter to Sumner on March 1: "It was honestly the atrocious tone of society on the occasion of your almost murder that first filled me with the desire to find this deep word of reproof." Criticizing the methods employed by the abolitionists against their erstwhile critics she argued that "the only way to treat effectually the evils of society is to treat them with sympathy. My whole study has been to find that deeper vein of consideration which should shew the reasons for the mistakes that men make, and the sins they commit."[41]

When Julia arrived home from Washington in the last days of May 1864, Chev showed his displeasure by being unusually critical and unreasonable in his demands, but she was determined that his objections should not deter her. That autumn she received an invitation to read a poem at the Bryant Centenary Celebration in New York. Chev, of course, was firmly opposed, but Julia went anyway, declaring in her journal that "internal necessity conquered external."[42] All through her diary for 1865 there are references to a continuing struggle with her family regarding the kind of life she insisted on making for herself.

When, on March 11, she was asked to read a poem at the Tufts University Commencement, it took her almost a week to work up the courage to ask Chev for permission to accept. When she did finally ask he naturally refused, insisting that it was his will and authority that must rule in the household.[43]

In April the wrangling over Julia's lecturing reached a climax. The news of Lee's surrender on the ninth, followed so quickly by Lincoln's assassination, seems to have thrown the whole Howe household into an emotional turmoil, but one that had more to do with family matters than with the end of the war. On April 23 both Chev and Flossy attacked Julia for the course her life was taking. The immediate cause was a proposed lecture before the Parker Fraternity. Flossy accused her mother of giving her father pain by insisting on delivering the lectures. Chev would not even listen to Julia's attempt to defend herself and dismissed the whole undertaking as mere display on her part. Julia, understandably, was deeply hurt by all this, and poured out her anger and frustration in her journal. She complained that she had been married for twenty-two years, during which time Chev had never approved of one act that she valued. "I never knew him to be so cruel and unjust as today."[44]

Somehow Chev managed to get hold of the journal and read the most recent entry. He begged her to tear the page out, claiming, probably with some justification, that her emotions had gotten the better of her. By this time Chev himself was in a more rational frame of mind, and he tried to explain to his wife that the reason he admired the work of such women as Florence Nightingale and Dorothea Dix, and was not critical of their being in the public eye, was that they were single. For a married woman to behave the way they did was quite another matter.[45] On the following day, Sunday, Julia spoke to her minister after the service about the trouble she was having with her family over her readings. Clarke apparently encouraged her to persevere despite the opposition from home, and several days later she gave

163

another lecture before the Parker Fraternity. Perhaps it was partly to punish Julia that Chev undertook early in the summer to sell Lawton's Valley without consulting her.

In any case the struggle between husband and wife continued, and was made even more difficult by Julia's uncertainty about the direction she wished her life to take. On June 3, 1865, she notes in her diary, "Literary affairs confused, I have no market. Chev takes away my voice and I do not see how or where to print. God keeps me from falling away from my purpose."[46] In these years money was very short and this partly explains the sale of Lawton's Valley as well as Julia's ambivalence about her future as a writer. Her published poems did add to the family revenue and she tried to get as much money for them as she could, often pestering her publisher, James T. Fields, to pay her more.[47]

Despite Julia's uncertainty about where this new career as a lecturer was taking her, she did not falter in her determination to go her own way. And it is clear that she was no longer motivated solely by personal ambition. A number of entries in her diary indicate that she now saw a strong religious justification for her new career. In one entry she referred to her speaking and writing as coming "in obedience to a deep, strong impulse"; in another, "If I am sent for and have the word to say, I should say it"; and in yet another, "I can only be good in fulfilling my highest function."[48] Her conscience, not her husband, was now her chief guide in such matters.

In the autumn of 1865 the Howes were forced to leave 13 Chestnut Street as the owners wanted it back. They did not return to South Boston. Instead, Chev purchased a house at 19 Boylston Place, a gloomy cul-de-sac whose only advantage was its proximity to the Boston Public Library. The whole family was reluctant to leave Chestnut Street. On the day of the move, Julia noted sadly in her journal: "This is my last writing in this dear house . . . where I have had three years of good work, social and family enjoyment. Here I enjoyed dear Sammy for six happy months — here I mourned long and bitterly for him. Here I read my six lectures on Practical Ethics. Some of my best days have been passed in this house. God be thanked for the same!"[49] The Howes lived in Boylston Place until 1868, when they moved back to Beacon Hill, this time to 32 Mount Vernon Street, an architecturally undistinguished house with a plain façade on the shady side of the street. This was the last of many houses in which all the Howes would live together. In 1871 the three oldest girls were married within a few months of one another. Meanwhile Harry, having graduated from both Harvard and MIT, had gone to Troy, New York, to earn his living as a scientist. Maud was the only child left at home.

Julia Romana had met her husband in Greece in 1867, when she had accompanied her parents there on a trip to distribute relief to the Cretan refugees who had been rebelling against Turkish rule. The sum of $37,000 had been raised in both Boston and New York, and Julia Romana's mother had helped by charging for her readings. (Chev did not seem to object to his wife's collecting lecture fees as long as it was for a good cause.) The Howes had set sail in March and had spent some time in Italy with Louisa before going to Greece. Louisa had lost her first husband and had married the American painter Luther Terry in 1861.

It had been many years since Julia had seen her sister and she undoubtedly found her changed, but not so changed as Rome itself. Julia had looked forward to this visit, the first since the long happy winter of 1850–1851, but she was very disappointed to discover that her old affection for the city could not be resurrected. In fact, it was not so much Rome that had changed as Julia herself, now a very different person from the unhappy, passionate young woman who had so lost herself in the romance of the ancient city sixteen years earlier. "Now, I must confess," she wrote in 1867, "that, after so many intense and vivid pages of life (the failure of John Brown, the sorrow and success of the late war) this visit to Rome once a theme of fervent and solemn desire, becomes a mere page of embellishment."

What had appeared sophisticated and romantic two decades earlier now appeared decadent, and Julia reprimanded the Americans then living in Rome, including Louisa, for attaching themselves to the "false superiority" of Roman society with its "smile of disdain for simple people." How superior she felt to the thirty-year-old Julia who had walked the ancient streets hunting for small jewelry and pictures: "I find the personage of those days poor and trivial." The only possible excuse, Julia now claimed, that anyone could have for spending time in Rome would be to study its art. But even art itself was now relegated to second place in her hierarchy of culture: "The inner convictions of heart, of conscience, may now be spoken in plain prose or sung in ringing verse. The prophet or reformer will impart his belief and his system best in its simplest and most direct form.[50]

Almost as soon as the Howes arrived in Rome, Chev, accompanied by Julia Romana and an American writer, Moncure Conway, departed for Greece. Julia worried about her daughter's safety without proper female companionship, but Chev insisted that it would be too expensive for them all to go. Julia had her doubts that this explained her husband's real motive for leaving her behind, and thought the actual reason might be due "to an indefinable fear of my predominance where he would wish to be the whole figure, which of course he would and ought to be."[51] A month later, however, she received a letter from Chev urging her to come and join him. She and Laura found him comfortably installed in a pleasant apartment in Athens, surrounded by Cretan refugees as well as by old men who had known him in the days of the Greek revolution and young men who knew his reputation and were anxious to make his acquaintance. Among the last was Michael Anagnostopoulos, who succeeded in persuading Howe to take him back to America and employ him as his secretary. Michael eventually married Julia Romana, shortened his name to Anagnos, and after his father-in-law's death succeeded him as director of the Perkins Institute.

Chev, who always missed his wife after more than a short separation, was delighted at first to have her with him in Athens. But his enthusiasm waned when he discovered that she was almost as much in demand as he was. Julia had hardly settled herself in her husband's quarters when she was asked to give a reading at the Acropolis to a number of Englishwomen. This was followed by other invitations to speak. Julia was naturally pleased with her success, but Chev was less so, particularly when people began to praise his wife's lectures in his presence.[52]

The Howes returned home in late October 1867 to find both their houses rented, so they settled themselves in the Doctor's Wing, an abode Julia still found unutterably dreary. As usual, it was hard for her to settle back into the routine of home life. She had found the months abroad very stimulating despite her newly critical view of Rome and indeed of all Europe. With all the children together again the old family discords broke out once more, and now Maud was old enough to join in. The cold, draughty rooms of the institute were almost more than Julia could bear, particularly since this was the first winter she had not spent in town in six years. One thing after another seemed to compound her misery. Soon after their return the Howes learned that Charles Sumner's wife had left him. Divorce was rare in those days, and despite, or perhaps because of, their own brush with the possibility of separation, both Julia and Chev were very upset by the news. The day the word reached them, Julia noted in her diary that "for men and women to come together is nature, for them to live together is art, to live well, high art."[53]

No sooner had news reached the Howes of Sumner's divorce than word came of John Andrew's death. "The benevolent cherub in spectacles," as Flossy described him,[54] had worn himself out as the wartime governor of Massachusetts working for the Union, and had died of a heart attack. Julia remembered him as one of her staunch friends and wrote a poem she hoped she would be allowed to read at his public memorial service. But Mrs. Andrew, who, one supposes, was not such a good friend of Julia's as her husband had been, told her that she would rather someone else read it. "I believe in God, but am utterly weary of man," Julia wrote after that rebuff.[55]

In these months Julia was also depressed by the thought of her own future. *Later Lyrics* was no longer selling well and to add to this discouragement a bad notice appeared in the *North American Review,* one she found "mean in motive and illiterate in criticism." She was not much better at accepting an unfavorable review than most authors. "No one of real culture," she complained of the reviewer, "handles in that way a book, which, whatever its faults, is literature and not merely ballad."[56] The fact was that Julia was never able to think of herself as anything but a first-class poet. Dreams of youth die hard, and this, coupled with the success of *Passion Flowers* and the unequaled popularity of the "Battle Hymn," meant that she often handled bad reviews with an extraordinary lack of grace. Her readings that fall did not go particularly well either. Discouragement seemed to pervade all her thinking. "I have so dreamed of high use," she complained to her journal, "that I cannot decline to a life of amusement or small occupation."[57]

"*I Am with You*"

*Now, I believe it is a woman's right to have a voice
in all the laws and regulations by which she is to be
governed.*
— Angelina Grimké, 1838

Julia Howe awakened on Tuesday morning, November 18, 1868, to find a cold east wind blowing out of Boston Harbor. Snow had fallen in the night, but now it was raining. Shortly before ten o'clock she left the house at 19 Boylston Place and made her way through the maze of streets in downtown Boston to Horticultural Hall. Slipping into one of the seats at the back of the auditorium, she hoped to remain unnoticed, but word had gone out the day before that Mrs. Howe might attend the meeting and perhaps address it as well. In any case there was something unmistakable about the short, stoutish woman, rather carelessly and unfashionably dressed. She was recognized almost immediately and persuaded, somewhat against her will, to join the others on the platform.

So began Julia Howe's first woman suffrage meeting and a commitment for the rest of her life to a cause which until then she had regarded with skepticism. Thomas Wentworth Higginson, whom she had first met before the war as one of the Secret Six supporters of John Brown, had persuaded her to go. He and Julia had seen a good deal of one another recently. Not only did

169

Higginson now live for most of the year in Newport, but they both belonged to the Radical Club, a group of Bostonians who assembled on the first Monday of every month to discuss one another's learned papers. A handsome, vigorous man, Higginson had commanded the first regiment of freed slaves during the war. With the return of peace he, like many onetime abolitionists, had taken up the cause of woman suffrage and was on the platform when Julia entered Horticultural Hall. So were a number of other respectable Boston people, including William Lloyd Garrison, Wendell Phillips, and Julia's own minister, James Freeman Clarke, all of whom had been leaders of the New England abolitionist movement before the war. Yet there was one person seated there who had for some time been the object of Julia's "imaginary dislikes":[1] Lucy Stone, a veteran leader of both the antislavery and suffrage movements and the organizer of this meeting.

The first Massachusetts woman to receive a college degree, Lucy Stone had joined Garrison's antislavery society as a lecturer shortly after her graduation from Oberlin. She caused considerable trouble by injecting the issue of woman's rights into the society's propaganda. In 1850 she had called the first national women's rights convention in Worcester.[2] During the war, domestic concerns as well as national ones interrupted her lecturing, but now in 1868 she had resumed her active career, taking part in various unsuccessful suffrage campaigns and helping to organize the American Equal Rights Association, which sought to secure the vote for both blacks and women. Lucy had the reputation of being one of the nation's best woman speakers. She was small, with a low but engaging voice, and people were deeply moved by the sincerity and eloquence of her speeches. But Julia Howe had built up an image in her mind of an arrogant, unladylike female who had in some way betrayed the essential womanliness of her sex.

As Julia herself willingly admitted, she had until recently

170

been rather contemptuous of other women, regarding them as inferior to men in matters of intelligence and common sense. In the years before the war many of the middle-class women she had seen around her had only confirmed her opinion. Few had had more than a rudimentary education. Their lives were restricted to home and church, and they thought of little but cooking, clothes and gossip. Many were adept at the art of flirting, but only a few — Julia considered herself to be among them — could converse on a given subject with any depth. But "the very flattery which men paid to women of some pretensions to learning or intellect was calculated," Julia later remembered, "to lead them to regard their own sex with a kind of contempt."[3] Furthermore, Julia's experience of her own upbringing and marriage had shown her the hazards of giving women too high an opinion of their talents. The question can be asked whether she had not perhaps been projecting Chev's criticisms of her own desire to lead a public life onto Lucy Stone and the other suffrage leaders.

Among Julia's papers is an undated manuscript entitled "The Woman's Rights Question," written sometime in the late 1840's or early 1850's, and read before an unidentified audience. She was apparently reluctant to deliver the paper and made it clear from the start that she had no intention of making a habit of public speaking. "I might perhaps like to wag my paw in a pulpit and even to exchange with Reverend Parker as some of my more ambitious sisters have done. But I should only dwarf myself, by appearing in Giant's Armour. . . . It shall content me playfully to cross words with him in a parlour fight." The essay is redolent with contempt for her sex as a whole. Women she considered to be both frivolous and lacking in common sense, and therefore it was best that they be protected by their husbands and the law. Blaming women for the abundance of superstition then existing in the world, she claimed that "priestcraft . . . in all ages and countries has found its strongest ally in the weakness of women."[4]

But her thoughts on this subject were beginning to undergo a marked change, even in the late '50's. One of her prewar poems, entitled "Florence Nightingale and Her Praisers," chastises men like her own husband for singling out exceptional women for praise, while many others with equal talents are prevented from exercising them by the narrow scope of opportunities open to women.

> *If you debase the sex to elevate*
> *One of like soul and temper with the rest,*
> *You do but wrong a thousand fervent hearts,*
> *To pay full tribute to one generous breast.*[5]

Beginning with the antislavery movement and continuing throughout the Civil War, Julia found herself working more and more with other women. While helping to organize bazaars or sew clothing for Union soldiers, she discovered hundreds of women like herself, who longed to be of service to others besides their families, but had been prevented from doing so by the isolated condition of the housewife. She had also come to the conclusion, as she came to know these other women better, that although she might be better educated, they were in no sense her intellectual inferiors. Until the war Julia's closest friends had all been men. Her intimacy with Theodore Parker and Edward Twistleton, and the intensity of her friendship with Horace Binney Wallace, surely arose out of a need for intellectual companionship, which she did not have with Chev and which she had not yet succeeded in finding among those of her own sex.

Julia's war experiences were only partially responsible for her changing attitude. Her study of philosophy, which recently had focused on the works of Kant, had convinced her that women were the moral and spiritual equals of men and could not therefore be their intellectual inferiors. Kant had placed particular emphasis on the freedom of the human soul and the consequent immorality of preventing any member of the human race from exercising his freedom. Influenced by such reasoning Julia began rather reluctantly to realize that if the ballot had been granted to the emancipated slave, surely the women of the North, who had greatly helped to open the door that admitted the slave to freedom, should be given the vote as well.[6]

In the years immediately following the Civil War the life of the middle-class American housewife was undergoing a considerable change. New inventions like the sewing machine, such developments as gas lighting and municipal water systems, and the availability of canned goods freed her from the more onerous household tasks. Immigration from Ireland and northern Europe provided an ever-increasing supply of cheap household help, all of which gave even the moderately well-to-do housewife considerably more leisure than she had heretofore enjoyed. More women were becoming better educated as a growing number of colleges opened their doors to them, and the exceptionally learned woman was no longer the rarity that Julia herself had been in the years before the war. Needing some outlet for their energies and some way in which to put their education and talents to work, these women began to come together in groups for purposes of culture and companionship.

Today we tend to think of women's clubs as primarily social organizations, but in the decades after the Civil War, clubs supplemented the almost exclusively male colleges and vocational institutions as educational centers. In clubs women acquired training and experience for new occupations. They learned to speak in public and make formal reports, and acquired facility in meeting and working with strangers. As Julia later recalled, until the war had brought them together, women had lived "in little bundles. They had their church and domestic circles, but beyond them their circles did not reach."[7]

In February 1868, Julia received an invitation to attend a meeting for the purpose of forming a woman's club in Boston.

Though not particularly enthusiastic about the proposal, she nevertheless agreed to attend the organizational meeting and gave a halfhearted assent to the measures agreed upon.[8] The club was first conceived as an opportunity for women to meet and relax together. The organizers decided to rent and furnish rooms, drew up a list of prospective members, and made plans for the opening meeting. The first official gathering of the New England Woman's Club was held in May with Julia presiding. A number of gentlemen came and one cannot help feeling that Julia was at least partially responsible for their presence since she would always be opposed to the idea of any woman's organization that in principle excluded men.

Man was indeed a faulty creature, she assured those assembled in Chickering Hall on that late May morning, "but we have largely partaken of his transgressions and have almost always been his accomplices." In the remainder of her short speech Julia claimed that women's organizations were subject to ridicule largely because of the discrepancy between "the magnitude of their legitimate aims and the smallness of their achievement." Yet, she insisted, "half the horizon of the world, social, moral and political," belongs to women "by simple human right."[9] Here was Julia Ward Howe essentially defending the cause of woman suffrage some six months before she reluctantly attended her first suffrage meeting. Having committed herself to the idea of the New England Woman's Club, Julia became one of its most active members. In 1870 she was elected president and she remained in that position until her death forty years later.

Thus war work, the study of Kant, and now the formation of the New England Woman's Club were gradually melting away Julia's suspicions of the women's movement. It is therefore not surprising that she was easily persuaded on that bleak November morning in 1868 to lend her support to the cause of suffrage. Having feared that the leaders of the movement were a coarse, unfeminine lot, she was surprised to find that Lucy Stone looked

174

very womanly indeed with her round, cheerful face. Her voice, Julia discovered, was soft and musical yet persuasive, her arguments were so "simple, strong and convincing" that when Lucy had finished her speech that morning in Horticultural Hall, and Julia herself was asked to contribute a few words, she began by saying, "I am with you."[10]

At the time of Julia's conversion to the suffrage cause, its organization was threatening to split in two. In 1866 the Fourteenth Amendment had been passed, granting the ballot to all male citizens over the age of twenty-one. Susan B. Anthony, Elizabeth Cady Stanton and other more radical suffragists were outraged by the inclusion of the word *male* in the amendment, and were convinced that it was just as important to grant the vote to women as to give it to blacks, perhaps more so. Lucy Stone and the moderates disagreed, and when the Fifteenth Amendment came up for discussion in 1868, proposing to prevent suffrage discrimination on the basis of "race, color, or previous servitude," they agreed not to press Congress to include the word *sex*, on the grounds that after the long and bitter war just ended, it was only right that former slaves should have the vote first. When Julia gave her short speech in Horticultural Hall that November morning, she admitted that she could not have supported woman suffrage until black suffrage was secured.[11] Julia was and always would be a humanist rather than exclusively a feminist. Granting the ballot to women and granting it to blacks were two aspects of a general movement for reform to ensure the continuing progress of civilization.

At the end of the three-day convention in Horticultural Hall the New England Woman Suffrage Association was formed and Julia was elected president. It may appear surprising at first that a woman who had previously had no connection with the suffrage movement should so quickly have assumed a position of such importance. In fact Julia was an excellent choice for the presidency, a position of honor rather than power. Her reputation as a woman of broad learning, earnest patriotism and social prominence gave the cause a respectability it had not had up to then. Tom Appleton, a very proper Bostonian who had little sympathy for enfranchising women, later told Julia's daughters, "Your mother's great importance to this cause is that she forms a bridge between the world of society and the world of reform."[12]

Meanwhile, other matters were widening the breach between radical and moderate suffragists. The most controversial issue revolved around differing views on marriage and sex. Elizabeth Cady Stanton had lately become an embarrassment because of her advocacy of abortion and birth control. She also felt that the blame for the evils of prostitution should be placed on society as well as on the individual. The moderates, who were determined that the movement should disassociate itself from any unorthodox views on marriage and relations between the sexes, criticized their colleagues for raising questions which seemed to them irrelevant.

Suffrage strategies, however, remained at the center of the dispute. At a meeting of the American Equal Rights Association in New York in May 1869, Mrs. Stanton introduced a proposal calling for a woman suffrage amendment to the Constitution; the moderates refused to support this move. The radicals, convinced that they had been betrayed by the male members of the association, who placed the cause of the blacks before that of women, proceeded to form their own suffrage organization for women only. They called it the National Woman Suffrage Association. None of the moderates were invited to attend the first meeting, and they therefore decided to form a group of their own.

In early August, Julia and other members of the New England Woman Suffrage Association circulated a letter which, among other things, stated that "without depreciating the value of Associations already existing, it is yet deemed that an organization at once more comprehensive and more widely representative than any of these is urgently called for." Later that month a call for a convention was issued for the purpose of forming the American Woman Suffrage Association, "which shall embody the deliberate action of the State organizations, and shall carry with it their united weight."[13]

The convention opened in Cleveland on November 24, 1869, with twenty-one of the thirty-seven states represented. Julia, who had already assumed a kind of spiritual leadership of the new organization, attended all the meetings and spoke twice. In words perhaps more appropriate to a sermon than an address before a political and social gathering, she talked of the progress of democracy and righteousness in the world. On the opening day she cautioned women "not to do injustice to others while seeking justice for themselves," thus clearly showing her disapproval of the single-minded feminism of the radical suffragists. Her second address, essentially a history of the women's movement, was, according to one reporter, faultless, and "moved the large audience deeply."[14]

Julia's debut as a suffrage speaker had occurred the previous February, when she addressed a legislative committee in the Green Room of the Massachusetts statehouse. In these early years of the state suffrage campaigns the Massachusetts legislature promised to be more amenable than most state governments to the matter of giving women political equality. Not only were they open to the idea, but they also made it easy for petitioners to get a hearing on a proposed bill every year if they wished.[15] Although Julia was thus assured a friendly audience at this, her first speech for suffrage, she went to the hearing burdened with the knowledge of Chev's strong disapproval. Not that he was opposed to woman suffrage; on the contrary, he approved heartily of giving the ballot to women and could see nothing standing in the way of its easy acceptance. But he refused to accept the idea of his wife's speaking in public. Julia went ahead nonetheless.

Many years later, looking back on the satisfaction she had derived from joining the suffrage movement, she recalled:

> For years past I had felt strongly impelled to lend my voice to
> the convictions of my heart. I had done this in a way from time
> to time, always with the feeling that my course in so doing was
> held to call for apology and explanation by the men and
> women with whose opinions I had hitherto been familiar. I
> now found a sphere of action in which this mode of expression
> no longer appeared singular or eccentric, but simple, natural,
> and under the circumstances, inevitable.[16]

Having committed herself to the cause of suffrage, all Julia's
arguments against the reform suddenly became so many reasons
in its favor. "All that I had felt regarding the sacredness and
importance of the woman's part in private life now appeared to
me equally applicable to the part which she should bear in public
life."[17] She came to see that all women, and not simply a superior
few, would be elevated through this reform. The argument was a
simple one, a matter of ideal justice: "When it was declared that
all men are born free and equal, it was certainly implied that all
women were so born. For the right postulated in this assertion is
the universal right of the human being."[18]

Already in her first suffrage speeches Julia spoke as the
prophet of the movement: "I, though no apostle, have good news
to tell you, news that shall make beautiful the feet of him who
brings them. And my news is this, the longest mission, the
deepest discord in the whole symphony of the human race approaches solution."[19] Woman suffrage, the key to woman's advancement, was also the key to the progress of the whole of
mankind. Julia spoke as peacemaker as well as prophet. "Our
errand," she declared in a speech before the American Woman
Suffrage Association in New York, "is one altogether of peace and
harmony. . . . We don't come here to ignore oppositions but to
reconcile them."[20]

Julia Howe was certainly no radical as far as the woman's
movement was concerned. She insisted over and over again that
she had no wish to alter the fundamental role of women as wives

and mothers, that she merely desired to make them intelligent companions for their husbands and wise instructors for their children. She assured the audience assembled at the first meeting of the American Woman Suffrage Association that she wished she could adequately express her belief "that the family is effectively to gain, not to lose by the extended activity of women."[21] She did believe that women should be trained to earn their own living, but she considered this mainly as a kind of precautionary measure, one with which Chev heartily agreed. For those women who did not marry and those who married but were suddenly left widowed and perhaps destitute, it was essential that they be able to support themselves.[22]

It was a common belief in the years before the Civil War that women were the moral superiors of men both in their role as mothers and as the guardians of religion in society.[23] Julia understood that this placing of women on a moral pedestal was basically a male subterfuge to keep women in an overprotected and restricted condition. "You are our subordinates," men say, "bound to serve and obey, and you should therefore have certain inestimable qualities which we do not feel obliged to possess." You should, men insisted, "be better than we."[24]

Julia did not agree that women were better than men. She felt they had been pretending a moral superiority which they did not in fact possess. However, women's particular situation in life did make it easier for them to achieve a superior moral state. First, women had the great advantage of being mothers and therefore the natural teachers of men; second, they had traditionally been the guardians of religious matters, at least in the home, and it followed that they should therefore set the religious tone of society; and finally she believed — and one wonders how well she knew her European history — that women shared a simplicity and a lack of sophistication about worldly matters which made them more receptive than men to ethical teachings.[25]

Like many other Victorians, Julia would continue to see

179

women as a class apart. They were equal to men, but their sphere was not the same, and the role demanded of them in their particular sphere implied that they shared certain characteristics. For example, as mothers it was natural that they should be peace-loving and opposed to violence and bloodshed. Because they had suffered the pains of childbirth, only women knew the true value of human life. Men, on the other hand, were naturally brutish, a quality they had developed in a more barbarous age out of the need for self-defense.[26] If women had been hindered in the past from achieving true equality in political, social and religious matters it was because they had been hampered by "an education disproportionate to the general attainments and needs of human society." The crusade for the advancement of women, Julia was convinced, had already begun to restore the balance between the two sexes.[27] Indeed, the effect of all these arguments seemed to imply not only equality but superiority. Wasn't Julia in effect determined to put her ideal new woman right back on the pedestal?

For several years after the formation of the American Woman Suffrage Association, Julia labored hard for the cause. She was elected foreign corresponding secretary of the association and consequently spent a great deal of time writing letters to leaders of the women's movement abroad. She was also made one of the editors of the association's new weekly, the *Woman's Journal,* and was expected to contribute editorials and articles on a variety of subjects. Here at last was an outlet for all of Julia's pent-up energies and ambitions. For years she had sat at home, scribbling and studying, watching Chev labor long and hard over his various causes. Now Julia Howe had a crusade of her own, and like other supporters of the American Woman Suffrage Association in those early years, she was full of optimism regarding the speedy attainment of its objectives.

In later life Julia recalled with pleasure a campaign in Vermont conducted in the winter of 1870 by the association. She went in early February, arriving in the sleepy little northern capital of Montpelier at 3 A.M. with the temperature hovering around zero.[28] The suffrage convention opened in the Village Hall that morning at ten o'clock with Julia, Mary Livermore (also a recent convert to suffrage), Lucy Stone and Henry Blackwell (Lucy's husband) giving the principal addresses.

Throughout the convention Julia went out of her way to say nothing that could possibly offend anyone. But much of what she did say bore little relation to the realities of life in Vermont. For example, she tended to make too much of the fact that most women led frivolous and unproductive lives, that they had been "educated to waste themselves on indifferent things."[29] As one woman wrote in the *Vermont Watchman,* "It touches our sense of the ludicrous to see people coming to the hard-working women of Vermont to tell us we are dying of ennui."[30]

The Vermont campaign lasted for several months and Julia returned to the state later in February, this time with William Lloyd Garrison. They traveled together from Boston up to Rutland on a train that stopped at every milk station. Since only popcorn and lozenges were served in the cars, they had to feast on words rather than food. After nine hours of almost incessant conversation — surely a testimonial to their enjoyment of each other's company — Julia was in danger of losing her voice. Fortunately, she managed to regain it sufficiently for the opening meeting that evening.

A large and appreciative audience had assembled in the Rutland Opera House. The Rutland *Daily Herald,* which, then as now, was more liberal than many newspapers in the northern part of the state, had given the speakers encouraging press coverage, pointing especially to the arrival of Garrison, "the Great American Liberator." His appearance "should of itself be sufficient to draw largely upon the presence of our citizens." And the paper assured its readers that "Mrs. Howe is a pleasing speaker, well worth hearing, one of the brightest thinkers of the age." Also mentioned was the large crowd she had drawn in Boston the previous Sunday, when she had spoken on the "Ethics of Culture."[31] It is curious that no mention was made during the entire time Julia was in Vermont of her authorship of the "Battle Hymn of the Republic."

The audience in Rutland was apparently more disposed to listen to a learned woman than the audience in Montpelier, and Julia again gave her Cleveland speech with its emphasis on class antagonisms between rich and poor women in the larger cities of the East Coast. What relevance this had for Vermont is questionable but she was listened to patiently enough. In reporting the convention to the *Woman's Journal* she referred to it as a "feast,"[32] and even the opponents of suffrage had to admit that the response had been good. Five hundred people had attended the last evening meeting; pamphlets had been distributed and a number of memberships to the Vermont Woman Suffrage Association were taken. At one in the morning a weary Julia and her friend Mr. Garrison climbed back on the train for the long ride home to Boston.

Both were convinced that their efforts had been effective and that Vermont would surely be the first state to adopt woman suffrage. But by the time Julia returned for her final campaign tour in March, she was aware that a considerable opposition to suffrage had arisen in the state, particularly in Burlington, where the last convention was to take place. She and her companions noticed immediately that the mood of the town seemed to be very hostile. Among other things a vulgar ballad had been circulated in which Julia, Mary Livermore and Lucy Stone were referred to as "three old crows." Julia recalled many years later: "We deliberated for a moment in the anteroom of our hall, I said "Let me come first in the order of exercises, as I read from a manuscript and shall not be disconcerted even if they throw chairs at us." As we entered some noise was heard from the gallery. Mr. Garrison came forward and asked whether we were going to be given a hearing or not. Instantly a group of boys were ejected from their seats by someone in Authority."[33] Julia then stood up and read her address through without interruption. She told her audience that she had come as peaceful ambassador, "not to destroy, but to build up." The Burlington *Free Press,* an antisuffrage newspaper, gave only snatches of her speech, which, it said, "went rather above the heads of most of the audience in some parts . . . but was listened to quietly and was as well heard perhaps as her voice in our City Hall could be."[34]

Julia's report of the Burlington convention in the *Woman's Journal* said very little concerning the unpleasant atmosphere her party had encountered there. Playing the part of peacemaker, she insisted they had received fair treatment from the press and the interest of the public had increased with every meeting.[35] Her report is in sharp contrast to those of the other speakers. Both Lucy Stone and Mary Livermore were outspokenly critical of the way certain Vermont newspapers had referred to the promoters of woman suffrage as professional agitators, determined to force an unwelcome burden on the shoulders of their Vermont sisters.[36] But Julia, who disliked being referred to as an agitator, was determined to maintain an attitude of cheerful optimism. In describing the last meeting of the convention, she concluded with the following words: "Our departure was a little hurried as the home-bound train was due at 9:30. We left delighted with the beauty of Burlington and confident that its consideration of woman suffrage would not end with our departure."[37] There was no question that the campaign had its effect on the minds of the women of Vermont, but it was equally evident by the time of the Burlington convention that enough opposition had been aroused to make the chances of adopting a suffrage measure most un-likely.

Of all the out-of-state speakers, Julia, though far from a favorite, was treated by most of the press with respect. Even the Burlington *Free Press* referred to her as a woman "who of course said nothing unladylike or undignified in the course of her re-marks." Whether she helped the cause of suffrage or not she surely learned a great deal from the experience. In Vermont, perhaps for the first time, she faced audiences who for the most part lacked sufficient learning to appreciate her scholarly essays. The sharp wit of Mary Livermore and the moving eloquence of Lucy Stone were more to their liking. Julia was aware that she was not the success as a suffrage speaker that she had hoped to be, but gradually she learned to overcome certain defects in delivery and content: "I became familiar with the order of proceedings, and learned to modulate my voice. More important even than these things, I learned something of the range of popular sym-pathies, and of the power of apprehension to be found in average audiences. All of these experiences, the failures, the effort, and the final achievement were most useful to me."[38]

By the late spring of 1870 the optimism shared by the leaders of the American Woman Suffrage Association had largely abated. The campaign to encourage the passage of suffrage amendments in the states had not fared as well as they had hoped, and with the dampening of their enthusiasm many of the supporters of suffrage tended to branch out in other directions and take up other causes. Julia followed this general pattern, and by the end of the year she was hard at work for two new crusades: the ministry of women in the churches and the promotion of peace.

Her interest in a woman's ministry had its roots in her friendship with Theodore Parker, who had favored the idea of women speaking in church long before she ever considered such a thing. Julia delivered her first real sermon from a pulpit in Harrisburg, Pennsylvania, in the spring of 1870. From that day on she preached whenever and wherever possible, although she was never officially ordained. In 1873 she organized her first woman preacher's convention in Boston, which resulted in the formation of the Woman's Liberal Christian Union.

184

Yet the cause that chiefly occupied Julia during the last part of 1870 was the promotion of world peace. In July she returned to Newport. The impulsive Chev, perhaps feeling guilty about depriving his wife of her cherished summer respite by the sea, had purchased a new house only half a mile downstream from Lawton's Valley. There at Oak Glen, as it was called, Julia heard late in the month of the outbreak of war between France and Prussia. Although the fighting did not last long, many considered it a totally unnecessary conflict, due largely to greed on both sides. Julia, like many of her countrymen, was unable to fathom the reasons for the war, but was appalled at the ease with which France was defeated. As she sat in her Green Parlor — Oak Glen, too, contained one — reading the newspaper reports, her thoughts turned frequently to the horrors of war and she became increasingly convinced that the Franco-Prussian conflict symbolized a return to barbarism. She describes in her *Reminiscences* how the question suddenly came into her mind: "Why do not the mothers of mankind interfere in these matters, to prevent the waste of that human life of which they alone know and bear the cost?" As a consequence of these thoughts she was overcome for the first time by "the august dignity of motherhood and its terrible responsibilities."[39] Becoming convinced that the women of the world must prevent this return to barbarism, she determined to initiate a woman's peace movement.

The 1870's were not propitious years for such a start, at least not in the United States. Americans were tired of crusades in general and war in particular. But Julia, with all the enthusiasm and idealism of the abolitionists in their crusade against slavery, plunged into a fury of activity, writing letters, speaking, organizing meetings, traveling all over the East Coast and eventually even to England to promote her cause. Her work for peace seemed to bring all her thoughts on Christianity, women and the progress of the human race into clear focus. Convinced that her appeal would "find a ready response in the hearts of great numbers of women throughout the limits of civilization," she decided to prepare an international congress of women to be held abroad at some future date.[40]

Meanwhile, much of her time was spent at her desk corresponding with prominent women in various countries. In September she published a little pamphlet entitled *An Appeal to Womanhood Throughout the World.* This was translated into a number of languages and copies were distributed throughout the globe. "Arise . . . Christian women of this day," Julia called to her sisters the world over. "As men have often forsaken the plough and the anvil at the summons of war, let women now leave all that may be left of home for a great and earnest day of counsel." Just as her "Battle Hymn of the Republic" had roused the fighting spirit of the North, so now, she hoped, would her *Appeal* rouse enthusiasm for peace.[41]

Back in Boston in October, Julia planned a meeting in New York to discuss the subject of convening a world congress of women in behalf of international peace. The meeting was held in Union League Hall on December 23 and featured addresses by Octavius Frothingham, pastor of the Third Congregational Unitarian Society of New York and a good friend of Emerson's, and by Lucretia Mott, the well-known Quaker and pioneer for women's rights. A friendly and courteous letter from John Stuart Mill was read: he supported Julia's peace efforts but disapproved of the idea of a separate congress of women.[42] The meeting in New York was followed by one in Boston in the spring of 1871, at which an American branch of the Women's International Peace Association was formed with Julia Howe as president. For the next two years she labored incessantly to organize her international congress, which she hoped would be held in London in 1872.

Julia's tireless efforts on behalf of peace was largely abortive. Such later pacifists as Edwin D. Mead gave her credit for initiating the postwar peace movement,[43] but in fact she was able to interest very few in her cause and those few were mainly Quakers. She did go to London in the spring of 1872, but her dream of a women's international peace congress never materialized. Later, she blamed the failure of the movement on the fact that too many women took Saint Paul's strictures against woman preachers literally. She was convinced that the women she had met favored the peace idea but were unwilling to work together because of a want of faith in themselves and each other. In vain did she point out to them that Saint Paul was also responsible for the statement that "a woman may prophesy wearing a veil."[44]

In the end Julia had more success with her peace idea at home than abroad. Upon returning from England in 1872 she conceived of a plan to hold annual Mothers' Peace Day festivals in various parts of the country as well as abroad. These festivals, to be celebrated on the second of June, may perhaps be seen as the predecessors of our contemporary Mother's Day, but that feast for florists, greeting card sellers and candy makers bears little resemblance to Julia Howe's original idea.

The first festival took place in Boston on June 2, 1873. The day dawned clear and bright, and the hired hall was, according to Julia, "beautifully decorated with many fine bouquets, wreaths and baskets, the white dove of peace rising above the other emblems." Garrison and Mary Livermore spoke, and when it was all over Julia confessed that she could not help a "few tears of joy here in my room and a cry of Glory to God in the highest which comes from my deepest heart. Oh joy! joy! I have been sometimes of late wondering whether I have done well to forsake the paths of literary distinction. I am answered now. Enough will throng there for their honors and delights of which I have had my share."[45] On that day eighteen festivals were held in various parts of the country, but the following year she could not arouse the same enthusiasm. "Puzzled about June 2," she confided to her journal in late May, and complained that she had no one to help her.[46]

"I Am with You"
זן

For the next decade or so the peace movement in Boston, such as it was, was Julia Howe's movement. It was she who wrote the necessary letters, hired the hall, and even paid the expenses. The annual meetings were attended faithfully by a number of friends and followers.[47]

A diary entry for May 27, 1871, underscores the importance she placed upon her "peace idea." "I am fifty-two years old this day and must regard this year as in some sense the best of my life. The great joy of the Peace Idea has unfolded itself to me. . . . I have got at better methods of working in the practical matters at which I do work, and believe more than ever in patience, labor, sticking to one's own idea of work."[48] Three years later at the annual meeting of the American Woman Suffrage Association in Detroit, a fellow suffragist noted the change that had come over Mrs. Howe in the last few years: Julia's words were now "more tender and trustful and less critical." Julia herself was struck by the aptness of these comments. "What she said does correspond to something in my own experience, something which I consider as a great and merciful deliverance."[49]

The Passing of the Chevalier

"He found the blind sitting in darkness, and he left them glad in the sunshine of the love of God.
— Edward Everett Hale

In the very years when Julia was moving into her wider career of service to mankind, her husband was becoming convinced that life was passing him by. Chev had always been restless. From the time of his marriage he had complained of wasting his life and in the late 1860's he wrote Sumner that he was convinced that the Lord had not made him to be a philanthropist. The life of the politician and journalist had always held great appeal for Sam Howe, and in the last decade of his life he made several fruitless attempts to obtain various posts in the American diplomatic service. He was a strong supporter of President Grant, and never appeared to be aware (nor did Julia) of the discrepancy between the man's skill as a military leader and his ability as a statesman. In 1869 Howe hoped for an appointment in Greece. Counting on the influence of Hamilton Fish, the new secretary of state, he was destined to be disappointed. But in 1871, another opportunity arose and Howe found himself supporting the President's ill-advised scheme to annex the Dominican Republic.[1]

Politically unstable and long the object of greedy glances

from American industrialists, financiers and politicians, the Dominican Republic seemed ripe for exploitation. Although the annexation scheme was supported by President Buenaventura Báez as a means of getting rid of his government's enormous debts, and by a number of Dominicans who hoped thereby to bring peace to their country, the chief promoters were a number of American speculators who had managed to obtain sizable concessions on the island. President Grant thought annexation a grand idea, and one sure to be popular with the American people. After a considerable struggle Congress finally passed a measure authorizing the appointment of a three-man commission to examine conditions in the Dominican Republic and make a recommendation for or against annexation.

Although Howe had taken no part in the public discussion and was aware that there had been "jobbery and trickery" in the whole thing,[2] he nevertheless favored the plan. As he later wrote in his "Memorandum on the Commission to Santo Domingo," he considered annexation a "sort of national duty to extend the benefit of our political institutions by peaceful means over the [West Indian] islands."[3] It was a view widely held by intellectuals of the time (and one Julia herself would hold during the debate over the annexation of the Philippines in 1898). He volunteered his services as a member of the commission and was duly appointed along with the Radical Republican Benjamin F. Wade and Andrew D. White, president of Cornell University. Howe made his first trip to the island republic in 1871 and discovered that the inhabitants, both black and white, desired annexation. He was completely charmed by President Báez, whom he found to be "a cultivated and distinguished gentleman and patriot." Báez assured the commission that his country was about to be invaded by the Haitians. At the same time, he cited various polls which indicated that more than ninety-eight percent of his people favored annexation. The commission went home convinced that the Dominicans desired union with the United States and certain that if the United States did not act to protect them some other country would.[4]

Sam Howe had been won over both by Báez and the intoxicating climate of the island. Reporters apparently followed the commissioners everywhere they went, and one reported with amusement the sight of the doctor riding about the peninsula on a bull. He was "curling up his feet and legs to keep them from the ground, and guiding the bull with one hand by a rope attached to a ring through the animal's nose, and applying the whip with the other . . .with his linen coat streaming in the air and his broad-brimmed hat covering his magnificent head."[5] The balmy air soothed his neuralgia and he went home feeling much restored and eager to repeat the visit.

Upon their arrival in the United States in late March, Howe and the other commissioners submitted to the Congress their report favoring annexation. Meanwhile, Senator Charles Sumner had launched a massive attack on the administration's unilateral interference in Dominican affairs, and when the report reached the Senate, it was put aside. No action on the matter was ever taken.

Later that year the same speculators, responsible for raising the issue of annexation in the first place, drew Howe into a scheme for leasing the town of Samaná Bay on the other side of the island from the city of Santo Domingo. Out of deference to the Chevalier, whom they hoped to persuade to join the board of directors, thus giving their project a respectability it did not in fact have, the promoters of the scheme agreed that one of the objects of the Samaná Bay Company was to improve the condition of the Dominican population by establishing public schools. Howe was naive enough to think the Samaná Bay Company an honest venture, and agreed to become not only a director but also to invest $20,000 of his own capital, half of which he had to pay in cash.

In early February 1872, Howe and Julia, Maud, a friend of

Maud's and three of his nieces sailed on the steamer *Tybee* from New York. Sam Ward was there to see his sister off and described her in a letter to Louisa:

> She has wrinkles and does not regard her plumage as she used to. Is full of her business but in subdued spirit. But her spirits are jolly and when I gave her for her trip a pretty writing case that I had bought for myself in London she clapped her hands with girlish glee. . . . From 2:30 to 4:30 she held a regular levée of mysterious people of all ages, but all with long hair and wild eyes, each of whom had something confidential for her ear. Chev was looking well and practical.[6]

After a rough sea voyage Chev and his several female companions reached the capital, Santo Domingo, and presently found themselves grandly installed in an old Spanish palace that had once been a convent. President Báez was treating the Howes as handsomely as he could in the hope that Chev would succeed in persuading the American government to agree to annexation. A guard of honor was kept in the courtyard of the palace and the whole of the second floor was at their disposal (the lower floor was reserved for their horses, who made rather noisy and troublesome neighbors). The Howes were also considerably bothered by fleas, but as Julia later recalled, they eventually "diminished this inconvenience, to which also we gradually became accustomed."[7] They quickly discovered that the best way to enjoy the beauty of the island was to go horseback riding, something Julia had not done since she was a girl in Newport. At first she was rather nervous about resuming this activity at such an advanced age — she was now fifty-two — but she soon regained her courage and before long was thoroughly enjoying her daily ride with Maud and the others. Their horses had a "peculiarly easy gait," and yet were "very swift and gentle."[8]

Julia had her first glimpse of President Báez some days after their arrival. The occasion was a High Mass in the cathedral in honor of the independence of the republic. Báez was seated at some distance from the Howes, but Julia was distinctly conscious of "a double, false face." To her he seemed a "man who would betray any time that suited his convenience." Later, a closer view changed her opinion. When he called at the palace the next day she was surprised to find him affable and intelligent, and was impressed by his knowledge of French. She berated herself in her journal that night for relying too much on first impressions when judging people.[9] That her first reaction was undoubtedly the more accurate does not seem to have crossed her mind. It would not have occurred to her to doubt Chev's judgment of a man. She had not doubted his appraisal of John Brown; in such matters her husband was infallible.

With five young women to amuse, Julia's days were filled with entertainments of one sort or another. Their visit coincided with Carnival and the Dominicans went out of their way to give their visiting American friends a good time. In return the Howes gave a ball in the old convent. Julia was, of course, almost giddy at the prospect. They could not possibly have afforded such entertainment at home, and as her daughter later summed up the situation, "To find herself at Carnival, the leader of a gay party, living in a spacious palace, supported by the guns and officers of an American warship, was an opportunity not to be missed."[10]

Perhaps the greatest pleasure Julia derived from her stay in Santo Domingo was the opportunity to preach every Sunday evening to a congregation of poor blacks. The services were normally held in the evening because, according to Julia, they "had neither clothes nor shoes fit for appearance in the daytime." The minister of this parish having died, there was no one who could preach to them, so Julia volunteered to give the sermon every Sunday for the duration of her stay. On Easter she decorated the poor little chapel with palms and flowers and treated her listeners to a sermon on Dante, which she later looked back upon as one of her better efforts.[11] How much the congregation understood of it all will never be known.

Julia did not return to Boston with the rest of the Howe party but instead left the island in early April of 1872. After a brief stopover in Boston to collect clothes and necessary papers she was on the ocean once more, this time to England to organize her peace congress. Although accustomed to traveling alone, she dreaded the prospect of this trip, partly because she doubted the success of her enterprise and partly because she hated to leave Chev and Maud for so long. She was particularly concerned about Maud, who at eighteen was a beautiful and pleasure-loving creature apparently without a serious thought in her head. Yet Julia had a particularly soft spot in her heart for this youngest daughter, who alternately entranced and tormented her. That April night as the little steamer pulled away from the island Julia took out her diary as usual: "The parting from Maud was very hard. Chev did not attend to me much, yet I shall miss him extremely, and his rough companionship and care." Two days later she added a little prayer: "May the purpose for which I undertake this painful and solitary journey be ever strong enough in my thoughts to render every step of it pure, blameless and worthy. . . . I dread unspeakably these dark days of suffering and confusion. To go is like being hanged."[12]

Once in London she attempted first to work through existing societies. She received little encouragement. At a meeting of the English Peace Society she was refused permission to speak on the grounds that a woman had never done so before. Nor were the English supporters of woman suffrage particularly interested in her attempt to found and foster what she called the Woman's Apostolate of Peace. They were too busy responding to the objection recently made in the House of Commons to giving women the vote, to pay much attention to Mrs. Howe.[13] In the end she hired a room in the Freemason's Tavern where she proceeded to give sermons on peace for five or six successive Sundays. Opportunities arose to speak elsewhere as well. She traveled to the Midlands and addressed meetings in Manchester, Birmingham and Leeds. Near the end of her stay she went to a peace congress in Paris as a delegate of the Women's International Peace Association, of which she was president.[14] In the end she felt the journey had been worthwhile even though its original purpose, that of organizing an international peace congress, came to nothing.

Of great comfort to Julia during the early part of her stay in England was the presence of Laura and her husband, Henry Richards, who were spending the last weeks of an extended honeymoon in London. Julia found Laura looking very well and happy, and "rather embellished than disfigured by expectant maternity."[15] Laura and Harry sailed for America in the middle of May. Julia missed them very much and determined to work even harder to make this separation from her family worthwhile.

On the last day of May she made a "delightful" excursion to Windsor with Edward Twistleton, who was now married to an American, Ellen Dwight. "He has all his old charm," Julia wrote of her friend, "exquisite taste and geniality, and a generous and loyal nature." On the eighteenth of June, he took her to the National Gallery, and at parting declared that "the good Father above does not often give so great a pleasure as I have had in these meetings with you." Julia was touched by this sentiment and wrote a secret letter to him in her journal that night: "Dear E.T., Thy splendid face always was to me a promise of some beautiful thing whose fulfillment might be on the other side of the silent river. This little bit of romance for myself."[16]

It was the last time these two friends ever saw one another, for Twistleton died two years later. Upon hearing of his death Julia affectionately recalled the comfort he had been to her: "In my most perplexed period, from 30–35 years of age, his pure, dear influence lifted me out of a terrible despair and skepticism — I mean a want of faith in human nature and myself, for of the Divine I have, never I think, been skeptical." Of their last meeting she remembered being "touched not flattered by his kind words. The time of intense personal attractions was ended for me."[17]

By the end of July, Julia was back in Newport, exhausted from her trip but delighted to hear that her first grandchild had arrived. Laura had been safely delivered of a baby girl named Alice. Julia was glad to be home, surrounded by family and friends once more. A few days after her return she took a walk around the garden with Chev, "whose talk is always so instructive." That evening she wrote in her diary, "Every break in our long continued habits shows us something to amend in our past lives."[18] As usual when they had been separated for a long period, Julia and Chev were delighted to see one another again, and this time the closeness seemed to last.

The house at 32 Mount Vernon Street in Boston was sold. Chev knew that he did not have much more time to live, and he wanted to spend as much of it as possible in the house he had loved the most. Living in South Boston was, as always, hard on Julia, but there was some solace in having Laura, Harry and the baby occupying the old wing while she, Chev and Maud lived in the new. Laura's babies came fast, and one of the pictures she remembered from those years was of her mother sitting at her desk "laboring at her endless correspondence; while beside her on the floor, the baby of the period was equally absorbed in the contents of the wastebasket." Another memory was the sight of Grandfather Howe, stooping in the doorway between the old and the new part of Green Peace, "a crowing child on his shoulders, old face and young alight with merriment."[19] In the summer Julia and Chev moved down to Oak Glen, and here the grandparents enjoyed another family of growing children, the Halls. Flossy and her husband, David Hall, who was a lawyer, lived in New Jersey in the winter, but nearly every summer Flossy brought her children to Newport for a long visit.

In these last years Chev appeared to give Julia far more

support in her various activities then he ever had in the past. In the fall of 1872, after her return from London, he helped her to compile a list of reference works on the woman question. He also seemed to make less of a fuss about her frequent lecture tours. But Chev was still opposed to Julia's speaking in public and was generally critical of the tactics of the suffragists. He wrote an old friend, George Finlay, in 1874:

> Mrs. Howe grows more and more absorbed in the public work of obtaining woman's suffrage; and, like most of her co-workers, shows more zeal then discretion; and, in my opinion, does more harm by subordinating domestic duties to supposed public ones. Surely women have the right of suffrage; and will obtain it soon; but zeal in pursuit of it, does not justify neglect of domestic relations and occupations; nor attempts to abolish those differences in our political and social sphere and duties which spring out of difference in the very organization of the sexes.[20]

The fact was that Chev no longer had the energy to oppose his wife as he once had: his health had been declining for some months. The first mention of it in Julia's diary comes on February 8, 1874: "Chev suddenly seriously ill, acute pain, threatening of pleurisy."[21] The previous year he had resigned his chairmanship of the Board of State Charities and had left the administration of the Perkins Institute largely in the hands of his son-in-law, Michael Anagnos. It was decided, therefore, that another trip to the Dominican Republic might be the best possible thing for his health. Julia was tired herself, and although she worried about leaving Maud unattended, she would profit greatly from the enforced rest. In January she had complained to her diary that the going back and forth to town exhausted her. She felt out of touch, as if she were losing her grasp on things that meant a great deal to her.[22]

197

After sailing once more on the *Tybee*, the Howes arrived safely in Santo Domingo on March 20. Julia was as "glad as a child" to be back, and proceeded to take advantage of her happy and frivolous state of mind by going out and buying a bracelet for Maud and an emerald ring for herself. The next day she felt "remorseful and foolish for having been so extravagant." After a few days in the city, the Howes moved across the island to Samaná Bay, where they occupied a little cottage about a mile from the town of Samaná.

President Báez had resigned in January and the new government was determined to rid the country of American influence. Consequently, shortly after Julia and Chev's arrival the Samaná Bay Company was ordered dissolved. The Howes witnessed the sad little ceremony of taking down the company flag. Just before the emblem was lowered Chev had his supporters stand around him while he made a short address. Julia observed that "the old Crusader never appeared nobler or better than on this occasion, when his beautiful chivalry stood in the greatest contrast to the barbarism and ingratitude which dictated this act." She was both proud of her husband and furious at the ingratitude of the Dominicans toward their American friends. To the bitter end, neither she nor Chev seems to have realized that he had been taken advantage of and that the purpose of the enterprise had been exploitation pure and simple, though she did claim to have had her doubts about the soundness of the whole venture: "In my secret mind I never saw how so motley an organization could pull together."[23]

The remainder of their stay was peaceful. Julia did not have the opportunity to preach as much as she would have liked. She spent most of her time with Chev, whose health did improve somewhat in the warm climate. But the weather was not as fine as it had been on their previous visit, and Julia became rather restless and dissatisfied with the sameness of their days. They had to give up a trip to Santiago because Chev did not feel up to it.

"It seems monotonous to look forward to three more weeks in this isolated place," Julia complained on April 15, but she realized that the enforced quiet was good for both of them. Chev's health was being restored, at least temporarily, and she was accumulating energy for the difficult months ahead.[24]

By the end of May 1874, the Howes were back in Boston and Julia was once more overwhelmed with work. Soon after their return Chev sent her down to Washington to plead with President Grant on behalf of the Samaná Bay Company. Chev had planned to go himself, but at the last moment he was not well enough. Julia had lunch at the White House on the tenth of June. She found the Grants very cordial and later described Mrs. Grant as "neither illiterate nor literary. . . .She seems very warmhearted and natural." .

During their meal together Julia spoke of the progress made by the Samaná Bay Company before its dissolution, even though she knew perfectly well that there had been little or none. Reluctantly the President suggested that a protectorate might be possible, but he never did do anything about it, and the matter was forgotten.[25] Howe himself looked back on the Santo Domingo episode as the last great adventure of his life. "Parts of it are like a romance," he wrote after his third visit to the island. "Parts read like the hopes and fears of the adventures of the pioneers of the East India Companies. Parts recall the South Sea Bubble, and parts the Spanish pursuit of Eldorado in Mexico and Peru; parts the French Buccaneers, while parts were enacted by lovers of chivalrous and dangerous adventure, imitators of the noble Quixot[e] whose high aim ever was to redress wrongs, put down evil doers, and lift up the fallen and oppressed."[26]

Chev's health declined rapidly during the remainder of 1874. That summer at Oak Glen, Julia spent hours playing whist with him, one of the few occupations that gave him pleasure in his last years. Despite increasing pain and weakness, he managed to complete his "Forty-third Report," summarizing his work at the Perkins Institute. But he became even more irrationally demanding as his strength declined and he realized that his life's work was finished. His strange and violent shifts of mood near the end of his life were probably caused by the brain tumor that eventually killed him. Cancer was an unmentionable subject at the time and the real cause of Chev's death was not discovered until many years later, when one of Julia's great-granddaughters read of it in a scrapbook kept by a teacher at the Perkins Institute.[27]

Julia, who had over the years learned to control her feelings, put up with Chev's fits of irascibility as best she could, although at times they were more than she could bear and she would pour her irritation into the pages of her journal. After one of these outbursts, though she was still angry she also felt somewhat remorseful and admitted: "I too have grave defects of character. God only knows which one of us departs most widely from his true will and way."[28] But there were good days as well as bad ones. "Chev very sweet and companionable yesterday afternoon," she wrote one day.

During the winter before his death she found life all but intolerable. He insisted on keeping the temperature of the house unbearably hot and became wildly indignant if anyone complained. There were times when she felt that without an "interval of entire freedom from care and responsibility of any kind," her sanity would go.[29]

All the time Chev was ill, Julia continued her work for suffrage, peace and the New England Woman's Club as far as she was able, and even added a new concern, the Association for the Advancement of Women (AAW). She had at first been rather unenthusiastic about this new organization, whose chief purpose was to bring women together from various parts of the country for annual congresses at which papers would be given on a variety of subjects and matters of mutual interest would be discussed. She thought the idea rather "vast and vague,"[30] but she quickly became one of the organization's strongest supporters and for nineteen years would be its president.

In the fall of 1875 an AAW congress was held in Syracuse, and the daughter of the local Episcopalian bishop, Ruth Huntington, later recalled the impression made by the "quantity of women's rights women" who invaded the town: "Some people were frankly apprehensive . . .others were curious." The day the congress opened, Miss Huntington and her friends settled themselves upon the back-slanting seats of the Wieting Opera House "with a sense of surrender to the forces of expansion and progress." There were all sorts of "live topics":

> Dr. Antoinette Blackwell speaking for the medical profession, quoted a French professor who had said that "there was no more danger for a woman in the dissecting-room than the ball-room." Mrs. Julia Ward Howe commended preparation in teaching and the familiarizing of parents with educational projects through mothers' clubs and neighborhood associations. We were excited at seeing Mrs. Howe, for her "Battle Hymn of the Republic" had virtually become a national hymn in wartime. And she was a most attractive personality in a soft dull-blue gown which set off her red-gold hair. There was no stressing of special grievances or causes. A local newspaper said that the subject of equal suffrage was "admirably shaded" during the sessions of the Congress. It was not intended to be a gathering of radicals, but of awakened and intelligent minds; a preparation for the tackling of greater issues to come.[31]

The AAW proved to be the perfect vehicle, as far as Julia Howe was concerned, for contributing to the education of women all over the country as well as for providing regular opportunities for women working in a variety of fields to come together to share their knowledge and ideas. The object of the association was to discover "practical methods for securing to women higher intellectual, moral and physical conditions" for the purpose of improving both social and domestic relations.[32] From the time of the first meeting of the AAW in 1873 until its demise in the 1890's, Julia contributed much of her time to organizing its annual congresses. She wrote letters and collected statistics. She gave papers and presided at meetings. One could almost have said that by the late 1880's Julia Ward Howe was herself the AAW.

Despite feeling guilty about leaving her husband when he was so ill, Julia managed to get away from time to time, leaving Laura and Harry to care for him. Earlier in the year she had gone to Washington, where she had organized the Washington Ladies Literary and Social Club. In fact, during these years she was very active forming women's clubs all over the country. On April 16, 1874, she heard with delight that "a number of intelligent Southern women are preparing to labor for the education of their sex."[33] Meanwhile she attended two legislative hearings on woman suffrage, one at the statehouse in Boston, another in Providence. She attended Radical Club meetings regularly, finding a talk by the transcendentalist John Weiss in January 1875, on the controversy between science and religion, very contemptuous of "the efforts of the orthodox to reconcile these oppositions, from which they cannot escape."[34] In April it was her turn to address the club and she read her essay "The Halfness of Nature," which had progress and the need for moral reform as its theme. "Of every human good," Julia told her audience of earnest Bostonians, "the initial half is bestowed by nature. But the value of this half is not realizable until labor shall have acquired the other half."[35] Julia was pleased to discover that her talk was well received: "Mssrs [Bronson] Alcott and Weiss both praised it warmly."[36]

The Howes spent the summer of 1875 in Newport. Julia hoped that the mild sea air would improve Chev's health but the change did little good, and by the time she left for Syracuse in October for the AAW congress, Chev was failing fast. She made one last trip that fall, this time to give a lecture in Maine in mid-November. On her return she found her husband no better, and more conscious than before of his approaching death. It was under these trying circumstances that she received what must have been a considerable shock from what amounted to a confession by Chev of a past love affair:

"I have had some sad revelations from dear Chev," she wrote in her diary on November 23, "of things about some of my own sex which really astonish me. From these I learn that women are not only sensual but lustful and that men are attracted rather than shocked by this trait. The privacy of offices, or at least their remoteness from domestic visitation, is eagerly made available by these women for the vilest purposes." This was Chev's way of telling Julia that during his years in the Perkins Institute he had been unfaithful to her. She had long suspected that this was true, but now having it all in the open meant that she could no longer close her mind to what had happened, no longer blame herself for the unworthy suspicions she had harbored on those evenings when Chev would leave for the institute and forbid her to come with him. "I could not help reviewing the great injustice done me," she confessed to her journal. "If thought has a grave may this ghost be laid and appear no more." But this was easier said than done. The last entry for the year shows the extent to which Chev's confession had revealed the "depth and vulgarity of evil in the human heart of which even my own errors had left me ignorant hitherto."[37]

If Chev's revelations troubled Julia deeply they apparently had a liberating effect on him. He became much more companionable. On December 8 she reported

> a most touching and comforting talk with dear Chev, in which I felt once more all the moral beauty which had been my faith and delight in him. I have solemnly sworn to him never to allude to anything in the past, which, coming up lately, has given us both pain. . . . I have reached the bottom of these years of estrangement in which there has been fault on both

sides and we shall begin to rebuild our life in common. My double bed is to be moved into his room so that we may have the comfort of being near each other in the dark and silent hours.[38]

"My Dear New Found." So began the Chevalier's last note to his wife, summing up in four short words the happy relationship that had characterized the last weeks of the Howes' life together. On January 4, 1876, a sudden attack sent him to bed for the last time. Five days later he was dead. The day after he died, Julia laid her bridal veil on the head of his bedstead and grieved to think that "in the place of my dear husband I have now my foolish papers. Yet I have often left him for them.[39]

Beginning Again

*The last day of a year whose beginning found me
full of work and fatigue. Beginning for me in a
Western railway car, it ends in a Roman palace.*
— Julia Ward Howe, Diary,
December 31, 1878

Chev's death affected Julia in a variety of ways. She mourned
him genuinely and missed his "rough companionship," and yet
she also experienced a certain relief after all the months of caring
for a cranky and demanding invalid. It would perhaps have been
natural for her to feel guilty for her own shortcomings as a wife,
and to an extent she did, but the last months of Chev's life had
witnessed a genuine reconciliation between them. Together they
had come to realize that there had been a "constant mutual
misunderstanding," which, Julia explained, had "made each of
us seem to the other something different from what each was in
reality."[1] Knowing there had been fault on both sides made her
own guilt somehow easier to bear, and although here and there
she mentions destroying some painful letters, her diary is relatively free from sentiments of remorse.

She apparently burned those of Chev's letters which had
given her pain, but some four years after his death she copied one
she had written about him shortly before the war: "He has terrible faults of character, is often unjust in his likes and dislikes,

arbitrary, cruel, with little mastery over his passions, incapable of enduring criticism or of profiting by it. He is much led by flattery and prizes above all a certain obsequiousness which always implies a want of character in those who show it. I know that there are rotten hearts that he will cherish to the grave and sincere ones whose affection will be little regarded by him." Yet even at the time of writing this letter Julia realized that she was painting an unjust picture of him, for she continued: "With all this, he is yet *un des hommes du bon Dieu*. I have told all his faults in these few lines, but if I should begin to speak of his perfection many pages would not suffice." She then explained that she had copied these lines "in order to impress upon my mind the injustice I fear I must often have done to the person of whom they speak."[2]

After months of patient nursing, the quiet period of mourning following Chev's death provided a welcome rest. "I consider this a very precious time for quiet thought and study," Julia wrote a month or so later, "and my experience is that such periods are often the preparation for busy and stirring times which follow."[3] The busy times came quickly enough. By March 9, exactly two months after Chev's death, she attended a hearing at the Massachusetts statehouse regarding a bill that would punish male and female nightwalkers equally.[4] For about a decade Julia, together with a number of suffragists, ministers and onetime abolitionists, had been concerned with what was then called purity reform. In several editorials for the *Woman's Journal* she had claimed that as long as prostitution existed and was condoned it would be impossible to "lift men and women out of the unhappy slough of sensuality." Julia, quite properly, could not understand how man could "offend against the laws of chastity without causing woman also to offend." She particularly deplored the aristocratic view, which demanded that the women of the upper class remain pure while the men "go down into the ranks of the people and bring disgrace where poverty has already brought ignorance and privation." Furthermore, she asked how can a man "frequent the purlieus of vice" and not contaminate his own family.[5]

Julia became closely involved with the antiprostitution movement for the next several years but never at the expense of her other activities, and by the late spring of 1876 she was once more occupied with all her organizations and causes. In April she attended a meeting of the South Boston Woman's Club and was elected president. At the beginning of June she was particularly busy with an endless round of meetings of social, religious and reform groups, for which five days (known as Anniversary Week) were set aside each spring. On the first of the month she attended a Woman Preachers convention; on the second she held her annual Mother's Peace Day celebration. The third of June found her at the New England Woman's Club, where, she confessed to her diary, she "was more jolly than altogether became my recent widowhood." But, as she admitted, the "magnetism of numbers" always intoxicated her.[6]

Family and financial worries were among her chief concerns in the months immediately following Chev's death. Julia Romana, the most sensitive and emotional of the Howe daughters and the most intimate with her father, was very shaken by his death, so much so that her mother feared she might never recover. Sam Ward had anticipated the troubled time when he wrote his sister a letter of sympathy. "Poor Julia Romana! What a blow this will be to her, who worshipped her hero father — brave as a lion and tender as a woman."[7] Julia Romana stayed with her mother at Green Peace until the middle of April, when she was reluctantly allowed to return to the institute. Julia was afraid her daughter would not improve away from home, and her fears were realized when Michael Anagnos reported that his wife was suffering from continued attacks of hysteria. Julia Romana returned to Green Peace once more, but in the middle of the summer of 1876 she wrote Uncle Sam that she was completely recovered.[8]

Financial worries were not as easily overcome, and would

continue to plague Julia for the remainder of her life. For a time
in the late 1860's she had been a relatively rich woman. Uncle
John had died in 1866, leaving her nearly $3,000 a year. Added
to this was a small annuity from her brother Marion's estate.
Then in 1873 Cousin Charlie Ward, the trustee in charge of
Julia's and her sisters' family inheritance, lost most of it in rash
speculation. By the time Chev died Julia had only slightly more
than two thousand a year of her own. But Chev could never
imagine that his wife was anything but a very rich woman in her
own right and he made no provision for her in his will. Furthermore he claimed that she was "amply able" to provide for their
son Harry, then temporarily out of work.[9] All his money was to
be divided equally among his daughters. The house in South
Boston, originally bought with Julia's money, was left in her
hands but it ended up costing her more in taxes than she could
collect in rent. Even so, Julia and her children decided almost
immediately that Green Peace should be rented and she and
Maud should move down to Oak Glen as soon as possible. Meanwhile, Laura and her husband left Boston to settle permanently in
Gardiner, Maine.

Julia spent a quiet spring and summer at Oak Glen in 1876,
but with the approach of autumn plans had to be made for the
coming year. Her first concern was, what to do with Maud, who
was still unmarried and whose life never seemed to have any
particular direction except the pursuit of pleasure and amusement; and her second, how to go about raising enough money so
that she and Maud could live in some degree of comfort. To solve
the latter problem she decided on an extended lecture tour that
winter, and to solve the former she decided to take Maud abroad
the following spring for a grand tour of Europe.

Throughout the month of November Julia was hard at work
writing a series of lectures for her trip west, and by early December she was off to Chicago. For the next two months she was
continually on the move.

Occasionally she stayed in hotels, but more often than not she was given a room in a private house. Sometimes these rooms were very comfortable, at other times she had to make do with the horsehair sofa in the parlor.[10] Her lectures for the most part were well attended. A newspaper in Kansas claimed that her audiences were the largest and most appreciative in the towns that had the "most well-appointed libraries,"[11] which suggests that she might be repeating the mistakes of her Vermont tour and talking over people's heads. In Topeka, Kansas, a group of legislators attended one of her talks, and afterward one of them was heard remarking, "Well I should be proud to see such a woman in the U.S. Senate."[12] She received one of her warmest receptions from the Chicago Woman's Club, where on January 17, 1877, she addressed a large and enthusiastic audience on the ethics of culture. Her lecture was followed by the usual singing of the "Battle Hymn," now a tradition at nearly all the gatherings she attended.

In Kansas, Julia took time off from her lecturing to visit the land Chev had bought there before the war. She wrote Laura that in Grasshopper she had met "an old gentleman named Winkle. . . . He says that Grasshopper is a fine place and that eighty acres of our land are splendid farming land. I feel much like bringing all of you out here where you could live and help build up a state."[13] Chev had also bought tracts near Lawrence and Burlington as well. None of this property, valuable though it might be, brought in any income; rather, it added to Julia's already heavy burden of taxes. Perhaps she thought the land would become more profitable if it were lived on. In any case it is hard to imagine that Julia ever took very seriously the idea of moving away from Boston. She would have been miserable so far from her clubs and other organizations, and Maud certainly would have objected to living in so remote and unfashionable a spot as Kansas.

Julia's financial situation was temporarily improved as a result of her lecture tour, and she had been able to leave Flossy,

Harry and Laura each a small amount of money, but she was nonetheless concerned with the expense of the trip abroad that she planned with Maud. She had hoped to be able to obtain a profitable newspaper correspondence while in Europe, but this was not to be. By the time she and her daughter returned to Boston in July 1879, she had incurred a debt of $3,500 with Baring Brothers in London.[14]

Julia was, in fact, extremely reluctant to leave on such an extended trip. At the time, Maud seems to have been totally unconscious of the sacrifice her mother was making on her behalf. Not until many years later did she realize that their European tour was made entirely for her sake and that her mother "was loath to leave the many interests of her Boston life."[15] Indeed, once in England, Julia's cares for Maud seemed to take up all her time. The days and nights were filled with an unending round of social engagements and visits, and among these came shopping expeditions to replenish Maud's wardrobe. Maud was delighted with everything, from their cheerful rooms, "gay with chintz hangings and window boxes of scarlet geraniums," to the whirl of London life. "The charm of that first London season," she later recalled, "was that we were made welcome in a dozen different circles and counted among our friends extreme conservatives and arrant radicals." Their existence reminded her of a "kaleidoscope," brilliant and shifting with "little bits of fashion, art, sport, philanthropy, politics, all jostling together and making a brilliant whole."[16] They had lunch with Lord Houghton, a well-known writer and philanthropist whom Julia had met on her honeymoon. He introduced them to William Gladstone, who was between terms as prime minister. Julia, though not easily intimidated, found the disputatious Gladstone rather frightening. She attempted in her usual learned fashion to discuss the influence of the Greek language on English, but was abruptly cut down with a curt "How? What? English words derived from the Greek?"[17]

The Howes' trip to Europe coincided with Ulysses S. Grant's triumphal world tour, the first such tour ever taken by a former President. At a banquet in London for the Grants, Maud and Lily Langtry shared the honor of sitting next to the general. This mark of attention was surely attributable to Maud's extraordinary good looks, which the English made much of. Maud herself admitted that the cult for beauty in London at the time "was unlike anything" she had known "before or since."[18] It is no wonder that Julia worried about her daughter, who was leading and enjoying precisely the kind of life she herself was becoming increasingly critical of: the pointless, pampered and extravagant existence of the British fashionable upper class.

Despite Maud's busy social life, Julia managed somehow to find time to see her own kind of people. She spoke as often as she could, attended prayer meetings and antivivisection meetings, visited hospitals with Henry James, spoke of Laura Bridgman, Chev's famous pupil, at the home of the lord mayor of London, and finally managed to snub Robert Browning at an evening party at Lord Houghton's. Browning had once been critical of some of her verses, with the result that Julia had developed an intense dislike for him. When the party was over she told her friend Lord Houghton how rude she had been to the poet and succeeded in making her host laugh with the remark, "If I could only write as badly about him as he writes about other people."[19]

The Howes left England in July and headed first for Prussia, where they had been invited to stay with Louisa Terry's eldest daughter, Annie, and her husband, Baron Eric von Rabe. Young Daisy Terry, Louisa's daughter by her second marriage, was there with her mother and remembered very well the impression Aunt Julia made on that visit: "A small woman of no particular shape or carriage, her clothes never taken care of, her bonnets never quite straight on her head; and yet there was about her presence an unforgettable distinction and importance. Her voice in speaking was very beautiful, her face had a sensitive gravity, a look of compassionate wisdom, until a twinkle of fun rippled over it and a naughty imp laughed in her eyes."

Daisy further noted that her aunt was "at first amused and then perhaps a little bored" by the Prussian military formality that prevailed at the von Rabes':

> The house party consisted of some fifteen or sixteen people of all ages, all closely related and at the end of every meal, every man present, from the oldest general to the youngest lieutenant, went round the room and solemnly kissed the hand of every woman. Aunt Julia thought she would introduce a little diversion into the rite; in the midst of all the ceremonious hand kissing she tripped across the room to where I stood and solemnly pulled my nose. There was a moment of consternation, nobody even smiled; the only thing to do was to pretend it had not happened.

Julia was, of course, mortified at her own behavior, and later confessed that it had not been at all funny. What had made her aunt put on such an odd little demonstration, Daisy wondered. Perhaps, she concluded, it was in "half-conscious tribute to Dr. Howe's fiery liberalism,"[20] not to mention a little of Julia's own.

Shortly after this incident occurred, Julia made the horrifying discovery that the otherwise amiable baron believed that dueling was the most efficient promoter of civilized society and the sword a more effective means of social control than the law. Julia's immediate reaction to these "barbarous opinions" was typical: she quickly gathered the ladies of the household together and subjected them to a reading of her essay "Is Polite Society Polite?" which deplored the traces of barbarism in modern society and stressed the need of respect for education and the law, and above all for human nature.[21] One supposes that Mrs. Howe was hoping thereby to reform at least a few of those backward Prussians, and what better way to begin than with the women!

The Howes left Prussia at the end of August 1877 and

traveled south to Geneva. There Julia was to be a delegate to an international congress that had been organized to protest the legalization of prostitution in Great Britain. The congress had been called by Josephine Butler, the leader of the English struggle against regulated vice. She hoped that as many American ladies as possible would attend, and since Julia had planned to be in Europe anyway at the end of September, she was a natural choice as delegate to what was described as "a general uprising of the moral and religious world."[22]

Although Julia was very impressed with the Geneva congress and particularly with the number of men of "first-class character and ability who attended it,"[23] she was upset at not being asked to speak until the last moment, an indication that she had acquired a considerable degree of self-importance in the years since she had first mounted the lecture platform. When at last invited to speak, she addressed the audience in clear, concise French, and later, when the congress had officially terminated, she spoke again, this time offering a number of criticisms. She remonstrated particularly with the men present for their failure to regard women as their equals, by laying too much stress on woman's frailty and her dependence on masculine support. Far from offending her hearers she apparently impressed them with her frankness and was urged to act as a spokesman for social purity to the Empress Augusta of Germany.[24] In Geneva she apparently saw the need of lightening the atmosphere somewhat by making a number of jokes in French.[25] These are not on record but such ad-libbing was obviously one of the secrets of Julia's magic. Many years later, when she gave a talk on Brook Farm to an audience in Brooklyn, a reporter from a local newspaper noted that she often "placed her manuscript aside" and "indulged in such a flurry of wit" that one regretted that "she didn't discard her prepared discourse and talk in her own natural and informal way."[26] But already in the mid-1870's her reputation as a speaker was singular. Couching her arguments in a high moral tone, she combined an air of learning and refinement with a willingness to speak out on any subject no matter how offensive it might at first appear to her audience. No one could accuse her of being unwomanly, and somehow she managed to make whatever cause she was defending seem a plausible one.

From Geneva the Howes went on to Paris. Julia was impressed with the changes which had taken place in France since she and Chev had last visited it, just before the revolution of 1848. She rejoiced that "the unreason of that time" had passed away and that "the people and their leaders are strong and calm." While in Paris she was asked to speak several times on the woman question, but before her first lecture she was carefully warned not to mention either woman suffrage or Christianity. "The first was dreaded," she later recalled, "because many supposed that the woman's vote, if conceded, would bring back the dominion of the Catholic priesthood, while the Christian religion to a French audience would simply mean the Church of Rome."[27]

Taking account of this warning she apparently impressed her audiences with the "extreme facility" with which she used the French language, her slight accent merely heightening the effect of her diction. One report spoke of the calmness of her speech, which flowed "gently, equally, harmoniously, revealing a mind which is always serious, often subtle and profound, always mistress of itself."[28] Besides lecturing on women, she also attended a congress on women's rights at which she was elected president, an honor which had all the appearances of becoming a habit. She also managed to found at least one club in Paris. She discovered a number of young American women, "students of art and medicine, who appeared to lead very isolated lives and to have little or no acquaintance with one another. The need of a point of social union for these young people" appeared to her as very great, so she invited a few of them to meet her at her lodgings, and after some discussion they succeeded in organizing a small club.[29]

Christmas found the travelers in Rome, where they settled
in with the Terrys at the Palazzo Odescalchi. On December 31,
Julia noted in her journal that the year which had begun for her
in a western railroad car had ended in a Roman palace and she
wished very much that she were back in the railroad car. Louisa's
life seemed to be totally absorbed in social matters, and Julia
found the endless afternoon teas and visiting tame and uninteresting. "I could indeed go through the West again," she wrote
Laura, "and do anything which has an object to it. But I find
myself indifferent about many things here which I once enjoyed
greatly."[30]

As it turned out, Roman social life came to an abrupt halt
shortly after her arrival there, when the whole country was
plunged into deep mourning for the deaths of King Victor Em-
manuel and Pope Pius IX. Julia, who inevitably found herself
half fascinated, half repelled by the pomp of the Roman Church,
could not resist going to visit the remains of the dead pontiff
lying in state in Saint Peter's, but when the new pope was elected
shortly afterward and Julia was shown a portrait of him, she
found his appearance unpromising. "The mouth is firm, the eyes
have that terrible cunning which always marks a man of ability
among the Romish priesthood."[31] As it turned out, Julia's reaction was unjustified. Leo XIII would do much to bring the
Roman Church in step with the modern world.

In early February 1878, Maud became seriously ill with
malaria, or what was locally known as Roman fever. For some
time her life was in danger, but by the first week of March she
was on the road to recovery, and in the late spring the two Howe
women left Rome to see more of Europe. Julia was finding
traveling with Maud somewhat of a trial. Like many beautiful
women accustomed to constant praise and attention, Maud
tended to become bored when she was not the center of an admiring circle. As a result Julia had taken to referring to her
youngest daughter as "the Duchess" and she confided to Laura

that she was feeling more and more "discomfited" about her. "A woman of her age and character," Julia insisted, "cannot live upon mere amusement, and if she could, one cannot always be sure of providing it for her." So far, Julia complained, the only places that had interested Maud were London and Rome, where she had been the center of a never-ending round of entertainments.[32]

The remainder of 1878 was spent in traveling through Italy and France and then in England again. In October, Julia wrote Laura that she was very tired of going about the world, "will see Egypt and then settle at home, if Maud will let me, and die."[33] As it turned out, the trip to the Middle East, including visits to Egypt and the Holy Land, were full of interest. Christmas Day found the two women on a little steamer heading up the Nile. The top deck had been suitably decorated with palms and one of the passengers, an English clergyman, had been prevailed upon to read the lessons and recite the litany. As the other passengers gathered for the singing of "Nearer My God to Thee," and "Hark the Herald Angels Sing," Julia had been amazed to discover what a great variety of the world's people were represented. Included were "two California gentlemen, two sons of a Sandwich Island missionary, two or three Italians, . . . an English couple belonging to the fashionable life," a clergyman of the same nation, who "gloried in the fact" that Dr. Johnson hated the Whigs, and finally an American, who could not visit the ruins "because his whole day is divided into so many glasses of milk to be taken at such and such times."[34]

"It was a good little time," Julia noted happily as the ship sailed up the majestic river. Her mind was wonderfully crowded with images. All the Book of Exodus seemed to come alive. Moses, Joseph and the Pharaoh "stole between us like impalpable shadows," Maud recalled. It seemed too that her mother left her at the first glimpse of the Nile and entered a world where the daughter could not follow.[35]

They continued on to Jerusalem, and on the ninth of January, 1879, Julia and Maud were in Bethlehem. On the tenth began a "perilous crossing of the hills which lead to the Dead Sea." They traveled mostly on horseback over mountains and through the desert, where the danger of Bedouin attack compelled Julia to hire an escort of Turkish soldiers. Despite the dangers, Maud noted that her mother seemed perpetually in a state of trance. "By the river Jordan, on the banks of the Dead Sea, on the Plains of Boaz, wherever we went, my mother was preoccupied and withdrawn. She seemed to be living over the earthly life of her Master, and those who had known and walked with him in these places. 'Christ has been here!' she murmured to herself over and over again, and seemed to think of little else."[36] But of all the places in the Holy Land, Jerusalem was Julia's favorite, crowded as it was with historical and religious associations. On January 16 she wrote in her journal: "Christ has been here — has looked with his bodily eyes on this fair prospect. The thought ought to be overpowering — *is* inconceivable."[37]

On July 15 the Howes were back in Boston after somewhat more than two years' absence. They went directly to the Perkins Institute, where Julia Romana, Laura and Flossie were waiting to welcome them home. After much embracing and tears of greeting the five women sat down and talked without stopping for seven hours.[38]

13

Boston in the Eighties

The Society of Good People is always Good Society.
— Julia Ward Howe,
"Is Polite Society Polite"

The Boston to which Julia returned with her daughter in the summer of 1879 had not changed appreciably in the two years since their departure, but it was certainly a very different city from the one she had come to as the young Mrs. Howe some forty years earlier. Over the course of four decades the population of the once tightly knit little seaport had grown from 100,000 to over 300,000. The shape of the city had changed also. Back in 1821 the Mill Dam, a causeway linking the end of Beacon Street with Sewell's Point in Brookline, was completed, and what had once been a clear sheet of water at the bottom of the Common, known as the Back Bay, became a dreary, stinking stretch of mud flats. By the middle of the century the increasingly unsanitary condition of the flats made it imperative that the area be properly filled in and built upon. Beginning in 1858 trainloads of gravel arriving every forty-five minutes from Needham, nine miles away, were dumped into the Back Bay. By the early sixties the first houses had gone up on Arlington Street facing the Public Garden, and by the time Julia and Maud returned, four blocks, stretching from Arlington to Exeter streets and from Beacon to Boylston streets had been built upon.

218

This new section of town, isolated as it was from the rest of Boston by the Garden to the east, the Charles River to the north and the railroads to the south, quickly acquired a character all its own. The houses were large and comfortable. Tree-lined Commonwealth Avenue reminded people of Paris, with its green mall and its spacious, even grandiose, houses built in the French manner with tall windows and high mansard roofs. The architecture of the Back Bay varied but the overall impression was both dignified and elegant.

Not only was Boston less compact geographically in 1879 but socially the once relatively homogeneous little city began to pull apart as the number of immigrants rose and the gap between the rich and poor widened. Increasingly, the well-to-do old Yankees were retreating with their fortunes to the safety of their brick houses on Beacon Hill, their brownstones on Commonwealth Avenue or out to the suburbs beyond.

Meanwhile, the great tide of prosperity that had swept over the rest of the nation in the years following the Civil War had only moderately affected Boston. Industry had not prospered there as elsewhere and financial setbacks had impaired her ability to compete with faster-growing cities like New York and Chicago. In 1872 a great fire had destroyed a large part of the commercial district, causing over sixty million dollars worth of damage, and immediately thereafter the Panic of 1873 had further crippled the city's financial power. Some old Bostonians thought the city was falling apart politically as well, particularly as the 1870's turned into the 1880's and Boston elected its first Irish mayor.

Despite these problems, Boston still considered itself the cultural capital of the nation. True, the towering figures of antebellum days were gradually disappearing: Thoreau and Hawthorne had died in the sixties; Garrison, Howe, and Sumner in the seventies; Longfellow and Emerson were still about and so was Wendell Phillips, although none of them would survive the eighties. Meanwhile a new generation had reached maturity, and if they were not of equal stature with the old, they nonetheless put much energy into maintaining Boston's reputation as the "Athens of America." One had only to look at the impressive public buildings being constructed in and around Copley Square in the newly developed Back Bay. There was Trinity Church, for example, considered by many to be the masterpiece of its architect, Henry Richardson. Built in 1869, this handsome Romanesque building provided a suitable place of worship for the Episcopal parish of Phillips Brooks, that energetic and cultivated preacher who so epitomized the new Boston vigor. At right angles to the new church was the Museum of Fine Arts, which had opened in the summer of 1876. One block away was the Boston Society of Natural History; equally close by were the new Harvard Medical School and the Massachusetts Institute of Technology.[1] By the mid-1880's Copley Square would be recognized as the intellectual and cultural center of Boston, and — to the local residents at least — proof positive of their city's continuing cultural prominence.

No sooner had Julia returned from abroad than she was called upon to give lectures on subjects relating to her travels. Trips abroad were very much the fashion and those who could not afford to go flocked to hear the experiences of the ones who could. But Julia's lectures were hardly travelogues, and she took advantage of the popularity of European travel to discuss a variety of themes. In October 1881, the *Woman's Journal* listed the lectures Mrs. Howe was prepared to deliver. They included "Paris: History Social and Political," "Greece Revisited," "Cairo and the Nile," and finally one entitled "Philosophy in Europe and America."[2]

One of these lectures was prepared especially for the Concord School of Philosophy, the summer school started by Bronson Alcott in his barn in 1879. A great crowd, the largest ever assembled there (one newspaper estimated it at fifteen hundred people), gathered at the Hillside Chapel, a few yards from the Alcott house, on a late July morning as Mrs. Howe prepared to give her lecture entitled "Modern Society."[3] Every seat was occupied and the aisles were filled with extra chairs brought over from a neighbor's house. Hundreds more gathered out on the lawn. Even the great Emerson himself had not attracted so many people.

Julia's lecture clearly indicated the direction her thinking had taken during her most recent travels abroad. For "Modern Society" was beyond all question a social critique aimed at extolling the progressive virtues of Julia's native land while deploring the reactionary tendencies she considered prevalent in European society. The lecture also showed her awareness of how small the world had become because of improved methods of transportation and the consequent ease with which people could come together. She was impressed by the growing internationalism that had been so evident at Josephine Butler's congress in Geneva and the women's rights congress in Paris. She had been amazed to discover the number of nations represented among the passengers on that little Nile steamer the previous Christmas. Great opportunities were now available to people all over the world, she assured her audience. Now it was possible as never before to compare human conditions and "choose the best out of the best." But, she warned, this would be no easy task, as it required the "wisdom to choose," as well as the "chance to see." And it was precisely the "wisdom to choose" that she found lacking among certain of her countrymen.

It was at this point in her talk that Julia launched into strong criticism of the worship of wealth, which she felt was causing so many in America to crown "low merit with undeserved honor," and to prefer the "barbaric love of splendor" to the simpler virtues of American life. This love of riches and the splendid trappings its possessors had insisted on acquiring had led to the increasing appeal of the dangerous attractions of

Europe. To see that this was so, one had only to look at the number of American girls who were trading their inheritances for the empty titles of the European aristocracy. How, she inquired of her listeners, could these "shallow souls" turn away from all our "Western splendors," and be "charmed into alliance with feudal barbarism and ignorance?" Such a prospect "rings the bell of alarm which is hung at the gates of paradise."[4]

Yet critical as Julia Howe was of much that she observed, she never doubted that America was the best nation on earth and that it stood as a beacon of progress for other countries to admire and imitate. Unlike Henry Adams, who looked about him in 1880 and concluded that his country, having reached its apogee in the decades before the Civil War, had been degenerating ever since, Julia looked about her and saw no reason to suppose that, just because things were not as they should be, they were not going to get better. After all, in many ways society was moving forward. One had only to look at the progress women had made in the last forty years; their legal disabilities were fast disappearing, more and more of them were being educated, and finally they were learning to work together for the improvement of society. If men, by contrast, were exhibiting a temporary retrogressive tendency in their current absorption with quick wealth, this was not to be wondered at. In any case, women were becoming wiser with each passing day and would soon reform them. These two themes, one critical, the other progressive, were to be essential ingredients of Julia's essays and lectures for the next thirty years. They became, in fact, a very satisfactory means of making sense out of the many disturbing new elements in American life. Julia could utilize them without resorting to pessimistic conclusions about the future. The prophets of doom like Henry Adams were too disturbing for most people's taste and Mrs. Howe's promise of a social millennium was hard to resist.

There was no question that the "Modern Society" lecture was a great success. Not only had the audience been large and enthusiastic but the Concord *Freeman* had been so impressed that it printed five columns of excerpts from the speech. As a finale Julia had recited her "Battle Hymn" and that night had confided to her journal that the compliments of Bronson Alcott and William Henry Channing "were quite enough to turn a sober head."[5] Even Louisa May, Alcott's novelist daughter, who had little patience with the abstruse philosophizing that tended to monopolize the sessions of the summer school and who spoke disparagingly of the high-minded ladies who came as students and "roosted on our steps like hens waiting for corn" — even she shared the general enthusiasm for Julia Ward Howe's lectures; she found them far more down to earth than most.[6] The popular acclaim brought financial benefits as well, and the earnings Julia made as a speaker were badly needed.

The first winter after their return, mother and daughter rented two rooms in Benedict Chambers, a respectable boarding house on Spruce Street, halfway down Beacon Hill. Though convenient to the shops and Julia's various clubs and organizations, the two rooms were hardly sufficient. As Maud recalled, not only did her mother's children and grandchildren, and "relatives to the last degree of cousinship," knock at their door and "demand hospitality," but many travelers visiting Boston also came there.[7] Whenever Julia and Maud decided to give an evening party it took a good part of the day to rearrange the rooms. In the bedroom one bed had to be put on top of the other and a screen placed in front of them. Julia's papers, which were invariably scattered all over the place, would have to be gathered up and stuffed into whatever receptacle could be found. Even after all this effort the rooms could only hold two or three extra people.[8] There was no question that Julia's style was being cramped.

Sam Ward eventually rescued the two from their confining quarters. At the end of the war he found he could be of use to the new Johnson administration and line his pockets comfortably as well. His friend Hugh McCullough, secretary of the treasury, needed someone who could maneuver the recalcitrant members of Congress into doing the administration's bidding, and Ward's little dinners in his shabby house on E Street soon solved the secretary's difficulties. Here a combination of succulent food, mellow wine and Sam's easy and stimulating personality could persuade almost any member of the House or Senate to support or oppose a given piece of legislation. It was not long before the King of the Lobby, as Sam came to be known, had established a considerable reputation for himself in Washington. However, Grant's election in 1868 brought Sam's career as a lobbyist to an abrupt end, and with no money coming in, Sam was soon in financial difficulties. Then, in the late 1870's, after nearly a decade of keeping his creditors at bay, he became solvent once more when an old friend from his California days decided to reward him for some valuable stock-market tips by seeing that Sam was well supplied with stocks and cash.[9]

But as usual, he could not hang on to his assets: his generosity combined with bad luck lost him this fortune in three years. Meanwhile, he saw to it that his friends, and particularly his relations, were well provided for. He paid off the mortgage on the Mailliard ranch in California — Annie and Adolphe had moved out there in 1868 — brought his sister Louisa and her daughter Daisy to America for a visit, and in April 1881 he bought Julia a house of her own at 241 Beacon Street.

Even before Sam gave Julia the Beacon Street house he had seen to it that she did not spend another cramped winter at Benedict Chambers. In the winter of 1880–1881 he paid the rent on a small furnished house on Mount Vernon Street, where Julia and Maud once more had room to entertain in style and where there was enough room for Louisa and Daisy Terry to pass the winter.

Sam had also managed to plan a surprise reunion for the three sisters, timed carefully to coincide with Julia's sixty-second birthday. Sam and Annie arrived first and Julia found her youngest sister very little changed. She was, as always, "a most tender and sensitive woman." Louisa appeared with gifts and greetings a little later and almost fainted with delight and astonishment when she saw Annie. It was the first time in twenty-five years that all four Wards had been together.[10]

Daisy Terry was delighted to be spending the winter with Aunt Julia, whom she had come to know well two winters before in Rome and whom she found to be "the best of company, witty and wise, merry and many-sided." The young woman and the old shared an enthusiasm for learned subjects and music, and called one another affectionately "Goethe" and "Schiller."[11]

Daisy's half-brother, Marion Crawford, was also in Boston that winter. A tall, blue-eyed, exceedingly handsome young man of twenty-six, Marion was on the threshold of his career as a novelist and had come to America in search of some means by which he could earn his living. Unconvinced at the time that writing was his vocation, he was thinking of becoming a singer. But Uncle Sam Ward, impressed by his nephew's gift for storytelling and willing to help him launch his career as a writer, procured him several book-reviewing jobs and commissions for magazine articles. Marion settled himself in a furnished room on Charles Street, around the corner from his mother and his aunt. As it turned out, he spent most of his days at 129 Mount Vernon, perhaps because he found working in the same house with his studious aunt more conducive to good writing habits than sitting alone in his own room. The following summer he stayed with the Howes at Oak Glen and wrote the novel that made him famous overnight. *Mr. Isaacs* was composed on a wooden table in Julia's Green Parlor, where each morning, if the weather was fine, Marion could be found filling page after page with his neat, careful handwriting. He would sit for hours at a time, hardly ever stopping to cross out or change even a word. Maud, impressed by her cousin's dedication to duty, would often sit at the other end of the table composing a story of her own.[12] Julia, meanwhile, would be upstairs working on her papers in the vain hope that nothing would interrupt her.

The move into 241 Beacon Street, which she was to occupy for the remaining winters of her life, took place on a December day in 1881. Although the house and many of its contents, including a good deal of refurbished furniture from Green Peace, were gifts from Sam, she found the business of setting up a house of her own very expensive. It was a comfortable if undistinguished brick dwelling built in the first years after the Civil War, when the extension of Beacon Street marked the beginning of building in the newly filled-in Back Bay. On the ground floor were the dining room and a reception room that Marion Crawford occupied as his quarters for the first two winters, "defending his time from the lion hunters and the interviewers," as Maud wrote.[13] Upstairs were two parlors, one behind the other. Julia fixed up the back one as a library. On the third floor were two bedrooms, one of which, Julia told Sam, was reserved for him. Maud was consigned a bedroom on the top floor. The house, though by no means large, was nonetheless adequate, but Julia wrote Sam that she thought it small for the money.[14]

As for Maud, the first two winters spent in the Beacon Street house she would remember as among the pleasantest of her whole life.

Sam did not have to encourage his sister to work hard; but he had spent a lifetime trying to convince Julia that her literary gifts were considerable and that she should give them more of her time. After reading an article she had written for the *Evening Traveller,* he dubbed her "Mr. Emerson's successor in New England" and urged her to charge a much higher figure for her public appearances.[15] Julia would have been delighted to receive more for her lectures than she did, but this was not always possible. Usually her public appearances brought her twenty-five dollars plus expenses, although sometimes she would get as much as a hundred dollars and at other times nothing at all. Her extended lecture tours brought in the most money, but these were interrupted by a lameness brought on by a fall at the institute in October of 1880. Periodically she would twist the knee again, and be ordered to stay home. Not until the late fall of 1883 was she once more able to go on an extended tour of the Middle West. Meanwhile there was plenty in Boston to keep her busy, if not affluent. In many ways she enjoyed her periods of enforced leisure: they enabled her to catch up on her correspondence and lecture writing. But they did make her financial situation very troublesome, and she was often forced to take out loans to meet her expenses.

One of the great excitements of the winter of 1881–1882 was Oscar Wilde's visit to Boston at the end of January. Hailed at the time as the apostle of the "aesthetic movement," Wilde was scheduled to lecture at the Music Hall. Sam Ward already knew him, and when Wilde expressed an interest in meeting Mrs. Howe, she invited him to lunch. She had gone to church that morning, and after a "lifting and delightful sermon" by James Freeman Clarke, she returned home only to be met at the door of 241 Beacon Street by an angry Maud, who chastised her mother for leaving her with all the arranging to do. Oscar came and "was delightful," Julia noted that evening in her diary, having found him "simple, sincere, and very clever." She gave a party for him after his lecture and was pleased with the way things had gone. "We all think him a man with genuine enthusiasm and with much talent."[16] Wilde was equally complimentary about Mrs. Howe. Accepting an invitation to dine with her *en famille* on a later date, he assured her that "there is no such thing as dining with *you 'en famille'* — when you are present the air is cosmopolitan and the room seems full of brilliant people; you are one of those rare persons who give one the sense of creating history as they live."[17]

If Julia Howe and Oscar Wilde enjoyed one another's company, there were those who disapproved of the friendship.

227

Thomas Wentworth Higginson, for one, was outraged that Mrs. Howe should entertain the author of "a thin volume of very mediocre verse," and chastised her in print for having invited such a person into her respectable home.[18] Julia, who was taking her accustomed delight in shocking respectable Boston with her unconventional taste in people, responded spunkily, also in print, that she was very glad to have had the opportunity of receiving Mr. Wilde at her house. "I also take exception to the right which Col. Higginson arrogates to himself of saying in a public way who should and who should not be received in private houses. To cut off even an offending member of society from its best influences and most humanizing resources is scarcely Christian in any sense."[19] To prove that she was not going to be intimidated by such busybodies as Mr. Higginson, Julia invited Wilde to come and stay with her that summer at Oak Glen. He drove out with Sam from Newport early in the afternoon of July 14, attired in knickerbockers, a salmon-colored scarf and a slouch hat, with the proverbial flower in his buttonhole. "The house is all slicked up uncommon," Julia wrote Maud. A number of friends were asked to tea in the Green Parlor, and Julia produced a round cake with a sunflower in the middle "composed of lemon peel and angelica." A small dinner party in the evening was pronounced a success by Marion Crawford, but Julia wished Maud had been there. "It seemed very hard without you."[20]

Several summers after Wilde's visit to Newport, Maud wrote an article for the *Critic* in which she described a typical day spent by her mother at Oak Glen. Julia would normally have breakfast at eight and follow it with a walk, then a long morning of work. Since letterwriting was the most burdensome of her tasks she would get that over with first and then settle down to whatever literary work had to be done. At one the mail arrived, signaling the end of the morning's labors. Her letters read, it was time for lunch, and this was followed in fine weather by coffee served in the Green Parlor. Here, shaded from the sun's heat by the boughs of the ancient mulberry tree, she might enjoy some good talk or reading aloud from newspapers. Then she would return to work for another two hours or so, after which she would take another walk or go for a drive.

The best time of the day always came in the evening, for Julia never worked at her papers once the light had faded, and after supper there was almost always dancing in the long parlor or out on the piazza. If the dancers stayed indoors Julia would play for them on the piano. The rugs would be rolled back and the furniture moved against the walls. On warm evenings Maud would play her guitar for them outside. As the days grew shorter and the evenings cooler one of the company would read aloud as well. Julia would limit the reading to light novels — she usually had had enough hard reading and thinking during the day.[21]

That this daily routine was frequently interrupted is evident from a letter Julia wrote her brother Sam:

> I sat down to my task at 10:00 a.m. Very bad gown & cap, but I think it does not matter as I am alone.
> 11:20 a.m. My neighbor, Mr. Caldwell of Redwood, calls in his gaiters, to propose to sell me his carry all. I change my cap and hastily come down. I am full of my work — he does not stay long. 12:15 a carriage at the door, & the Wm. G. Welds alight, for a friendly visit. I wipe my pen and go down. They remain for half an hour, & the Welds' dog almost kills one of my ducks. 1 p.m. Mrs. King of Georgia (Louisa Woodward) is announced. This time I give it up, change my dress and go down for an intimate chat. This old friend does not often visit me. She leaves at 2 p.m. when I take a slight dinner determined to finish my stint before dark. But lo, at 4 p.m. the jolly John St. Griswold drives up to the door, with two friends. Again the pen is laid down, & I descend to receive him. In spite of all this I did make some way with my work, industriously scribbling in every available interval of time.[22]

229

The routine of life at Oak Glen was interrupted further by frequent trips to Boston for meetings or lectures, to Concord for Julia's annual address before the School of Philosophy, or perhaps to northern New England for a suffrage campaign. Yet the three or four months spent in Newport represented relative peace and quiet compared to the endless round of activities that comprised Julia's life in Boston.

14

"We Have Been the Scatterers of Seed Not the Harvesters"

In legislating or philosophizing for woman we must neither forget that she has an organization distinct from that of man, nor must we exaggerate the fact. Not 'first the womanly and then the human' but first the human and then the womanly, is to be the order of her training.
— Thomas Wentworth Higginson,
Common Sense About Women

Although Julia's devotion to the cause of woman suffrage had abated somewhat during the 1880's as she became involved with other concerns, she nevertheless continued to answer calls to speak at conventions, to work for the new goal of municipal suffrage, to preside over meetings and banquets, and finally to defend the cause before the Massachusetts legislature. Of all these activities she apparently enjoyed best the challenge of meeting the arguments of the antisuffragists at the annual legislative hearings in the statehouse on Beacon Hill.

Back in 1875, shortly before his death, Chev had told his wife that the cause of woman suffrage lacked one element of success "and that is opposition. It is so distinctly just that it will slide into popularity."[1] At that time what opposition there was confined itself to a few male voices raised in protest, but by 1882 the first woman opponents of suffrage had organized themselves into the Boston Committee of Remonstrants, with "Lizzie" Homans, an old friend of Julia's, as their leader. Julia welcomed the opponents of suffrage. Always ready for a good argument, she attacked them with some of her best speeches, which have a clarity and directness often lacking in her more formal addresses.

At one hearing her antagonists, most of whom were well-to-do women of high social rank, repeated the old argument that the vote would place an unnecessary burden on women. Julia replied with the often ignored, but valid, contention that "many of the women who join us in petitioning for suffrage are women who earn their own living, often supporting their families, including an aged father or impecunious husband. They teach, write, sew, cook, do their own housework and care for their children, and they know that they could find the little time required to give their vote. . . . You ladies do not cook your dinner, nor make your own clothes, nor sweep and dust your mansions, nor sit at the weary desk of the teacher day in and day out, and yet you have not time to vote. And because you have not, you with your delicate fingers would wring from the hard hand of labor its only guarantee of freedom."

In the same speech Julia attacked another favorite argument of the opponents of suffrage: that the ballot by calling into being a whole army of ignorant immigrant women, would increase the number of undesirable voters. "On this point I desire to appeal to you gentlemen," she said, addressing the legislators:

You were chosen and sent here by the rank and file of the community. Were you the choice of ignorant voters? Did the vicious element of the community come to the front in your election? If, with the others, the hod carrier, the railroad and the factory operative, had the power to elect a decent and creditable legislature, why should not the school teachers and shop girls and servant maids of Boston, with all these ladies to help them, be able to do as well?[2]

232

Julia attended hearings on other questions besides woman suffrage, including the plan of separate prisons for women, the discussion of how male procurers of prostitutes should be punished, the removal of the many legal restrictions imposed on married women, and the placing of matrons in police stations. All these claimed her attention. Her approach to reform in these years reflects the idealistic outlook of other liberal reformers of the late nineteenth century. She would gladly have agreed with Edward Bellamy, the utopian socialist, who wrote in the late 1880's that "the dawn of a new day is near at hand" and that "the full day will swiftly follow."[3] In the late spring of 1881, she addressed herself to the subject of reform before the annual meeting of the New England Suffrage Association. "Reformers and teachers," she told her audience, "have for the basis of their work the belief that human beings generally are capable of rising to the discernment of the highest good, and of becoming inspired with a zeal for its general recognition. Yet they know that to bring men and women to this largeness of thought is the hardest work in the world." It was men, not institutions, who needed reforming. "Man is born irrational," she claimed. "Every individual of every generation has to be trained and lifted out of his childish irrationality."[4]

It is evident from this speech that although Julia can be considered liberal in her support of certain institutional reforms, she was, at the same time, conservative in her insistence that men, not institutions, were what really needed reforming. But Julia was by no means alone in adhering to this rather contradictory view of how social progress was to be achieved. Although she and a number of Protestant Christians in Boston, including her own minister, James Freeman Clarke, shared a humanitarian optimism about the future of society, they could not quite dismiss the old Calvinist view that man was by nature evil. Furthermore, although they were willing to believe that evil sprang as much from the environment as from man himself, they also felt

233

strongly that a proper social equilibrium could only be maintained through voluntary cooperation and that government interference in the workings of society should be minimal. Moderate Social Gospelers, like Clarke and his parishioner Mrs. Howe, felt that men and women should help one another through education and association to build a cooperative society characterized by clean government and lack of racial and religious bigotry. Sympathetic as they were to the economic plight of many of the working class and to the need for cleaning up the slums, these Christian reformers had few concrete suggestions to make beyond espousing a kind of voluntary community effort.[5]

If Julia and other Christian reformers of her day failed to find any concrete solutions to the working and living conditions of the laboring class, she at least did her best to solve what she considered to be the economic plight of middle-class American women. By the mid-1880's Julia was becoming increasingly concerned with the industrial value of women's work. During the very years when their educational and employment opportunities were widening, opposition from a number of quarters became increasingly strident: such female independence threatened the sanctity of the home. It was declared that women could not do men's work. Neither physically, intellectually nor emotionally were they suited to any form of labor except that of caring for their husbands and children.

One such critic was Charles W. Elliott. In an article for the *North American Review* entitled "Woman's Work and Woman's Wages," he claimed that men's occupations were unsuited to women and that the female worker could never labor as diligently nor produce as much as the male worker without severe damage to her health, her brain, her nervous system, and most particularly her reproductive functions.[6] Such arguments were common enough, as Julia well knew, but she also knew them to be totally illogical. Elliott never once mentioned, for example, the hardships that women endured who worked as domestics in the houses of the well-to-do.

> The cook roasts slowly over the kitchen fire until her nerves become so irritable as to render her ill-temper proverbial. The parlor-girl stands on her feet month in and month out. She runs up and down, carries heavy dishes, goes out on errands, when, according to the professors of sexual hygiene, she ought to be comfortably tucked up in bed, with someone to wait upon her. The laundress washes, irons, and scrubs the floor till she is full of rheumatic aches and pains, which may or may not be peculiar to women. The seamstress, if she sews all her life, is fortunate to escape consumption or spinal disease.[7]

In her rebuttal Julia further pointed out the disadvantages women faced in a free labor market. Not only did they enter it far less well equipped than male workers — they had fewer opportunities for education and fewer kinds of work were open to them — but their political disfranchisement imposed on them a basic inferiority. "A very little study will show Mr. Elliott two things, viz.: that women are usually paid at a much lower rate than men are for doing the same work with the same ability, and also that in an enfranchised community the laborer is able to make a more intelligent and effectual protest against underpayment than he can make where he does not share the political power vested in his employers." The vote, not unionization, was the means by which the inequalities of the labor market could be rectified.[8] It is evident from this article that Julia had little firsthand knowledge of the conditions of the laboring poor. The only working-class people she had ever really known were domestics, and the horrors of factory life, which were only just beginning to be publicized in the late nineteenth century, had not yet reached her.

If she did not fully comprehend the problems shared by both men and women of the working class, she was aware of some of the inequalities suffered by women of all classes. In her article she objected to the absolute distinction made by Elliott between men's work and women's work. "Men can sew, embroider, wash, cook, dress hair, upon occasion. Women can teach, preach, keep accounts, set type, write books, paint and model. They can even dig, carry stones and split wood. The question in determining what either shall do is first: 'What needs to be done?' and secondly: 'Who is there to do it?' "[9]

Julia had an opportunity to study the question of the industrial value of women at close hand when she was appointed the chairman of the Woman's Department at the World's Industrial and Cotton Centennial Exposition, which was due to open in December 1884 in New Orleans. She had undertaken a similar task when she had headed the Woman's Department of the Merchants and Mechanics Fair in Boston the year before, but the New Orleans exhibition was to be national in scope and would require far more organization. The period between December 1884 and June 1885 comprised a unique chapter in Julia Ward Howe's life. Though it placed heavy physical, mental and emotional demands upon her, she discovered organizational talents she never knew she possessed.

Her appointment as head of the Woman's Department was greeted with considerable enthusiasm by both the managers of the fair and by her fellow New Englanders. The Boston *Traveller* had much praise for the appointment, citing Julia's gifts "as the more remarkable that they comprehend so many different and diverse fields."[10] But there was less enthusiasm among the women of New Orleans. They deplored the prospect of this Yankee woman's assuming a position they felt should rightfully have gone to one of them.[11] The fact that Mrs. Howe was the author of the Union's most stirring hymn made her even less desirable. But

Julia herself was either happily unaware of the antagonism or determined to make the best of the situation.

The managers had been wise in one respect; if they had mistakenly chose a northern woman, they at least had chosen one who would do her best to befriend her southern sisters when she reached New Orleans. Here was the sort of challenge to which Julia rose happily. She had not spent the last decade encouraging those of her sex to associate with one another for nothing, and now she had an opportunity not only to get southern and northern women to work together but also to show these southerners that their Yankee sisters were not a group of flaming radicals. The woman's movement had made little headway in the South and Julia hoped the association with northerners might help to break down some southern prejudices against both the vote and a wider role for women.

Troubles of various sorts confronted her almost from the moment she stepped off the train in New Orleans on an unusually warm December day. Shortly before her arrival a critical article had appeared in the *Picayune* accusing her of sectionalism in the appointment of her staff. "It would have been a graceful thing," the article pointed out, "if Mrs. Howe had paid our New Orleans ladies the compliment of selecting one or two of their number to serve on her staff, and she has shown herself lacking in courtesy by failing to do so."[12] It was perhaps impolitic of Julia not to have chosen at least a few southern women for her staff, and her reasons for this omission can only be guessed at. With only two months between the time of her appointment and the opening of the exposition she had had almost no time to organize such matters. Furthermore, since she did not know any southern women she probably considered it more prudent to wait until her arrival in New Orleans before making any choices. In any case as soon as she did arrive she called together the woman representatives of the various states and quickly selected a number to be on her staff. In fact, she succeeded so well in winning over the malcontents that by mid-January the women of New Orleans claimed they were "proud to serve under such a leader."[13]

Staff problems were only the beginning, however. At the time of her appointment in October she had been promised $50,000 to cover her expenses. Upon arriving at the fair grounds she discovered that the space set aside for her department's exhibit was by no means ready for occupancy. The roof leaked and neither stands nor partitions had been erected. Nor was the necessary money to complete the arrangements forthcoming. Never one to be daunted by difficulties, she gathered the various lady commissioners about her and announced that if the necessary funds were not to be had from the management they would simply have to raise what they could themselves. Women have been known to build churches with the help of a thimble and a teapot, she assured her fellow officers by way of encouragement, and "we must devise some entertainments to put money into our treasury."[14]

The first such fund-raising effort was a lecture by Julia. On the evening of January 17 Warlein Hall was packed to capacity as Mrs. Howe once again trotted out her lecture "Polite Society" — for the first time south of the Mason-Dixon Line. She was worried that this particular address might be too "homely" for a southern audience "accustomed to rhetorical productions," but as she later noted, "Every point in the lecture was perceived and applauded and I felt more than usually in sympathy with my audience."[15] A second entertainment, organized by Julia and, billed as a "Soirée Creole," was also a success, and the final event, a "Musical Matinee," netted the department some fifteen hundred dollars. The money thus raised enabled the women to set up the exhibits and prepare for the opening of the Woman's Department, which was scheduled for March 3, 1885.

The exhibit, when finally completed, was an extensive one, representing the work of women from thirty-five of the forty-eight states. Maud had personal charge of the book exhibit. Besides this there were a variety of inventions by women, including a model ventilator that had been tested in the Boston State House. There were paintings, exhibitions of handiwork, dairy products, and vegetables, and even some samples of ore from mines owned by women.[16] Julia was particularly fond of showing visitors a heavy iron chain forged by a woman blacksmith,[17] proof as far as she was concerned that women were as physically able as men to perform most tasks.

When the Woman's Department was formally opened on March 3, the gallery of the Government Building, where its exhibits were held, was "bright with flowers and gay with flags."[18] Julia gave the major address and stressed for her audience the importance "from an industrial point of view" of a separate exhibit of woman's work. "There are few manufactures," she assured her listeners, "in which the hand and brain of women have not their appointed part. So long, however, as this work is shown merely in conjunction with that of men, it is dimly recognized, and makes no distinct impression." She not only stressed the value of such exhibits in disproving the common contention that women were a "non-producing class," but also underscored the importance of such enterprises in providing the opportunity for women of different sections of the country to work together. "Greater and more important than the acquisition of skill is the cultivation of public spirit."[19]

Financial difficulties and personnel problems continued to plague Julia and her staff for the remainder of her stay in New Orleans. By the end of February it was obvious that the necessary money promised the Woman's Department by the management of the exposition was not to be paid. Contrary to expectation, visitors had not flocked to the fair in large numbers. New Orleans was a long way from the bustling centers of the Northeast and Middle West, and Americans had yet to develop a taste for traveling long distances — except perhaps to Europe — simply for the pleasure of it. Furthermore, since early December it had rained almost every day, making the approaches to the exposition grounds a sea of mud and impeding transportation. Added to these difficulties was a series of strikes, first by the streetcar operators, which further reduced attendance, and then by construction workers, which delayed the opening of exhibits already behind schedule.[20]

On January 6 the sun made one of its rare appearances and people flocked out from New Orleans to the fairgrounds, but by that date the management was already in serious financial trouble, expenses having exceeded estimates by some $250,000. Of the $50,000 promised to Julia's department, only $3,900 had been received by the end of January. A month later both the management and Julia herself were petitioning Congress to grant them an appropriation sufficient to keep the exhibition open. Julia's, in fact, was the only department to petition Congress on its own, and eventually, with the help of Senator Hoar of Massachusetts, the sum of $15,000 was added to the congressional appropriation expressly "for the relief of the Woman's Department."[21]

With funds on the way she thought her financial problems were solved, but when the exposition closed on the last day of May the money had still not come from Congress. By this time the cold, rainy winter had long since turned into a hot, muggy Louisiana summer. By the middle of May, Julia, worn out by her continued efforts to raise money and the relentless heat, was severely ill. Somehow she had managed to borrow money here and there to keep her department going and to pay off at least some of its debts. The women of New Orleans with only a few exceptions had come to admire this tireless lady from Boston who had managed to raise nearly $2,500 by the end of April. Despite the severity of her illness Julia refused to go home, claiming that occasional doses of champagne and ice were all she needed to recover, and indeed by the end of May she was well enough to carry on and managed to find time as well to lecture to the students of all-black Leland University.

Throughout the postwar years she had continued to concern herself with the welfare of the blacks. Back in the late 1860's, when she had first joined the suffrage movement, she had supported the Fifteenth Amendment, which gave Negroes, but not women, the vote. Her greatest pleasure that first winter in Santo Domingo had been preaching to her little congregation of blacks, and beginning with this first postwar visit to the South she would visit their universities and speak in their churches whenever the opportunity arose. Although there is no record of how she felt on the subject it is unlikely that Julia would have been anything but critical of the growing racism among the suffragists of the late nineteenth century. Like Susan B. Anthony she continued to believe that both Negroes and women had the same inalienable rights as other American citizens and she was surely horrified at those northern suffragists who supported the enfranchisement of southern women precisely because it would increase the white majority in the electorate.[22]

In mid-June the money from Washington finally arrived and Julia was free to go home. The last day of the month found her comfortably settled at Oak Glen in "a rapture of repose, rather lonely but very soothing."[23] Seated in her Green Parlor and looking back over her work with the Woman's Department, Julia concluded that it had been rather "like having a big nursery to administer, with children good, bad and middling."[24] Her role as "nanny" had often been a trying one, she recalled, and if there were those who had praised her efforts, citing her courage and perseverance in overcoming the endless obstacles that arose, others had been less complimentary and had accused Mrs. Howe of undue arrogance in her management of the woman's exhibit. Apparently there were times when Julia's red hair did get the better of her. A New Orleans paper spoke of her "overbearing disposition and uneven temper."[25] The fact was that a number of the woman commissioners were often impossible to work with, and Julia regarded the newspapers' pleasure in describing any little flare-up among the ladies as vulgar and abusive.

Whether or not the New Orleans press was justified in its criticism, Julia herself appears to have been satisfied on the whole with the success of the exhibits and with the "able and faithful" services of the officers of her staff and the great majority of woman commissioners. She also believed that the exposition had promoted goodwill by bringing together women from all over the country. The "friendly relations," she wrote in her report, which grew out of this association "still bind together those who are now thousands of miles apart, but who, we may hope, will ever remain united in a common zeal for promoting the industrial interests of women."[26]

Although the exhibits were indicative of a wide variety of occupations in which women were employed, some felt that the displays were not really representative of women's work in the nation as a whole. One reporter claimed that in order to discover the real industrial capacity of women it was necessary to visit the various state exhibits. What he meant, of course, was that there you would find examples of the products made in factories where, with the exception of household domestics, by far the greatest number of women were employed. The work in the Woman's Department, however, was "largely the product of over-hours work, the nice things made by the housewife to render her home dainty and attractive."[27]

Julia herself had been disappointed with the "superfluous and unsatisfactory" character of much of the work exhibited by the various states,[28] but she never came to terms with the real reason why this was so. Whether she was unaware of the great numbers of women employed in factories in the 1880's or disapproved of factory work for women, and there is evidence to support the latter, Julia never really concerned herself with the employment problems of laboring-class women beyond encouraging them to become household servants. She was most conscious of the problems faced by middle-class women and particularly by women of the upper middle class, whom she considered undereducated and overprotected with few marketable skills and even less knowledge of how to acquire them. Yet she knew from experience that circumstances all too often forced such women to earn their own living. "Among the most piteous social tragedies of American life are the sudden changes of fortune which befall women bred in the lap of luxury and endowed only with expensive tastes and inefficient habits."[29] After New Orleans, Julia was convinced more than ever that all women should receive training in some useful occupation and all should acquire proficiency in handiwork and the household arts. At least a skillful housekeeper could take in boarders or go into domestic service. A woman with some education could become a teacher or a writer. Moreover, even those who need never face the threat of financial misfortune should acquire some useful skill.

This problem absorbed much of Julia's time for the next year or so. Not surprisingly she felt that an organization was needed. As the women's clubs, the AAW (Association for the Advancement of Women), the Women's Christian Temperance Union and the suffrage societies had all brought women together for the furtherance of one cause or another, so should some kind of group be formed to study women's industrial capacities and interests. This organization would not only provide a means of exchanging ideas but it would also increase communication between rich and poor women.

Julia's proposed Industrial Council of Women never did come into being despite her efforts to interest women in the idea through a series of articles in the *Woman's Journal.*[30] She had hoped to get considerable cooperation from the former women commissioners at the New Orleans exposition. Because they represented the various states and territories, they would have been the natural foundation for such a national organization. But the

243

plan met with little encouragement. A few women sent reports to the *Woman's Journal* describing the employment of women in their districts. Others sent in comments and suggestions regarding the various occupations women might undertake to earn a living, but the nationwide response to her appeal for an organization never materialized.

Perhaps the reason for the lack of interest was that few women laboring to support themselves or their families were very excited by the prospect of an organization that purported to concern itself with the problems of all working women, but in fact seemed to place the greatest emphasis on finding jobs for impoverished gentlewomen and on keeping the idle rich busy with some useful pursuit. Like many other older reformers of the late nineteenth century Julia never did manage to confront the working women's real problems, notably unequal wages and poor working conditions. To alleviate the conditions of the slums was one thing, but to interfere in the relations between worker and employer was a different matter entirely. Back in 1870 she had written: "The attempts made to avert competition and effect a monopoly in the labor interest, would, if successful, dwarf and impoverish our country. Work and wages are both important; but work is the first necessity."[31]

If Julia Howe's efforts to organize women interested in employment problems failed, she nonetheless continued to be of real service to the woman's movement in countless other ways. Sometimes even her silence on certain questions was influential. While in New Orleans she had been very careful not to mention the subject of woman suffrage, knowing the unpopularity of the cause in that section of the country. But according to at least one southern woman the very fact that Mrs. Howe was known as being strongly in favor of giving women the ballot made a lasting impression, particularly since her silent support was strengthened by the distribution of ten thousand leaflets at the exposition by the Massachusetts Woman Suffrage Association.[32]

"We Have Been the Scatterers of Seed Not the Harvesters"
אא

In the spring of 1888 Julia had headed west for the most extensive and triumphant lecture tour of her career. Although one excuse for going was a long-overdue visit to her sister Annie in California, the real purpose was to earn some money. She began her journey with a visit to Maud in Chicago,* and then proceeded on to Washington Territory, a part of the country she was most eager to visit since women now had the vote there. Life in the Pacific Northwest was still very primitive and Julia had to put up with numerous discomforts during her stay. Apparently she enjoyed herself thoroughly anyway and wrote back home that she intended to make a yearly visit to that part of the world.[33] In Walla Walla she gave a lecture in a small opera house located directly over a stable and "smelling of same." Three days later she was in Paser Junction, where she shared a three-quarter-sized bed with a Mrs. Isaacs who had traveled with her from Walla Walla. Riding in the Pullman the next day to Tacoma seemed like a "return to high society." On May 5 she was in San Francisco.

Her nephew John Mailliard boarded the train in Oakland and she recognized him immediately "from his likeness to his mother." After a few days of rest at the Mailliard ranch and long talks with Annie she began lecturing in California. Her repertoire covered a fairly wide range of topics, from reminiscences of pre-war days to a discussion of "Women in the Greek Drama." She was occasionally surprised to discover that an audience would prefer to hear her lecture on women rather than one on Emerson or Aristophanes. On May 14, she worried for fear that her lecture "Woman as a Social Power" would not "be suitable for a chance audience," but then was surprised to find that they liked it better than her talk on Longfellow and Emerson. In California, as elsewhere in the United States, merely the presence of this dignified and eminently respectable woman, who had achieved

---

*Maud was living there with her artist husband, Jack Elliott, whom she had married the previous year.

such fame, was enough to convince many that suffrage was not the disreputable cause they had thought it to be. The standing ovations, the cheers, the waving handkerchiefs, which seemed to greet her wherever she went, particularly in California, were surely proof of this. The whole experience was so intoxicating that she returned two years later for a second visit, only to be disappointed because her reception was not as enthusiastic.[34]

But if California let her down on this second and last visit, Boston rarely did. By the late 1880's Mrs. Julia Ward Howe had become a recognized institution and no meeting was a success unless she spoke at it. In old age — she turned seventy in May 1889 — she much resembled Queen Victoria. Small and shapeless in build, she invariably wore a black or lilac satin gown covered by a flowered silk cloak and a small lace cap that was nearly always slightly askew. Her speaking manner was quiet and refined.[35] It was her very womanliness, the clear speaking voice, the air of quiet distinction, that seemed to appeal to all who saw or heard her, and although she never succeeded completely in winning over Beacon Street, she thoroughly charmed the rest of the city of Boston.

Yet Julia could be outspoken when she wished. She continued to speak often in support of woman suffrage, and if she was not filled with the holy fire of other speakers for the cause, she won over many who would have been put off by more emotional rantings. She dreaded the prospect of addressing a chapter of the conservative Daughters of the American Revolution in the early 1890's, knowing that she "must speak of suffrage in connection with the new womanhood, and anticipating a cold and angry reception." But to her great surprise her words "which were not many," were "warmly welcomed! Truly the hour is at hand."[36]

Unfortunately, the hour was not at hand, although many suffragists were hopeful in the early years of the nineties that most states would enact at least partial suffrage. Women acquired the vote in Wyoming in 1890, in Colorado in 1893, and in Utah and Idaho in 1896. But these were small victories compared to the succession of defeats suffered between 1870 and 1910. Massachusetts was a case in point. There had been near victories in the 1870's; the state senate voted heavily in favor of a constitutional amendment granting suffrage to women, and in 1879 the School Suffrage Act enabled women to vote for school committees. Both of these events led to considerable optimism on the part of the suffragists of Massachusetts. Knowing that their worst obstacle was not the vote in the house, but the statewide referendum that would necessarily follow the passage of a constitutional amendment, they decided that their best hope lay in a simple legislative victory. Since the legislature had shown itself to be cold to the idea of a presidential suffrage bill, the leaders of the movement decided to concentrate on municipal suffrage instead.

Earlier attempts to give women the vote in city elections had met with little success, but changing urban conditions in the late eighties made the idea seem more feasible. Nationwide labor unrest, together with a stream of immigrants that poured into the cities and created slums out of once prosperous neighborhoods, had disturbed the urban middle class and made them suspicious of any mention of radical reform. Because the idea of woman suffrage did have radical overtones it seemed wiser not to stress suffrage as a right that belonged to women simply because they were citizens and to put greater emphasis on the social benefits of enfranchisement. Women after all were considered natural housekeepers; might they not turn their talents to the task of cleaning up the cities? Furthermore, as the accepted guardians of morality, once possessed of the ballot they would surely vote to replace corrupt city bosses with responsible officials. From such arguments, which no longer viewed woman suffrage as an end in itself but as a means for securing other reforms, it was only a short step to limiting the vote to middle-class women who could be relied upon to uphold the ideals of good government, that is, a short step to favoring a form of class suffrage.[37] In the eighties, however, the consequences of this shift in emphasis were not evident, and Julia Howe, among others, tended to support municipal suffrage as an entering wedge that would lead one day to full voting rights for women. The fact that middle-class women might counteract the votes of the working-class women, many of whom were recent immigrants and therefore susceptible to corrupt influences, was only one more reason for favoring woman suffrage.[38]

In the spring of 1892, when the drive for municipal suffrage in Massachusetts was at its height, Julia spoke before a joint special committee of the legislature. In commenting on the failure of men to improve urban conditions she cited their inability to keep the streets clean or to guard the public health, not to mention the fact that on a nationwide scale they had failed to "keep our commerce honest, our diplomacy respectable." Women, she claimed, possessed gifts that made them particularly well suited to achieving reforms in the cities. They not only had a sense of "prevision," but they were concerned with the minor responsibilities of life and therefore were excellent at handling detail.[39]

Despite her housekeeping arguments, municipal suffrage was never passed, one reason being the growing alliance between prohibition and suffrage. Temperance women had relatively little interest in suffrage as an abstract right, but the drive for municipal suffrage with its emphasis on the correction of urban problems did appeal to them as a possible aid in their efforts to oppose the liquor interests.[40] Although most suffragists favored this alliance of the two reforms, Julia Howe did not. She felt strongly that women as a body should not pledge themselves to any particular cause — excepting of course, suffrage.[41] Time would show her judgment to be correct. Although the cooperation between the two movements did at times bring the legislature close to passing a municipal suffrage bill, by the midnineties this alliance between the two reform groups had the effect of uniting the liquor interests with labor and with much of the Democratic party against woman suffrage.

Julia, however, was less concerned with ideological shifts than with organizational changes. In 1887 the two national woman suffrage associations — the National and the American — began moving toward unification. This had come to seem desirable for several reasons. For one, members were increasingly aware that the two were ideologically closer than they had been in the 1870's. For another, recent social upheavals, combined with the failure of the Stanton-Anthony (or National) wing to achieve national suffrage reform, had the effect of moderating their radical stance and encouraging them to concentrate more on winning over the states. Then, too, the National Association, being better organized, had far outstripped its rival in membership. The growing strength of the antisuffrage forces provided a final encouragement, making it imperative that suffragists work more closely together to educate and arouse public opinion.

The low attendance at the annual convention of the American Woman Suffrage Association in Philadelphia in 1887 encouraged those present to pass a resolution favoring unification. Alice Stone Blackwell, the daughter of Lucy Stone and Henry Blackwell, was the person chiefly responsible for persuading the older members of the association, like her own parents, Mary Livermore, and Julia Ward Howe, of the feasibility of such a union.[42] Julia apparently went along with the decision because she was willing to sign her name to the announcement of the first convention of the newly formed National American Woman Suffrage Association to be held in Washington in February 1890, and agreed to attend the convention. She was also undoubtedly prepared to be ignored by the leaders of the old National Association, since their members outnumbered those of the American. Two years earlier Susan B. Anthony had suggested that neither Julia Howe nor Mary Livermore be considered for official positions in the new organization as neither held their reputations solely as suffragists.[43] This may appear as an extraordinary statement until one realizes that the enmity between the leaders of both organizations was still strong. They were forced by circumstance and not friendship to join forces, and it was true that many suffragists did feel that Julia was not single-minded enough about the woman's movement. Some contemporary feminists still dismiss her for this reason.

The proceedings of the opening meeting of the newly formed National American Woman Suffrage Association on February 17 confirmed Julia's worst suspicions. The western delegates tried to override the easterners and elect Elizabeth Cady Stanton president. Julia gave an account of the proceedings in her diary: "Mrs. Colby claimed to represent Washington State and gave five votes for Mrs. S. The Ohio delegation voted solid for her. I did not fancy them too much. The Mormon delegation claimed fifteen votes, all for Mrs. Stanton. I was very tired and very much irritated at finding myself and my friends rampantly overridden by the rough westerners. Meditated upon many foolish things to say and do, but mercifully did not follow up my disturbed impulses." Mrs. Stanton was duly elected, but not, Julia noted, by a very large majority.[44]

Julia was not merely bothered because the leaders of the American Association would have to give up their power in the new organization to old radicals like Stanton and Anthony; she also resented the increasing influence of the western suffragists at the expense of the old guard. Furthermore, she distrusted the modern tendency to bureaucratization and consolidation as well as the new leaders who supported them. She belonged to a simpler age and could not therefore understand the need for these organizational changes. Nor was she alone in feeling this way; many progressive reformers of the late nineteenth century, appalled and confused by the dislocation brought about by the tremendous growth and expansion of the postwar decades, wanted to return to smaller and more cohesive groups.[45]

The same thing was happening among the women's clubs. Except for the loosely defined AAW, which had grown out of the club movement but had no official ties to it, the women's clubs had never before had any kind of national organization. The move for federation was begun by Sorosis of New York, the archrival of the New England Woman's Club. Sorosis took itself very seriously not only as the most important of all the women's clubs in the country, but also as the oldest, a claim which the New England Woman's Club was always contesting. Although the old sense of rivalry came into play here, as it did in the consolidation of the suffrage associations, some of Julia's objections to the idea of federation were well grounded. Above all she was concerned lest such a union should threaten the existence of her beloved AAW, which in the late 1880's was having troubles of its own. Second, she feared that such large associations would severely restrict the possibility of democratic rule "owing to the want of opportunity for deliberation in concert." She wrote a Mrs. Bragg in May 1889 that "the quieter and more thorough organizations of women don't want to be swept into these 'big things' which assume like the Catholic Church to be universal, but which mean, as it does, to give universal domination to a few wily people."[46] Julia had always considered papal control of the Catholic Church the prime example of European corruption. She was convinced, for example, that Pope Leo XIII was fundamentally a crook, and that cumbersome institutions like the Catholic Church by their very size permitted corrupt men to rule. She may also have feared that a general federation would perpetuate the increasingly conservative character of most clubs. By the 1880's most of them were generally opposed to woman suffrage.

When the first meeting of the General Federation of Women's Clubs was held in the spring of 1890 Julia had managed to convince a majority of the members of the New England Woman's Club not to send a representative. A year later, however, the pressure in favor of joining the federation was too great even

251

for Julia to overcome, and on a day in late May 1891 she attended the second annual meeting of the new organization in Orange, New Jersey. She found herself being hailed as "the woman who wears upon her brow the triple crown of poet, scholar and reformer." The warmth of this greeting naturally broke down some of her resistance and she graciously replied that "when I see these Western and Southern lions coming to lie down with us Eastern lambs, I am inclined to think we must be already living in the millenium without knowing it."[47] The club lions were apparently a good deal friendlier than the suffrage variety.

Despite the warmth of her reception Julia maintained strong reservations towards the idea of federation. During the very years when the General Federation of Women's Clubs was bringing women together from all over the country to attend their biennial conventions, Julia was having difficulties with her own AAW. By the late eighties she was carrying almost the entire burden of planning the annual congresses. In September 1889 she wrote her good friend Ednah Dow Cheney, who had been a loyal supporter of the AAW from the beginning, that she was "much surprised at the way my officers stand back leaving me to work as I can, almost without assistance. . . . All the helpful machinery of our Association seems to have given out, and that at a very important moment when we ought to make our best showing in order to hold our own, and not be driven from the field by the larger movements that we know of."[48]

What really seemed to disturb Julia was the fact that Sorosis and the National Woman Suffrage Association were together trying to "put themselves before the world as centers of authority on the Woman Question."[49] Certainly the almost immediate success of the General Federation of Women's Clubs — by 1892 it would have twenty thousand members representing nearly two hundred clubs — was a threat to the AAW.[50] Julia kept the latter going until 1898 and even made attempts to revive it after that; she could never quite admit that it had served its purpose now that the women's clubs had a national organization of their own. In her *Reminiscences,* published in 1899, she gave her own reasons for the demise of the AAW:

> Some of our most efficient members have been removed by death, some by unavoidable circumstances. More than this the demands made upon the time and strength of women by the women's clubs, which are now numerous and universal, had come to occupy the attention of many who in other times had leisure to interest themselves in our work. The biennial conventions of the General Federation of Women's Clubs no doubt appear to many to fill the place which we have honorably held and may in some degree answer the ends which we have always had in view.[51]

Perhaps, though, it was not the General Federation's success that was responsible for the declining interest in Julia's AAW, so much as the increase in the number of young women who were attending college, and the growing importance of settlement houses in the work of civic reform. The old educational and reform functions of the AAW had by then been taken over by other institutions whose approach was both more organized and more professional, and thus more in tune with the new progressive spirit of the age.

Certainly one very important reason why Julia was reluctant to see the termination of the AAW was that it had been in many respects *her* organization. Elected president for the first time in 1876 she remained president through the last congress in 1897. During the last ten years or so of the AAW's existence it was largely she who organized the meetings and corresponded with the various clubs urging them to send delegates. She derived great pleasure from the congresses themselves as well as the journeys to the cities in which the meetings were held.

The last AAW congress was held in Springfield, Massachusetts, in November 1897. Julia gave the concluding address, which emphasized the great good accomplished by the congresses:

> Progress has been in the direction of definite statements of the great needs of society, and of practical suggestions of the way in which these may best be met. The quiet study of social problems may not make a great noise in the world but without it the world will not be greatly helped. Existing laws, customs and prejudices need to be viewed in a historic spirit and submitted to a careful analysis. This is because the things which most deserve to be held fast in the social economy are so twined about the stuff that impedes progress.[52]

Julia feared correctly that the moderate but reformist spirit of the Association for the Advancement of Women would not be continued by the more conservative General Federation of Women's Clubs, many of whose members were outspokenly opposed to suffrage and other reforms. For example, at the Los Angeles biennial of the General Federation in 1902 a move was made to make race a condition of membership in order to encourage southern clubs to join the fold. Julia was not present but the delegates from the Massachusetts Federation led an attempt to block the move. They were badly outvoted, and a local paper voiced the satisfaction of most clubwomen with the decision. "The color line has been passed with little friction, and the question is now a buried issue. The unity of the Federation has been preserved, and North and South have forgotten their difference in a new and stronger union, the result of mutual courtesy and concession."[53]

Such a compromise of principle would never have occurred at a congress of the AAW; Julia would have seen to that. What little power she had once wielded in the various national woman's organizations was fast disappearing. She remained important to the suffrage and club movement, but less and less as a spokesman and organizer and more and more as a figurehead, which after all was now perhaps the role that suited her best.

By 1896, with the election of McKinley as President, the movement for woman suffrage along with other reforms entered a period of decline. The Massachusetts Woman Suffrage Association, which had been the backbone of the old American wing had lost many of its old members and few new ones joined. Most younger women were more interested in the club movement or the Women's Christian Temperance Union. Julia too, by the late 1890's, turned her attention from suffrage to other matters as she entered the last decade of her long life.

15

Mine Eyes Have Seen the Glory

Yes, I've had a lot of birthdays and I'm growing very old,
That's why they make so much of me, if once the truth
were told.
And I love the shade in summer, and in winter love the sun,
And I'm just learning how to live, my wisdom's just begun.
— Julia Ward Howe, 1907

As the years passed and the eighties became the nineties and the nineties turned into the new century, Julia Ward Howe became more and more a recognized national institution. This small, white-haired woman could hardly enter a crowded hall or auditorium without the whole audience rising to greet her. More and more she was accorded the respect normally reserved for royalty and there were frequent references in the press to Mrs. Howe's resemblance to Queen Victoria, whose birthday was only three days earlier than her own.[1] The autumn before her death she was the only woman officially invited to attend the grand Fulton-Hudson celebration in the Metropolitan Opera House in New York City on the night of September 27, 1909. A reporter from the New York *Times* could not help noticing the "friendly interest" with which Mrs. Howe was observed throughout the evening as she sat on the great stage in her low easy chair surrounded by distinguished guests of every nationality. When the time came for her to read her poem, "Fulton," she was escorted to the front of the stage; whereupon "the audience, as if by common impulse, jumped to its feet, to applaud her warmly as she came forward, remaining standing while she read."

The *Times* reporter compared her to Queen Elizabeth I and Queen Victoria, assuring his readers that the two English monarchs had "never had the spontaneous, instinctive, chivalric obeisance which American audiences now pay to Julia Ward Howe. . . . She fills the national imagination as no other woman has, by her identification with a great chapter in human liberty and by her constancy in support of human uplift."[2]

Only two years earlier Julia had been accorded an even greater honor when she became the first woman to be elected to the American Academy of Arts and Letters. Her friend Higginson was the person chiefly responsible for her nomination, and on February 5, 1907, she received a letter from him proclaiming "victory at last. . . . It was carried through by the two editors of the *Century* and Mark Twain, with maybe a little help from your humble servant."[3]

But it was in Boston that Julia was really loved. Here people of all ranks and races, of all creeds and colors, regarded her as their friend and benefactor. No important birthday celebration, memorial service or other public gathering of the type cherished by Victorian Boston was complete unless she were seated in a place of honor on the platform. The autumn before her death the Boston *Transcript,* having taken note of the great number of meetings at which she had recently been seen, concluded that "all the big occasions still seem to need her."[4] Everywhere Julia went she always had a word to say. Sometimes this consisted of a poem written especially for the occasion or a short speech prepared in advance. At other times she would speak impromptu. Invariably she was listened to with rapt attention.

"The secret of her power," said one reporter, who was trying to impart something of the flavor of her speeches to his readers, "is that she has been a great believer, expecting good and finding it."[5]

As Julia neared eighty her ability to withstand the fatigue of a long lecture tour lessened considerably. Her children were very conscious of the strain it put upon her, and by the early 1890's she referred a number of times to pressure from her daughters to slow down. "Please," she implored Laura in one letter, "don't write Maud to worry her about my lecture outings. I have enjoyed them, and the money earned has been a *great help.*"[6] Indeed, money problems continued to plague her for the remainder of her life, although there were times when she earned enough to help out various members of the family as well as pay her own expenses. "Flossy and I have put our dear Sam [Florence's oldest boy] through Harvard College on the footing of a gentleman," she wrote Louisa in the early summer of 1893, "with good rooms, good clothes and everything proper. We even gave him a little spread on Class Day for relatives and intimates."[7]

When Sam graduated from Harvard, however, the terrible Panic of 1893, which caused mills, factories and mines all over the nation to shut down, was ushering in the worst depression the nation had yet seen. In August 1893, the month in which more industries closed than in any other, Julia wrote Laura from Oak Glen that it seemed an "anxious summer with distress and perplexity in the air. So severe a financial crisis must leave its traces upon the country for a long time."[8] In New England the hardest hit industries were clothing, leather and wool. The result was severe unemployment in Massachusetts in early 1894. "Men died like flies under the strain," wrote Henry Adams, "and Boston grew suddenly old, haggard and thin."[9]

Julia's own finances were not really affected until 1896, when the burden of caring for her properties on a reduced income made her wonder if she could afford to open her Beacon Street house that fall. But somehow or other enough funds were scraped together and by the end of October she was back in Boston, noting in her diary that she was "very homesick for sky and trees."[10] During the remainder of the nineties Julia still added to her small and inadequate income by lecturing. Many of her lectures were given locally or in Massachusetts or nearby states, but several times a year, as long as her strength held out, she would venture further afield. Sometimes, though, she could not lecture at all. In the spring of 1897 a bout of lameness kept her at home from the end of May to late June, and this at a time when her finances were particularly troublesome. Early in 1899 she confided to her diary that she was "fighting the wolf hand to hand."[11]

But as her eightieth birthday approached it became increasingly evident that she could no longer count on lecturing to keep her solvent. In the closing months of 1898 she went on a week's speaking tour through New York State. One morning she was forced to rise at 5:30 in order to catch a train from Syracuse to be in Buffalo in time to lecture. She managed to get through her talk with no difficulty, but afterward suffered from a severe attack of vertigo, which forced her to return home.[12] The following autumn her doctor, William Wesselhoeft, insisted that she must no longer attempt long lecture tours, though he sympathized with the frustration he realized this would cause her. "I know very well," he wrote her, "that you cannot *rest* like other people, and you will always work. I want you to work as long as you can, but I do not want you to undertake tasks which younger women would be unable to execute."[13]

With her lecturing curtailed, Julia was forced to find some other way of supplementing her income.[14] An obvious solution was to write more, and this she did, but a volume of her essays, entitled *Is Polite Society Polite?*, which came out in 1895, did not sell very well. "Unfortunately," she wrote Laura, "I cannot comfort myself as I once could by thinking that I am above the level of the general public. Clearly my writings don't interest them." Since her mother continued to write verse, Laura apparently suggested that she put together another book of poems, but Julia hesitated, unwilling to bury them "in another dead book."[15] They were published nevertheless, but her fears were at least partially realized when *Later Lyrics* met with only a moderate response. People apparently much preferred Mrs. Howe in person to Julia Ward Howe in print. The good response that greeted her *Reminiscences* in 1899 was of small consolation and only confirmed the fact that people were more interested in Julia herself than in her ideas.

Thomas Wentworth Higginson, who shared so many platforms with Mrs. Howe during these last years of her life, perhaps explained better than anyone the lack of interest shown in her published works. Her poems, he said, were rarely concentrated enough (the "Battle Hymn" and a few others were exceptions): "They reach the ear attractively, but not with positive mastery." Higginson had the same criticism of much of her prose. Her *Reminiscences* he found much too brief, with "groups of delightful interviews with heroes squeezed into a single sentence." Her lectures on the other hand he found "better arranged and less tantalizing."[16] Many years earlier Julia herself had confided to Higginson that she feared her writings were like "a pair of tongs that could not quite reach the fire."[17]

In the last years of her life she made fewer references in her journals and letters to money problems. This was partly because various relatives and friends gave her financial help. Indeed, her son Harry, by then a distinguished professor of metallurgy at Columbia, sent her a regular allowance. She also had more than her usual success in selling articles to magazines and newspapers, and though she no longer traveled far from Boston, her lectures and public appearances at home became if anything more frequent. As her daughters put it: "In these years an added burden was laid upon her, in the general and affectionate desire for her presence on all manner of occasions. The firemen must have her at their ball, the Shoe and Leather Trade at their banquet, the Paint and Oils Association at their dinner. Their festivities would not be complete without her; she loved them, went to their parties, had the right word to say, and came home happy, her arms full of flowers."[18] Not only was she called upon to attend numerous civic and social occasions but she herself added new causes and new associations to the ones she already served.

In the 1890's the immigrant question was of paramount concern to Julia and others. For decades countless numbers of foreigners had been climbing out of steerage and swarming onto the docks of Boston Harbor, and for decades Bostonians had struggled with the problem of absorbing these newcomers. In the 1840's it had been the Irish who fled their homeland to the miseries of wretched tenements and long hours in the factories. They had brought little with them but their allegiance to Roman Catholicism, a faith which above all others offended the sensibilities of Julia and other Protestant Bostonians. Beginning in the eighties, however, the Irish were being outnumbered by a new wave of immigrants from southern and eastern Europe. These newcomers, who were also Catholic, suffered not only from the usual handicaps of lack of money and marketable skills but also from ignorance of the English language.[19] Even in good times Boston found it hard to cope with this daily influx of men, women, and children from abroad, and resentment of the newcomers naturally increased in the face of labor unrest and depression in the eighties and nineties. As one labor spokesman put it, "We sympathize with the oppressed of the Old World, but we . . . are as a country . . . in the position of any other asylum whose dormitories are full up. . . . We cannot go abroad and hope to lift up the labor of the world."[20]

If labor leaders were concerned with the effect of immigration on the unemployment problem, a number of Bostonians were more troubled by the effect the new arrivals from southern and eastern Europe were having on the racial makeup, not only of Boston, but of the nation as a whole. Henry Cabot Lodge, the patrician congressman from Massachusetts and a longtime student and admirer of his own English heritage, was morbidly sensitive to the revolutionary social consequences which he was convinced would be the result of the new immigration. Consequently, in 1891 he proposed that every adult male wishing to emigrate to the United States be given a literacy test in the language of his native country. Lodge made little headway until 1894, when congressional elections gave both houses Republican majorities. That same year the Immigration Restriction League was formed in Boston and Lodge's crusade was further helped by the increasing hardships brought about by the depression.[21]

A number of Republicans, including Julia Ward Howe, were very much opposed to any form of immigration restriction. For Julia such a measure ran counter to traditional American hospitality. Roused to indignation by Lodge's proposal she wasted no time in sending off a letter of protest to the Senate.[22] Whether or not her letter had any influence, the Lodge immigration bill did not pass and it would be another sixteen years before a similar measure came before the Congress again.

Although strongly opposed to immigration restriction Julia had long been concerned with the dangers aliens presented once they arrived on American soil. Convinced that the Roman Church was determined to keep its grip on the minds and purses of the new arrivals, most of whom came from Catholic countries, she insisted that some means be devised whereby such pernicious influences could be counteracted. Furthermore, since many of the new immigrants were of peasant stock and had had little or no education, she feared that giving them the vote would allow them to use their "new opportunity with unscrupulous selfishness." True citizenship, she believed, was moral citizenship, and a person could only acquire that when he had some idea of the character of the state, of its value to the individual and of his obligation to obey its laws. And finally, Julia was concerned lest the ideal American character be lost if little Irelands, little Italys and little Polands were tolerated. "The condition of their being allowed to come," she noted in her diary in 1891, "should be that they become Americans." That same year, speaking before a congress of the Association for the Advancement of Women in Grand Rapids, Michigan, she proposed that every foreign voter pass a citizenship test before casting his first ballot. "A simple manual of American history and of American rules of government should be devised. . . . in this way we may at least make some provision for putting together the framework of our society."[23]

The Americanization approach to the problem of absorbing immigrants more fully into society would be taken up with enthusiasm by various groups, including the settlement houses, the Daughters of the American Revolution, and the North American Civic League for Immigrants, founded in Boston in 1908. The movement would develop a broad program for educating them and helping them to become acclimated, but it never developed a real following among the American public until after World War I, when it changed and became more concerned with questions of loyalty and less with the immigrants' social and political adjustment.[24]

Apart from the issue of aliens in America the 1890's witnessed a rising interest on the part of a number of liberal-minded Bostonians, including Julia Howe, in the welfare of oppressed people the world over. Their concern focused on victims of tyranny, from the murdered Chinese Christians in the Boxer Rebellion to the Russians crushed by Tsarist autocracy. As was usual when a group of Bostonians became concerned over a cause they formed an organization. For example, in 1897 they founded the Society of American Friends of Russian Freedom for the purpose, Julia claimed, of aiding "by all moral and legal means the Russian patriots in their effort to obtain for their country Political Freedom and Self-government." She was one of the leaders of this new association, and other officers included such worthies as Thomas Wentworth Higginson and James Russell Lowell. The society, or at least its officers, met regularly and their efforts reached a climax in February 1905, when a great meeting was held in Faneuil Hall to celebrate the general strike of Russian workers following the massacres of Bloody Sunday. Julia herself rose up in the crowded hall to exclaim, "How glorious is this uprising!"[25]

The mid-nineties found Julia working hard to rally support for yet another oppressed people, the Armenians, thousands of whom were persecuted by the Turks in 1895 and 1896. Chosen president of the Friends of Armenia, a society formed for the purpose of disseminating news and information about the Armenians through the American press, Julia devoted a great deal of her time to the cause and even considered making a trip to England and Russia to speak to Queen Victoria and Tsar Nicholas II respectively on behalf of both peace and Armenia. Henry Blackwell was apparently her most enthusiastic supporter in this venture. Others, particularly members of her family, were opposed.

But Julia was determined to go if she could be of use. Accordingly, in May 1896 she wrote Senator Hoar, the influential Republican who had aided her in securing funds for the Woman's Department of the New Orleans Exposition a decade earlier, asking if it would be possible to obtain official support for her venture. "If I could see the Queen of England and the Czar of Russia," she told Hoar, "I might do something to induce the two great sovereigns to forget their differences so far as to agree upon effectual measures of protection for the Armenian people. "It seems a laughable proposition to say that a little old woman, greatly a stranger to diplomacy, could accomplish anything of the kind. . . . My own idea is, not that I could accomplish anything by interviewing crowned heads, but that I might possibly help public opinion to crystallize around some good plan of action."[26] There is no record of a reply from Senator Hoar. In any case Julia's family persuaded her to abandon the venture.

If Julia's efforts to intervene with the crowned heads of Europe on the part of Armenia failed, she apparently did succeed a year later in helping to persuade Pope Leo XIII to intervene in Cuba. Civil war had broken out on the Caribbean island in February 1895, partly as a result of the American tariff, which imposed a duty on raw sugar and created real economic suffering, and partly because of Spanish misgovernment. Regrettably, both the Cubans and the Spaniards indulged in atrocities against one another, but the sympathy of most Americans was with the Cuban rebels. The "yellow press" of New York, the *Journal* and the *World,* did their best to whip up public sympathy for the patriots by exaggerating the Spanish atrocities.

One of the most sensational war stories involved the rescue of a young Cuban woman, Evangelina Cisneros. Evangelina's uncle, the president of the insurgent republic, was captured by the Spanish authorities and imprisoned on the Isle of Pines off the Cuban coast, where his niece was allowed to join him. According to Spanish authorities, Miss Cisneros proceeded to murder the governor of the island and she was consequently carried off to prison in Havana. The New York *Journal* claimed that the reason the young Cuban woman had killed the governor was that he had offered to protect her family at the price of her honor. The *Journal* went on to assert that Miss Cisneros told her friends of the "brute's" suggestion, whereupon they took it into their hands to seek revenge by murdering him. Whatever the truth of the tale, the *Journal* played it up for all it was worth and enlisted the aid of a number of prominent women, including Julia Ward Howe, in their endeavor to rescue Evangelina from Spanish hands. Julia was at Oak Glen when the request came from the *Journal* that she petition the pope and encourage him to dissuade the Spanish government from imposing a twenty-year sentence of exile and imprisonment. Julia was happy to comply and Pope Leo apparently responded to her request by recommending clemency. However, the Spanish authorities firmly denied the truth of the

Journal's account of the affair and refused to release Miss Cisneros. At this point the newspaper took matters into its own hands and sent a reporter to Havana to rescue the girl and put her safely on a ship bound for New York. A great reception greeted Evangelina on her arrival and she was invited to Washington to call on President McKinley.[27]

Whether Miss Cisneros had in fact murdered the governor of the Isle of Pines, her story as told, and in part engineered, by the *Journal* aroused the sympathy of thousands of Americans for the cause of the Cuban insurrectionists. As for Julia's part in the affair, there was no question that she was only too ready and willing to believe that the desperate condition in which most Cubans found themselves was largely the responsibility of the Spanish authorities. Surely in her mind, Spain, the most Catholic of all Catholic countries, was associated with the decadence and barbarity she so easily attributed to the Roman Church. She would find it only natural that the government of such a backward country would be guilty of the most brutal policies.

In the spring of 1898, Julia was in Rome, paying a last visit to the city that once had so captivated her with its ancient charms. While there, she learned that the "splendid little war" between Spain and the United States was under way. Her sister Louisa Terry had died the previous October and Julia had made this last journey abroad, partly to comfort the widower, and partly to be company for Maud, who was finding life with her artist husband Jack difficult and uncertain. Julia's niece, Daisy Terry Chanler and her husband Wintie, a grandson of Sam Ward's, were also spending the winter in Rome, but when the war broke out in April, Wintie left to join his friend Teddy Roosevelt's Rough Riders.

Julia was still in Rome when word reached her of the American naval victory over Spain off the Philippines. She was delighted by the news,[28] but once back in Boston she was puzzled and uncertain about the future status of the islands. A reporter who heard her speak before a convention of Massachusetts editors remarked, "It was easy to read between the lines that she didn't favor turning the Philippines back to Spain"; neither would she allow them to "float like a derelict in the Far Eastern seas, the prey to savage internecine strife and foreign rapacity."[29] The question of Philippine annexation was much discussed that winter in Boston. Many of those whose opinions Julia respected were opposed to annexation but Julia herself seemed resigned to the inevitable: "I don't quite see that we ought to," she wrote Maud, "but think we shall."[30]

Julia's enthusiasm for the American victories in the war against Spain comes as a surprise when one recalls that a few decades earlier she had come out so strongly in favor of world peace. Her crusade for peace in the 1870's had been inspired by her disgust at the senseless greed exhibited by two supposedly civilized nations in the Franco-Prussian War. The writer of the "Battle Hymn" had always been a believer in just wars, and in the 1890's the word *justice* appears frequently in her lectures and writings on matters of foreign affairs. In an article on the Armenian massacres, she declared: "I am an advocate of peace, and in my younger days I traveled far and wide to advance its sacred claim. But it is not peace to sit still while villages are burning and streets are running with blood."[31]

Julia's world-vision of the nineties focused no longer on women united for peace but rather on a unified Christendom, more particularly a unified Protestant Christendom, protecting their own in heathen lands. The wars of midcentury, the Franco-Prussian and the Crimean, were needless holocausts. But the Boxer Rebellion in China, the Cuban civil war, the revolutionary uprisings in Russia, and finally the struggles of the Armenians against the Turks, were all symptoms of a worldwide struggle of backward peoples to rise up against oppression. "As we would help our fellow man, against the wild beasts of the forest, or the desert," she continued in her article, "we must help him against the most cruel beast of all, the human tiger. I say let Christendom unite to make the repetition of such scenes impossible. This cannot be done without armed authority, but it can be done without bloodshed." How she proposed to rescue oppressed peoples from tyranny without bloodshed is hard to fathom, particularly since she apparently had no objection to what she termed the "brutal but effective" methods the British used in putting down the Boxer Rebellion in China. "I sometimes think God allows her [Great Britain] to be unprincipled for the good of mankind," she wrote Ednah Cheney. "But really, wherever she plants herself, she brings some of the greatest blessings of civilization."[32]

The publication of Julia's *Reminiscences* in 1899, coinciding as it did with the approach of the new century, gave her an irresistible opportunity to look back at the legacy which the nineteenth century was bequeathing to the twentieth:

> Let me say at the very beginning that I esteem this century, now near its close, to have eminently deserved a record among those which have been great landmarks in human history. It has seen the culmination of prophecies, the birth of new hopes, and a marvelous multiplication both of the ideas which promote human happiness and of the resources which enable man to make himself master of the world. Napoleon is said to have forbidden his subordinates to tell him that any order of his was impossible of fulfillment. One might think that the genius of this age must have uttered a like injunction. To attain instantaneous communication with our friends across oceans and through every continent; to command locomotion whose swiftness changes the relations of space and time; to steal from Nature her deepest secrets, and to make disease itself the minister of cure; to compel the sun to keep for us the record of scenes and faces, of the great shows and pageants of time, of the perishable forms whose charm and beauty deserve to remain in the world's possession — these are some of the

achievements of our nineteenth century. Even more wonderful
than these may we esteem the moral progress of the race; the
decline of political and religious enmities, the growth of
good-will and mutual understanding between nations, the
waning of popular superstition, the spread of civic ideas, the
recognition of the mutual obligations of classes, the advancement of women to dignity in the household and efficiency in
the state. All this our country has seen and approved. To the
ages following it will hand on an inestimable legacy, an im-
perishable record.[33]

The idea of a millennium of unified Christendom became
crystallized in Julia's mind during the last years of her life. She
regarded two events in 1907 as particularly significant for the
future of the human race: the Hague Peace Conference, called by
Tsar Nicholas II in June; and the Fourth International Congress
of Religious Liberals, which convened in Boston in the last week
of September. Julia was not asked to speak at the congress, nor,
for that matter was any other woman, showing, as the *Woman's
Journal* pointed out, that "spring comes slowly up this way, even
among religious liberals."[34] She did, however attend the big
evening meeting on the twenty-fourth, and as she entered the
hall the immense audience rose and gave her an ovation.

The following spring she published an article in the *Christian Register* entitled "Religious Progress in the Last Two Generations," in which she spoke of the "great degree of religious toler-
ance which has come to prevail among religious people," of a
reawakening of concern for religion, and finally of the "great
Congresses of Religion in this Country," which "have borne witness to the wonderful growth of religious sympathy. . . . Behind
these events I seem to discover something even more wonderful
than they. I find this in the fact that the believing and worship-
ping world is beginning to find out that beneath all differences of
doctrine or discipline there exists a fundamental agreement as to
the simple, absolute essentials in religion."[35]

269

אﬡ

Then, on the night of April 2, 1908, there occurred an extraordinary episode, which can best be described in Julia's own words. She had been suffering from a bad case of bronchitis and had been confined to bed for some days, when she awoke suddenly, her head filled with amazingly vivid ideas. Such occurrences were by no means unusual. The "Battle Hymn" had come to her in this way, as had many of her other poems. But this was somehow different, and from the beginning she referred to the episode as her "midnight's vision."[36] According to her daughters, in the days and weeks that followed, she wrote out bit by bit what she had experienced, finally scrawling on the envelope containing it, "An account of my vision of the world regenerated by the combined labor and love of Men and Women." As she described it:

> Men and women of every clime [were] working like bees to unwrap the evils of society and to discover the whole web of vice and misery and to apply the remedies and also to find the influences that should best counteract the evil and its attendant suffering. . . . All were advancing with one end in view, one foe to trample, one everlasting goal to gain. . . . And then I saw the victory. All of evil was gone from the earth. Misery was blotted out. Mankind was emancipated and ready to march forward in a new Era of human understanding, all-encompassing sympathy and ever-present help, the Era of perfect love, of peace passing understanding.[37]

Word of Mrs. Howe's vision spread quickly among Bostonians. Accounts of it appeared in many local newspapers and she was asked to speak of it on various occasions that spring and summer. Modern readers, aware that World War I loomed only a few short years away, can hardly approach Julia's prophecy with anything more than a smile and shrug of the shoulders, but to her contemporaries, conscious of the ever increasing skepticism around them, Julia's optimism, founded as it was in a deep and fervent faith, was both comforting and irresistible.

But for all of Julia's faith in a Christian millennium, she had few illusions about the imminence of woman suffrage. She told a reporter from the New York *Globe* only four months before her death: "I believe I shall live to see women in New York and some of the other states enfranchised, but not in Massachusetts. I'm sorry, but I believe it will take longer here because Massachusetts women as a rule adhere too strongly to old-time conventions."[38] Nevertheless she continued to work for the reform, and the year before her death became the center of a controversy on the subject.

Mrs. Humphry Ward, the English novelist and social worker, had written a letter to the London *Times,* in which she stated that the suffrage movement in the United States was a failure, in large part because of the organized opposition of American women to the reform. Part of the letter was published by Lyman Abbott, a Congregational clergyman and editor of the *Outlook,* an organ of progressive Christianity. Julia, who had had occasion to cross swords with Abbott at an earlier suffrage hearing, was of course incensed by both the letter and Abbott's obvious delight with it. Although she can hardly have been surprised by Mrs. Ward's sentiments — the lady was an old acquaintance and had recently founded the Women's National Anti-Suffrage League in England — she was rightly concerned that such a letter, written by a woman who was much admired in America, might have an adverse effect on the suffrage cause. Her feelings of outrage were no doubt intensified by the remembrance of her last meeting with Mrs. Ward — a friendly reunion in Boston just a few months before.

Julia promptly sat down and wrote a reply to Mrs. Ward and sent it off to the *Times.* Firmly denying Mrs. Ward's assertion that the opposition to suffrage was stronger than its support, she pointed out that the women who took an active part in promot-

271

ing suffrage were much more numerous than those who were actively opposed.[39] Lyman Abbott then proceeded to summarize Julia's arguments in the *Outlook,* turning them around in such a way as to support Mrs. Ward's contention that the woman suffrage movement in America was indeed a failure. One sentence in Mrs. Howe's letter Abbott claimed "to be conclusive against any present extension of the suffrage. 'In America most women are still indifferent on the question of suffrage.' " For Abbott as for most antisuffragists the strongest argument against giving women the ballot was this very indifference: "To impose the suffrage on people who wish to be relieved from it ought to be an unthinkable proposition."[40] This was an ancient subject of dispute between the suffragists and the "antis," and Abbott was undoubtedly correct in claiming that most women were indifferent to obtaining the ballot. The suffragists simply retorted that the vote was woman's right and she should have it whether she wished it or not. For the next few months a verbal battle raged in the suffrage and antisuffrage press, with the former standing up for Julia and the latter for Mrs. Humphry Ward.

Lyman Abbott, essentially a fair-minded man despite his disapproval of giving women the vote, devoted a large part of the *Outlook* on April 3, 1909, to the question of woman suffrage, including a photograph of Julia on the cover, and an article inside matched by one of his own. Julia's, entitled, "Woman and the Suffrage," listed twelve good results that would follow the enfranchisement of women; one would be the closer binding together of families, rather than their disruption, as some of the opponents of suffrage claimed. Lyman Abbott's article and another published the following week entitled "The Professions of Motherhood" essentially defended the importance of woman's private role as wife and mother, and claimed that she had neither the desire nor the responsibility to assume the burden of government which use of the ballot implied. The National American Woman Suffrage Association was so delighted with Julia's piece in the *Outlook* that they had it printed and distributed as a pamphlet. The "antis," not to be outdone, did the same with both of Abbott's articles. The last note was sounded by the *Woman's Journal* on May 22, 1909: "Convincing as Mrs. Howe's article has been pronounced, it may be doubted whether Dr. Abbott's will not make even more converts to our side."[41]

This final verbal battle with the "antis" was not Julia's last effort for the suffrage cause. Shortly before she died she determined to disprove a further claim by Mrs. Humphry Ward: that woman suffrage had proved a failure in those western states that had adopted it. She took a census of ministers, politicians and newspaper editors in the suffrage states to ascertain their opinions. She left no record of how she chose her sample, but the results of her poll were published only one week before her death. She had received a total of 624 replies, 62 of which were unfavorable, 46 in doubt and the remaining 516 in favor.[42] It was characteristic that Julia's last act for the cause that had initially drawn her into public life was both progressive in its method — her reliance upon statistics — and optimistic in its conclusions. She would not live to see women get the vote but surely she had done her part to make woman suffrage possible.

The last years of her life were largely spent quietly at home on Beacon Street or at Oak Glen. Surrounded by family and friends she was rarely alone; and in the last year or two there was always at least one daughter or granddaughter about. Laura's daughter spent all of nine winters living with her grandmother, and years later wrote a memoir of those happy times.[43] She recalled that when her grandmother appeared at the breakfast table each morning there was at once "merriment and sunshine. She might say, on coming down, 'I have been in the depths, I have been submerged and you must pull me out!' — but at once, over the newspaper, over the letters, over this and that tiniest happening, the flame of merriment sprang up and sparkled. . . . The only naughty thing in her was that she would hold and cling, shrinking a little — much as she thirsted for the high privacy of her books in her own room — from going there in solitude."

During all the years devoted to so many causes hardly a morning passed without Julia's spending some time with her books. Rosalind well remembered the rows of them lining one wall of the reception room from floor to ceiling, "black leather-bound volumes, gold-lettered." Here could be found the complete works of Fichte, Goethe, Schopenhauer, Kant and Hegel, together with "the worn volumes of the classics, in the original, and also in translation: Aristotle, Herodotus, Plato, Horace; but not so much Latin, more Greek." Upstairs, Julia's study was "heaped and piled with papers, pamphlets, books; they were on every chair. . . . It never seemed to interrupt her to have us come and go with any needed message or errand, she was in-interruptable. She looked up with a welcoming smile . . . then vanished again up the starry, sunny heights where her books led her." It was in the mornings also that she did her writing.

In the afternoon she always practiced a little piano; then came tea and a few friends for company or reading aloud. The evenings, Rosalind remembered, were the best times. Then more friends came to call or there was more reading aloud. When Rosalind read, her grandmother would sit "leaning forward, tense, every fibre absorbed in listening." The one thing Julia could not bear was any "financial calamity to hero or heroine: "No, stop! I cannot bear it!" and Rosalind would have to skip that part. When friends came there would be games or talk. For the most part Julia would sit quietly paying careful attention to what each person said. "Her listening was so intent," Rosalind recalled, "that each guest spoke his best."

Rosalind last saw her grandmother at the time of a family wedding. Rosalind had not been well and Julia arranged that she should rest after the wedding in the same room with her. "She [Julia] lay very quiet . . . until she thought I was asleep; and then I heard soft paroxysms of laughter shaking her, as she tried to restrain them." Some moments later, when Rosalind thought a suitable amount of time had passed, she inquired of her grandmother, "What are you laughing at?"

"Oh, the most foolish thing in the world," came the reply, between the paroxysm that still shook her. "Darling, I am trying to translate 'The Cat and the Fiddle' into Greek." Julia's unquenchable sense of humor was what those who knew her in old age remembered best about her.

Happily for Julia, she passed the last months at Oak Glen, her favorite spot. Every fall she had dreaded the return to Boston, fearing that she might never see her beloved sky and trees again, but on June 23, 1910, she and Maud moved down to Oak Glen for the last time. The journey from Boston had, as usual, been a fatiguing one, but immediately upon arrival Julia made straight for the piazza and her favorite high-backed rattan chair. There she sat all afternoon, reading, "but not feeling quite at home," she wrote that night in her journal. The house had been given a shiny new coat of yellow paint, which made it seem unfamiliar to her. Also Maud had thought it best to move her mother downstairs, a change which Julia did not approve of, but succumbed to nonetheless. The long summer days passed quietly enough with reading and writing. Her last project, besides her survey of the effects of suffrage in the western states, was to write a paper titled "On What Religion Really Is." Her daughters noticed that she spoke more in these last months about the past, "the figures of her childhood and girlhood being evidently very near to her."[44]

Then in October came the last of Julia's three honorary degrees. She had received the second from Brown the year before, where her appearance so moved a gentleman spectator that when she came forward to receive her hood he compared the effect it had on him to the arrival of Lohengrin in the swan boat in the first act of Wagner's opera.[45] To receive her third degree, from Smith College, Julia had agreed rather reluctantly to travel to

275

Northampton, but once on the way her usual high spirits returned. Fortunately, golden autumn weather prevailed, and on October 5 "she was dressed early in her white dress covered by the black gown. She placed her mortarboard over the proverbial white lace cap and was wheeled into the hall and lifted up, wheelchair and all, onto the platform." Opposite the platform, Maud recalled, "a curving gallery of white-clad girls, some two thousand of them, rose . . . and with them the whole audience. They rose once more when her name was called, last on the list of those honored with degrees; and as she came forward, the organ pealed, and the great chorus . . . broke out with "Mine eyes have seen the glory of the coming of the Lord."

It was the last time Julia heard those words sung.

The trip back to Oak Glen was uneventful. Julia was not even tired. Her son Harry came for the weekend, and as usual in the evening mother and son sat at the piano and sang German songs. On Tuesday she went to her club, the Papetrie, a successor to the old Town and Country, and enjoyed herself as always. Driving home in the unusually warm autumn evening Julia asked that the top of the carriage be put down so that she could enjoy the simultaneous setting of the sun and the rising of the full hunter's moon. The next day she woke up with a slight cold, but made nothing of it. Then the cold turned into bronchitis. For a few days it seemed that she might pull through, but on Sunday evening she was heard to say, "God will help me!" and again as morning approached, "I am so tired!" A few hours later she was dead.[46]

On October 19, a damp, cheerless autumn day, funeral services were held at Oak Glen; then the body was taken to Boston by train for services in the flower-filled Church of the Disciples. Hundreds had gathered to watch as the white coffin was carried up the aisle by eight of Mrs. Howe's grandsons. Afterward, the funeral procession made its way slowly out to Cambridge, passing through Harvard Square, where a small crowd had gathered in the drizzling rain. At the gates of Mount Auburn Cemetery, some two hundred men, women and children were waiting with bared heads to see the cortège pass through, and at the grave the blind children from the Perkins Institute sang one last tribute before the coffin was lowered into the ground. Meanwhile, three thousand miles away in San Francisco, a small ceremony was held at the base of a monument dedicated to the sailors who had fought at Manila Bay. Here a group of men and women, led by the members of the Susan B. Anthony Club, the mayor and the Thirtieth Infantry Band, looked up at the flag flying at half-mast and began solemnly to sing "The Battle Hymn of the Republic."[47]

Chapter References

Abbreviations Used in the Citations

FHH	Florence Howe Hall, ed., *Julia Ward Howe and the Woman Suffrage Movement*
HPHL	Howe Papers, Houghton Library, Harvard University
HPLC	Julia Ward Howe Papers, Library of Congress
HPSL	Julia Ward Howe Papers, Schlesinger Library, Radcliffe College
HS	Harold Schwartz, *Samuel Gridley Howe*
JWHD	Julia Ward Howe, Diary
JWHS	Julia Ward Howe, Scrapbooks
R&E	Richards and Elliott, *Julia Ward Howe*
REM	Julia Ward Howe, *Reminiscences*
SGH	Samuel Gridley Howe
SW	Lately Thomas, *Sam Ward*
WJ	Woman's Journal

1
Wards and Cutlers

1. Bayard Still, "New York in 1824: A Newly Discovered Description," *New York Historical Society Quarterly* 46 (1962):147, citing Samuel Haynes Jenks in the Nantucket *Inquirer.*
2. Dickens, *American Notes and Pictures from Italy* (New York: Oxford University Press, 1957), 86–87.
3. Julia Cutler Ward to Sarah Mitchell Cutler, May 18, 1820, HPHL.
4. REM, 35.
5. Tharp, *Three Saints,* 21.
6. Julia Cutler Ward to Sarah Mitchell Cutler, Mar. 22, 1803, HPHL.
7. Her supporters included Dr. John Witherspoon, who had been the pastor of her church in Scotland and was now president of Princeton.
8. For a good summary of Isabella Graham's philanthropic activities, see Edward T. James, ed., *Notable American Women, 1607–1950.*

9. A Swedish naval officer who visited New York in the years following the War of 1812 remarked on the decorum that was preserved in such places, run by "quality folk" who joined their guests for dinner every afternoon and gathered around the parlor fire with them afterward for a game of cards or some other form of amusement. Bayard Still, *Mirror for Gotham: New York as Seen by Contemporaries from Dutch Days to the Present* (New York: New York University Press, 1956), 90.

10. Julia Cutler to Samuel Ward, Jan. 27, 1812, HPHL.

11. Julia Cutler to Samuel Ward, Mar. 26 and Sept. 2, 1812, HPHL.

12. Julia Cutler Ward to Sarah Mitchell Cutler, May 17, 1814, HPHL.

13. Tharp, *Three Saints,* 27.

14. Julia Cutler Ward to Sarah Mitchell Cutler, July 24 [1823], HPHL.

15. Julia Cutler Ward to Sarah Mitchell Cutler [1822], HPHL.

16. REM, 10.

17. Julia Cutler Ward to Samuel Ward, Sept. 11, 1822, HPHL.

18. V. 1 of Freeman A. M. Hunt, *Lives of American Merchants* (New York: Derby and Jackson, 1858) contains a chapter on Samuel Ward.

19. Unidentified newspaper clipping dated Nov. 29, 1839, in the Samuel Ward Papers, New York Public Library.

20. REM, 53–54.

21. R&E, 1:29.

22. John W. Francis, *Old New York or, Reminiscences of the Past Sixty Years* (New York: Middleton, 1866), 254.

23. REM, 24.

24. Quoted in R&E, 1:26.

25. REM, 49.

26. Ibid., 46.

27. Ibid.

28. JWH, "Reminiscences," clipping of a magazine article, undated but probably written sometime in the late 1850's or early '60's for the *Cosmopolitan Art Journal,* in JWHS, v. 9, HPSL.

29. WJ, Sept. 9, 1894, 281.

30. Julia Cutler Ward to Sarah Mitchell Cutler, Sept. 8 [1824], HPHL.

31. Charles E. Rosenberg, *The Cholera Years: The United States in 1832, 1849, and 1866* (Chicago: University of Chicago Press, 1962), 17–18.

32. Hone, *Diary,* 1:65.

33. For details on this and other cholera epidemics, see Rosenberg, *Cholera Years,* and also Douglas T. Miller, *Jacksonian Aristocracy: Class and Democracy in New York, 1830–1860* (New York: Oxford University Press, 1967), 94.

34. Quoted in SW, 47.

2

New York Girlhood

1. REM, 44–45.

2. JWH, "Memoirs" (1882), HPHL.

3. REM, 43.

4. In Germany, Cogswell had charmed Goethe into donating a set of his works to Harvard College. Later he would help John Jacob Astor found the Astor Public Library.

5. JWH, "Freely Ye Have Received, Freely Given," sermon, HPLC, folder #83.

6. For a discussion of Julia's earliest poems and a few samples of them, including this one, see R&E, 1:33–35.

7. Cardini was a friend of the Garcia family, who had performed the first opera in America. He taught voice according to the Garcia method.

8. JWH to Samuel Ward, July 8, 1837, HPHL.

9. REM, 60.

10. Ibid., 20.

11. Ibid., 44.

12. Ibid., 58–59.

13. SW, 72.

14. JWH to Sam Ward, Aug. 11, 1836, quoted in Elliott, *This Was My Newport,* 53.

15. JWH to Samuel Ward [1837], HPHL.

16. JWH to Samuel Ward, n.d., HPHL.

17. JWH, "Matilda thou has seen me start" [1837], HPHL.

18. Joseph Greene Cogswell, "autograph diary letter," HPHL.

19. R&E, 1:55.

20. Ibid., 1:51–52.

21. Sam Ward to Samuel Ward, July 16 [183–], HPHL.

22. JWH to Henry Ward, Jan. 31, 1838, HPHL.

23. For the best discussion of Samuel Ward's banking activities during the Panic of 1837, see SW, 79–80.

24. REM, 54.

25. Ibid.

26. Russel Blaine Nye, *Society and Culture in America, 1830–1860* (New York: Harper & Row, 1974), 285–286.

27. JWHD, Oct. 2, 1899, HPHL.

28. JWH, untitled poem, HPLC, MS box #5.

29. JWH, "The World Lost in Darkness and Sin," sermon, HPLC, folder #58.

30. REM, 62; and "Freely Ye Have Received" (see n. 5).

31. Mary Ward to JWH, Feb. 26, 1842, HPHL.

32. JWH, "Ralph Waldo Emerson the Author," HPLC, folder #18.

33. Ibid.

34. JWH to Anne Ward, n.d., HPHL.

35. Quoted in R&E, 1:58.

36. Quoted in SW, 112.

37. Ibid.

38. REM, 149; H. W. Longfellow to Sam Ward, Jan. 21 and 30, 1842, Longfellow Papers, Houghton Library, Harvard University.

39. Quoted in Tyack, *George Ticknor and the Boston Brahmins,* 151.

40. JWH to Louisa and Anne Ward, n.d., HPHL.

41. Quoted in R&E, 1:69.

42. Tharp, *Three Saints,* 83.

43. JWH to Louisa and Anne Ward, n.d., HPHL.

44. Hone, *Diary,* Jan. 24, 1842, 2:582.
45. John Forster, *The Life of Charles Dickens* (London: Chapman & Hall, 1872), 149.
46. Hone, *Diary,* Feb. 19, 1842, 2:589.
47. JWH to Mary Ward, n.d., HPHL.
48. REM, 80.
49. JWH to Mary Ward, n.d., HPHL.

3
The Chevalier

1. The sources for Julia Ward's first meeting with Samuel Gridley Howe and the progress of their courtship include REM; R&E; Tharp, *Three Saints.*
2. REM, 82.
3. The principal source for SGH's career up until the time of his meeting with Julia Ward is HS.
4. Richards, *Samuel Gridley Howe,* 71.
5. REM, 87.
6. Horace Mann to SGH, May 20, 1841, quoted in HS, 94.
7. SGH to Charles Sumner, Dec. 6, 1841, quoted in HS, 152.
8. SGH to Horace Mann, postmarked Dec. 28, 1841, quoted in HS, 153.
9. Quoted in SW, 127.
10. JWH to Louisa and Anne Ward, n.d., but presumably the winter of 1842 since the party for Dickens is mentioned.
11. Hone, *Diary,* June 8, 1842, 1:605.
12. Quoted in R&E, 1:75 (source of quote not given).
13. Mary Ward to JWH, Oct. 3, 1839, HPHL.
14. Sam Ward to SGH, Mar. 4, 1843, HPHL.
15. Sam Ward to SGH, Mar. 9, 1843, HPHL.
16. Sam Ward to SGH, Apr. 4, 1843, HPHL.
17. Ibid.
18. The explanation of Julia Ward's financial situation at the time of her marriage is given in SW, 126–127.
19. HS, 42.
20. SGH to Charles Sumner, Sept. 11, 1844, HPHL.
21. Quoted in Wagenknecht, *Longfellow,* 216
22. H. W. Longfellow to Sam Ward, Mar. 15, 1843, Longfellow Papers, Houghton Library, Harvard University.
23. SGH to Charles Sumner, Mar. 5, 1843, HPHL.
24. JWH to Sam Ward, letter announcing her engagement, n.d., presumably Feb. 1843, HPHL.

4
Honeymoon in Europe

1. Tharp, *Three Saints,* 98–99, and *Until Victory,* 190.
2. Tharp, *Until Victory,* 191.

3. JWH to Louisa Ward, Friday [May] 12 [1843], copy courtesy of the Richards family.
4. Ibid.
5. REM, 90.
6. Ibid.
7. Quoted in SGH, 113.
8. JWH to Laura E. Richards, Jan. 10, 1905, HPHL.
9. JWH to Louisa Ward (see n. 3 above).
10. Ibid.
11. JWH, "The Present Is Dead," poem dated June 4, 1843, HPHL.
12. SGH to H. W. Longfellow, Apr. [1843], HPHL.
13. Dickens, *American Notes and Pictures from Italy* (New York: Oxford University Press, 1957), 29–45.
14. JWH to [Sam Ward], June–July, 1843, HPHL.
15. REM, 108.
16. JWH to [Sam Ward], June–July, 1843, HPHL.
17. Quoted in R&E, I:83.
18. Quoted in SGH, 114.
19. REM, 96–97.
20. JWH to Louisa Ward, July 2, 1843, HPHL.
21. SGH, 114–115.
22. REM, 116.
23. JWH to Louisa Ward, July 29 [1843], copy courtesy of the Richards family.
24. REM, 103–105.
25. SGH to Charles Sumner, Oct. 6, 1843, HPHL.
26. REM, 122.
27. Baker, *Fortunate Pilgrims,* 62–69.
28. SGH to Charles Sumner, Feb. 1, 1844, HPHL.
29. Quoted in Baker, *Fortunate Pilgrims,* 114.
30. SGH, 117–118.
31. JWH to John Ward, Dec. 13, 1843, HPHL.
32. JWH to John Francis, June 15, 1844, HPHL.
33. For Theodore Parker's views on women, see H. S. Commager, *Theodore Parker,* 180–181.
34. The poem is in HPHL.
35. R&E, I:96.
36. Tharp, *Three Saints,* 109.
37. Apparently the house had been settled upon Emily Astor Ward and therefore the Astors considered it theirs. See SW, 134.
38. REM, 123–124.
39. SGH to Charles Sumner, Jan. 17, 1844, HPHL.
40. SGH to Charles Sumner, Mar. 16, 1844, HPHL.
41. Postscript to a letter from JWH to John Francis, June 15, 1844, HPHL.
42. The poem "Parting from a New Friend," quoted on p. 78, was written only a month after Julia Romana's birth.
43. For more information on Thomas Crawford at this time, see Van Wyck Brooks, *The Dream of Arcadia,* 88–89, and Tharp, *Three Saints,* 109–114.
44. Tharp, *Three Saints,* 119–120.

45. REM, 133.
46. Ibid., 136.
47. Ibid., 138.
48. Ibid.
49. JWHD, Apr. 24, 1865, HPHL.
50. JWH, "The Darkest Moment" [1844], HPHL.
51. JWH, "The Dawning of Light," begun in Rome and finished in England [1844], HPHL.

5

Early Years in South Boston

1. REM, 149–150.
2. SW, 141.
3. JWH to Louisa Ward Crawford, July 23, 1845, HPHL.
4. Ibid.
5. JWH to Louisa Ward Crawford, Oct. [1845], HPHL.
6. R&E, 1:111–112.
7. Richards, *Stepping Westward*, 7.
8. JWH to Louisa Ward Crawford, Oct. 1846, HPHL.
9. JWH to an unidentified recipient, n.d., JWHS, HPHL.
10. JWH to Sam Ward, Dec. 1844, HPHL.
11. JWH to Louisa Ward Crawford and Anne Ward, Sept. [1844], HPHL.
12. JWH to Anne Ward, "Saturday the 13th" [1845?], HPHL.
13. REM, 150.
14. M. C. Crawford, *Romantic Days in Old Boston*, 307–313.
15. JWH to Anne Ward (see n.11).
16. REM, 214–215.
17. Crawford, *Romantic Days*, 309–310.
18. Ibid., 244–251.
19. JWH to Louisa Ward Crawford, May 15, 1847, HPHL.
20. The quarrel between Sam Howe and Sam Ward over Julia's money is referred to in Howe's letters to Charles Sumner and in letters from both Julia and Sam Howe to Sam and John Ward. See HPHL.
21. JWH to Louisa Ward Crawford, Tuesday [March 1845?], HPHL.
22. JWH to SGH, Oct. 1846, HPHL.
23. JWH to Louisa Ward Crawford, Mar. 31, 1847, HPHL.
24. JWH to Anne Ward Mailliard [1847], copy courtesy of the Richards family.
25. The main sources for the description of Green Peace and the home life of the Howes are R&E, v. 1; Richards, *When I Was Your Age* and *Stepping Westward*; Elliott, *Three Generations*.
26. JWH to Louisa Ward Crawford, May 15, 1847, HPHL.
27. JWH to SGH [1846], HPHL.
28. JWH to Anne Ward Mailliard, Dec. 15, 1849, HPHL.
29. For a complete discussion of Ward family finances at this time, see SW, 126, 144–147.

30. JWH to Louisa Ward Crawford, Sept. 20, 1847, copy courtesy of the Richards family.
31. JWH to Anne Ward Mailliard [1848], HPHL.
32. Ibid.
33. JWH to Anne Ward Mailliard [1844], HPHL.
34. REM, 206–208.
35. H. S. Commager, *Theodore Parker*, 115.
36. REM, 245.
37. JWH, "The Ethical Office of the Drama" (essay), HPLC, folder #24.
38. Ibid.
39. Richards, ed., *Letters and Journals of SGH*, 2:393.
40. REM, 244.
41. Ibid., 150.
42. Ibid., 153.

6

Passion Flowers

1. R&E, 1:130–131.
2. JWH to Anne Ward Mailliard, quoted in R&E, 1:132.
3. For information on the marriages and later lives of Anne and Louisa Ward, I have largely relied on Tharp, *Three Saints*.
4. Sam Ward's unsatisfactory relation with his in-laws is discussed most thoroughly in SW, 139–141, 144–147, 173–174.
5. The chief source for this Roman winter is REM, 188–204.
6. REM, 192.
7. R&E, 1:134.
8. REM, 191.
9. Baker, *Fortunate Pilgrims*, 189.
10. REM, 195.
11. Ibid., 196.
12. G. E. Hatvary, "Horace Binney Wallace: A Study in Self-Destruction," 137–149.
13. JWH, "Via Felice" (poem), in *Words for the Hour*, 52–56.
14. REM, 203–204.
15. Fanny Longfellow to Emmaline Wadsworth, Sept. 3, 1851, *Selected Letters*, 182.
16. JWH to Anne Ward Mailliard, Dec. 15, 1849, HPHL.
17. JWH to Edward Twistleton, June 7, 1851, HPHL.
18. JWH, "Rome," *Passion Flowers*, 8–25.
19. HS, 159–160.
20. H. S. Commager, *Theodore Parker: Yankee Crusader*, 214–217.
21. JWH to Anne Ward Mailliard [1851], HPHL.
22. Tharp, *Three Saints*, 167–168.
23. JWH to Anne Ward Mailliard [1851], HPHL.
24. JWH to Anne Ward Mailliard, "Wednesday the 17th" [1851], HPHL.
25. JWH to Anne Ward Mailliard, Nov. 8 [1851], HPHL.

26. Theodore Parker to JWH, Sept. 2, 1850, HPHL.
27. JWH to Anne Ward Mailliard, Nov. 25 [1851], HPHL.
28. JWH, "Tribute to a Faithful Servant," *Passion Flowers,* 141–146.
29. Samuel Longfellow, ed., *The Life of Henry Wadsworth Longfellow, with Extracts from His Journal and Correspondence* (Cambridge: Houghton Mifflin, 1891), 2:236.
30. JWH to Anne Ward Mailliard [1852], HPHL.
31. Fanny Longfellow, *Selected Letters,* 189.
32. From the diary of H. W. Longfellow, quoted in Tharp, *Three Saints,* 176.
33. Theodore Parker, "Daniel Webster," in H. S. Commager, ed., *Theodore Parker: An Anthology,* 246–247. The "7th of March" refers to Webster's famous speech during the debate in the Senate over the Compromise of 1850. Regarded until then as a Free Soiler, Webster aroused the wrath of the abolitionists by his appeal on behalf of the Union at the expense of concessions to slavery.
34. REM, 164–165.
35. Commager, *Parker: Yankee Crusader,* 114.
36. REM, 305.
37. R&E, 1:141n.
38. JWH to Anne Ward Mailliard [Feb. 25, 1853], HPHL.
39. JWH to Anne Ward Mailliard, Dec. 3, 1852, HPHL.
40. JWH to Anne Ward Mailliard [1850's], HPHL.
41. JWH to Horace Binney Wallace, Jan. 7, 1853, HPHL.
42. JWH to Louisa Ward Crawford, Feb. 18, 1854, HPHL.
43. JWH to Auguste Comte, Feb. 15, 1853, HPHL.
44. JWH to Anne Ward Mailliard, Feb. 16, 1853, HPHL.
45. R&E, 1:148.
46. Quoted in S. Longfellow, ed., *Life of Henry Wadsworth Longfellow,* 2:238; one of the parties is described in a letter of JWH's to Anne Ward Mailliard, May [1853], HPHL.
47. Richards, *Stepping Westward,* 26–28.
48. JWH to Anne Ward Mailliard, "Monday, December" [1853], HPHL; W. S. Tryon, *Parnassus Corner,* 222.
49. JWH to Anne Ward Mailliard (see n. 48).
50. JWH to Anne Ward Mailliard, Dec. 29 [1853], HPHL.
51. R. W. Emerson to JWH, Dec. 1853, in R&E, 1:139–140.
52. New York *Tribune,* Jan. 10, 1854.
53. JWH, "Mind Versus Mill-Stream," *Passion Flowers,* 80–85.
54. JWH to Anne Ward Mailliard, "Tuesday 7th" [1854], HPHL.
55. JWH to Louisa Ward Crawford, July 23, 1854, HPHL.
56. JWH to Anne Ward Mailliard [1854], HPHL.

7

Prelude to War

1. HS, 195–196. I have relied on this work for nearly all my information on Sam Howe's involvement in the Kansas question. See Ch. 12, "Kansas Agitation," 195–216.

2. Quoted in John A. Garraty, *The American Nation: A History of the United States to 1877*, 2d ed. (New York: Harper & Row, 1971), 455.
3. JWH to Louisa Ward Crawford and Anne Ward Mailliard, May 29, 1856, HPHL.
4. New York *Evening Post*, May 21, 1856, quoted in David Donald, *Charles Sumner and the Coming of the Civil War*, 283.
5. Quoted in Donald, 286.
6. SGH to Charles Sumner, May 25, 1856, quoted in HS, 203.
7. REM, 239.
8. Sam Ward to JWH, Mar. 30, 1857, HPHL.
9. Fanny Longfellow, *Selected Letters*, 208–209.
10. JWH to Samuel Gray Ward [1857], HPHL.
11. JWH to J. R. Lowell, n.d., HPHL.
12. Martin Duberman, *James Russell Lowell* (Boston, Houghton Mifflin, 1966), 177–178; James C. Austin, *Fields of the* Atlantic Monthly, 101–111.
13. JWH, "The Sermon of Spring" (poem), in *Words for the Hour*, 9.
14. JWH, "Recollections of the Antislavery Struggle," in *Cosmopolitan* 7 (1889): 279–286.
15. I learned this from a talk with Julia's great-granddaughter Julia Ward Stickley.
16. SGH to Theodore Parker, Nov. 1854, in Laura Richards, ed., *Letters and Journals of SGH*, 2:404.
17. JWH, letter to the New York *Tribune*, Aug. 18, 1859. Julia was commissioned in the mid-1850's to write a series of letters from Newport. They are unsigned but unquestionably hers.
18. JWH to Anne Ward Mailliard, May 26, 1859, HPHL.
19. REM, 253–254.
20. Ibid., 256.
21. Louis B. Filler, *The Crusade Against Slavery, 1830–1861* (New York: Harper & Bros., 1960), 239–241.
22. REM, 254.
23. HS, 221–222.
24. Ibid., 227.
25. David M. Potter, *The Impending Crisis, 1848–1861* (New York: Harper & Row, 1976), 373.
26. REM, 255–256.
27. Ibid., 256.
28. Ibid.
29. JWH to Anne Ward Mailliard, Nov. 6, 1859, HPHL.
30. .HS, 234–246.
31. Ibid., 237–240.
32. JWH to Anne Ward Mailliard [1859], copy courtesy of the Richards family.
33. JWH to Anne Ward Mailliard, Dec. [1857], HPHL.
34. REM, 233.
35. Allan Nevins, *The Emergence of Lincoln* (New York: Scribner's, 1950), 2:484–486.
36. Garraty, 464.
37. JWH to Theodore Parker, May 18, 1859, HPHL.
38. JWH, *A Trip to Cuba*, 12–13.
39. Ibid., 234.

40. REM, 236.
41. HS, 261.
42. SGH to Theodore Parker, May 17, 1859, HPHL; REM, 235.

8

Battle Hymn

1. SGH to Charles Sumner, Apr. 5, 1860, HPHL.
2. HS, 252–253.
3. Quoted in SW, 250. I have relied on Thomas's book for most of my information concerning Sam Ward's activities during the Civil War.
4. SW, 273.
5. HS, 252.
6. JWH to Anne Ward Mailliard, [May] 24, 1861, HPHL.
7. Quoted in Robert C. Albrecht, "The Theological Response of the Transcendentalists to the Civil War," *New England Quarterly* 38 (1965):21–34.
8. For Northern attitudes toward the war see George M. Frederickson, *The Inner Civil War: The Northern Intellectuals and the Crisis of the Union* (New York: Harper & Row, 1965).
9. REM, 270.
10. Ibid., 273–274.
11. For a good description of Washington at this time, see Margaret Leech, *Reveille in Washington, 1860–1865* (New York: Grosset and Dunlop, 1941).
12. REM, 275.
13. I have quoted not the original version but the slightly amended and more familiar one she sent to the *Atlantic Monthly* and which was also published in her *Later Lyrics*, 41–42. The original version reads:

Mine eyes have seen the glory of the coming of the
    Lord
He is trampling out the wine press where the grapes of wrath are stored,
He hath loosed the fateful lightnings of his terrible
        swift sword,
    His truth is marching on.

I have seen him in the watchfires of an hundred
        circling camps
They have builded him an altar in the evening dews
        and damps,
I can read His righteous sentence by the dim and flaring lamps
    His day is marching on.

I have read a burning Gospel writ in fiery rows
        of steel
As ye deal with my contemners, so with you my grace
        shall deal

287

*Let the hero born of woman crush the serpent with
his heel
Our God is marching on.*

*He has sounded out the trumpet that shall never call
retreat,
He has waked the earth's dull sorrow with a high
ecstatic beat,
Oh! be swift my soul to answer him, be jubilant
my feet.
Our God is marching on.*

*In the whiteness of the lilies he was born across
the sea
With a glory in his bosom that shines out on you
and me,
As he died to make men holy, let us die to make
men free
Our God is marching on.*

An extra verse was added and later dropped. For a facsimile of the first draft, see R&E, 1:190 (facing).

14. Isaiah's verses had also inspired Macaulay, and Edmund Wilson suggests that Julia had read his *Songs of the Civil War,* and had seen a parallel between the Northern cause in 1861 and that of the Cromwellian army striking the forces of popery and royalism:

    *Oh! wherefore came ye forth, in triumph from the North,
    With your hands, and your feet, and your raiment
    all red?
    And wherefore doth your rout send forth a joyous shout?
    And whence be the grapes of the winepress which ye tread?
    Oh, evil was the root, and bitter was the fruit,
    And crimson was the juice of the vintage that we trod;
    For we trampled on the throng of the haughty and the
    strong
    Who sat in the high places, and slew the saints of God.*

    See Wilson's *Patriotic Gore: Studies in the Literature of the American Civil War* (New York: Oxford University Press, 1962), 93–94.
15. For various interpretations of the "Battle Hymn," see Edward D. Snyder, "The Biblical Background of the Battle Hymn," *New England Quarterly* 24 (1951): 231–238; and Wilson, 91–96.
16. Quoted in James C. Austin, *Fields of the* Atlantic Monthly, 104.
17. REM, 275–276.
18. JWHD, Oct. 9, 1899, HPHL.
19. R&E, 2:189.
20. Entry of July 21, 1870, *Journals of Ralph Waldo Emerson,* ed. by E. W. Emerson and W. E. Forbes (Boston: Houghton Mifflin, 1913), 10:325.

9

Family Life in the Sixties

1. Richards, *Stepping Westward*, 48.
2. *Boatswain's Whistle,* Nov. 10–16, 1864.
3. JWH to Louisa Ward Terry, Sept. 2, 1863, HPHL.
4. R&E, 1:216.
5. Hall, *Memories Grave and Gay,* 4.
6. Richards, *When I Was Your Age,* 36.
7. Richards, *Stepping Westward,* 123.
8. Hall, *Memories Grave and Gay,* 201.
9. JWH to Annie Ward Maillard, Mar. 1862, HPHL.
10. Hall, *Memories Grave and Gay,* 27.
11. Richards, *Stepping Westward,* 57.
12. Hall, *Memories Grave and Gay,* 168.
13. Florence Howe Hall, "Mrs. Julia Ward Howe — Her Connection with the Women's Clubs," clipping from *America* [c. 1889], HPHL.
14. Hall, *Memories Grave and Gay,* 166.
15. Richards, *When I Was Your Age,* 62–64.
16. Richards, *Stepping Westward,* 30.
17. R&E, 1:154.
18. Hall, *Memories Grave and Gay,* 138–139.
19. Ibid.
20. REM, 258.
21. Hall, *Memories Grave and Gay,* 111.
22. Richards, *Stepping Westward,* 113–114.
23. SW, 311.
24. Elliott, *This Was My Newport,* 59.
25. JWHD, 1863, HPHL. For more details about Sammy's short life and a description of his illness and death, see JWH, "The Last Letter to Sammy," ed. by Deborah P. Clifford, *Harvard Library Bulletin* 25 (1977): 50–62.
26. JWHD, May 20, 1863, HPHL.
27. "The Last Letter to Sammy," 60.
28. JWHD, May 23, 1863, HPHL.
29. R&E, 1:195.
30. JWHD, Sept. 24, 1863, HPHL.
31. For a discussion of liberal Christian theology see Alstrom, *A Religious History of the American People,* 779–781.
32. JWH, "The Ideal Church," *Christian Examiner* 79 (1865): 67–83.
33. REM, 305.
34. Quoted in Walter Muir Whitehill, "John Brown of Pottawatamie in Boston, 1857," *Proceedings of the Massachusetts Historical Society* 69: 262–273.
35. JWHD, Jan. 17 and 20, 1864, HPHL.
36. JWH, "Duality of Character," unpublished essay, HPHL.
37. JWH, *Later Lyrics,* 18.
38. For a thorough discussion of the effect of the war on the thinking of the northern intellectuals, see Frederickson, *The Inner Civil War.*

39. JWHD, May 11, 1864, HPHL.
40. JWHD, May 14–20, 1864, HPHL; JWH to Charles Sumner, Feb. 23, 1864, HPHL.
41. JWH to Charles Sumner, Mar. 1, 1864, HPHL.
42. JWHD, Nov. 5, 1864, HPHL.
43. JWHD, Mar. 11–19, 1865, HPHL.
44. JWHD, Apr. 23, 1865, HPHL.
45. JWHD, Apr. 23–24, 1865, HPHL.
46. JWHD, June 3, 1865, HPHL.
47. Tryon, *Parnassus Corner,* 265–266.
48. JWHD, May 11, 1864; Mar. 23, 1865, Mar. 26, 1865, HPHL.
49. JWHD, Nov. 3, 1865, HPHL.
50. JWH, *From the Oak to the Olive,* 28–63.
51. JWHD, May 1, 1867, HPHL.
52. JWHD, July 9–13, 1867, HPHL.
53. JWHD, Oct. 26, 1867, HPHL.
54. Hall, *Memories Grave and Gay,* 147.
55. JWHD, Nov. 23, 1867, HPHL.
56. JWHD, Oct. 30, 1867, HPHL.
57. JWHD, Nov. 21, 1867, HPHL.

10
"I Am with You"

1. REM, 375.
2. The first women's rights meeting had actually been held in Seneca Falls, N.Y., in 1848, but there had been no elected delegates.
3. Report of an interview with JWH in the Rochester *Post Express,* Oct. 21, 1890, clipping in JWHS, 3:101, HPSL.
4. JWH, "The Woman's Rights Question" (speech), HPHL.
5. Quoted in FHH, 12.
6. REM, 373.
7. Report of an interview with JWH in the Rochester *Post Express,* Oct. 21, 1890. See n. 3.
8. REM, 375.
9. Address of JWH written at the time of the founding of the New England Woman's Club, New England Woman's Club Papers, Schlesinger Library, Radcliffe College, folder #43.
10. REM, 375.
11. Boston *Daily Evening Transcript,* Nov. 18, 1868.
12. Quoted in R&E, 1:360.
13. Stanton, *The History of Woman Suffrage,* 2:756–757.
14. Ibid., 766.
15. Merk, "Massachusetts and the Woman Suffrage Movement," 1:33.
16. REM, 376.
17. Ibid.
18. Speech of JWH, clipping from Boston *Herald,* Sept. 25, 1880, JWHS, 3:25, HPSL.

19. JWH, suffrage speech (labeled "early"), HPHL.
20. JWH, speech given on May 11, 1870, at an American Woman Suffrage Association meeting in New York, WJ, May 21, 1870, 156.
21. JWH, speech given at the Cleveland Convention [1869], HPHL.
22. WJ, Nov. 28, 1885, 380; report of the Editorial Convention in Boston, 1890, clipping from JWHS, v. 4, HPSL.
23. Welter, "The Cult of True Womanhood," 151–174.
24. JWH, "The Moral Initiative As Belonging to Women," FHH, 130.
25. JWH, "Why Are Women the Natural Guardians of Social Morals?" FHH, 93–112; "Behold I Create All Things New," HPLC, folder #2.
26. JWH, "How Can Women Best Associate," WJ, Oct. 25, 1873, 342.
27. JWH, "The Rights of Women," clipping in JWHS, 5:47, HPSL.
28. For a more complete discussion of this particular suffrage campaign in Vermont, see Deborah P. Clifford, "An Invasion of Strong-minded Women: The Newspapers and the Woman Suffrage Campaign in Vermont in 1870," *Vermont History* 43 (1975): 1–19.
29. *Vermont Watchman and State Journal,* Feb. 2, 1870.
30. Ibid., Feb. 7, 1870.
31. Rutland *Herald,* Feb. 21, 1870.
32. WJ, Mar. 5, 1870.
33. REM, 380–381.
34. Burlington *Free Press,* Mar. 11, 1870.
35. Her report was quoted in the Burlington *Free Press,* Mar. 9, 1870.
36. WJ, Apr. 9 and 30, 1870.
37. Quoted in the Burlington *Free Press,* Mar. 9, 1870.
38. REM, 377.
39. Ibid., 328.
40. Ibid.
41. The appeal is cited in its entirety in R&E, 1:302–303.
42. WJ, Dec. 31, 1870, 416.
43. Edwin D. Mead, *Julia Ward Howe's Peace Crusade.*
44. WJ, Sept. 7, 1872, 282; REM, 337.
45. JWHD, June 2, 1873, HPHL.
46. JWHD, May 27, 1874, HPHL.
47. R&E, 1:318.
48. JWHD, May 27, 1871, HPHL.
49. JWHD, Oct. 16, 1874, HPHL.

11
The Passing of the Chevalier

1. For SGH's involvement in the Dominican Republic question I have relied almost exclusively on HS, 291–320.
2. HS, 296.
3. Ibid.
4. Ibid., 296–303.

5. Quoted in HS, 300.
6. Sam Ward to Louisa Ward Terry, Feb. 10, 1872, HPHL.
7. REM, 349.
8. REM, 357.
9. JWHD, Feb. 27–28, 1872, HPHL.
10. R&E, 1:325.
11. REM, 351.
12. JWHD, Apr. 7 and 10, 1872, HPHL.
13. JWHD, May 10, 1872, HPHL.
14. REM, 331; R&E, 1:315.
15. JWHD, May 8, 1872, HPHL.
16. JWHD, May 31 and June 18, 1872, HPHL.
17. JWHD, Oct. 27, 1874, HPHL.
18. JWHD, Aug. 6, 1872, HPHL.
19. R&E, 1:340.
20. SGH to George Finlay, Aug. 13, 1874, HPHL.
21. JWHD, Feb. 8, 1874, HPHL.
22. JWHD, Jan. 27, 1874, HPHL.
23. JWHD, Mar. 25–31, 1874, HPHL.
24. JWHD, Apr. 15, 1874, HPHL.
25. JWHD, June 9 and 10, 1874, HPHL.
26. Quoted in HS, 319–320.
27. This was told me by the great-granddaughter in question, Julia Ward Stickley.
28. JWHD, Apr. 1, 1874, HPHL.
29. JWHD, Dec. 23, 1874, HPHL.
30. REM, 386.
31. Ruth Huntington Sessions, *Sixty-Odd: A Personal History* (Brattleboro, Vt.: Stephen Daye, 1936), 98–102.
32. Quoted in R&E, 1:373.
33. JWHD, Apr. 16, 1875, HPHL.
34. JWHD, Jan. 18, 1875, HPHL.
35. JWH, "The Halfness of Nature," HPLC, folder #6.
36. JWHD, Apr. 26, 1875, HPHL.
37. JWHD, Nov. 23–Dec. 31, 1875, HPHL.
38. JWHD, Dec. 8, 1875, HPHL.
39. JWHD, Jan. 10, 1875, HPHL.

12

Beginning Again

1. JWHD, Apr. 30, 1876, HPHL.
2. JWHD, Apr. 2, 1880, HPHL.
3. JWHD, Feb. 6, 1876, HPHL.
4. JWHD, Mar. 9, 1876, HPHL.
5. WJ, June 28, 1873, 204; July 5, 1873, 212.
6. JWHD, June 3, 1876, HPHL.

7. Sam Ward to JWH, Jan. 10, 1876, HPHL.
8. Sam Ward to JWH, July 20, 1876, HPHL.
9. JWHD, Jan. 15, 1876, HPHL.
10. JWHD, Dec. 10, 1876–Feb. 12, 1877, HPHL.
11. St. Louis *Globe Democrat*, Jan. 16, 1877, clipping in JWHS, 3:31, HPSL.
12. Ibid.
13. JWH to Laura Richards, Jan. 4, 1877, copy courtesy of the Richards family.
14. JWH to Laura Richards, Sept. 18, 1879, copy courtesy of the Richards family.
15. Elliott, *Three Generations*, 135.
16. Ibid., 139–146.
17. REM, 411.
18. Elliott, *Three Generations*, 147.
19. JWHD, May 26, 1877, HPHL.
20. Margaret Chanler, *Roman Spring* (Boston: Little Brown, 1934), 49–51.
21. JWH, *Is Polite Society Polite?*, 3–33.
22. Quoted in Pivar, *Purity Crusade*, 83.
23. JWH, letters to the Chicago *Tribune*, 1878, HPSL.
24. WJ, Oct. 13, 1877, 324–325.
25. JWHD, Sept. 22, 1877, HPHL.
26. Report of JWH's lecture on Brook Farm, clipping in JWHS, v. 4, 69 HPHL.
27. JWH, manuscripts of letters to the Chicago *Tribune*, 1878, HPHL; REM, 419–420.
28. Quoted in WJ, Aug. 10, 1878, 252.
29. REM, 421. According to her daughters this was the American Girls' Club.
30. JWH to Laura Richards, Mar. 8, 1878, copy courtesy of the Richards family.
31. WJ, May 4, 1878, 140.
32. JWH to Laura Richards, July, 1878, HPHL.
33. JWH to Laura Richards, Oct. 22, 1878, copy courtesy of the Richards family.
34. JWH, *Modern Society*, 44.
35. Elliott, *Three Generations*, 184.
36. Ibid., 185.
37. JWHD, Jan. 16, 1879, HPHL.
38. JWHD, July 15, 1879, HPHL.

13
Boston in the Eighties

1. Whitehill, *Boston: A Topographical History*, 168–173.
2. WJ, Oct. 15, 1881, 332.
3. Boston *Daily Advertiser*, July 30, 1880, 1.
4. Howe, *Modern Society*, 47.
5. Warren Austin, "The Concord School of Philosophy," *New England Quarterly*, 2 (1929): 199–233; JWHD, July 29, 1880, HPHL.
6. Austin, 222.
7. Elliott, *Three Generations*, 195.
8. JWHD, Feb. 24, 1880, HPHL.

9. SW, 336–408.
10. JWHD, May 27, 1881, HPHL; SW, 408.
11. Chanler, *Roman Spring*, 87.
12. Elliott, *Three Generations*, 197.
13. Ibid., 199.
14. JWH to Sam Ward, Apr. 13, 1881, HPHL.
15. Sam Ward to JWH, Aug. 4, 1882, HPHL.
16. JWHD, Jan. 29–30, 1882, HPHL.
17. Oscar Wilde to JWH, n.d., quoted in Elliott, *This Was My Newport*, 100.
18. Quoted in SW, 442.
19. New York *Daily Tribune*, Feb. 18, 1882.
20. Elliott, *This Was My Newport*, 100.
21. Extracts from Maud Howe Elliott in the *Critic*, reprinted in WJ, June 8, 1887, 193.
22. JWH to Sam Ward, Oct. 21, 1883, HPHL.

14
"We Have Been the Scatterers
of Seed Not the Harvesters"

1. JWH, speech before the Brooklyn Woman Suffrage Association, JWHS, v. 3, HPSL.
2. JWH, speech before the Massachusetts Legislature, quoted in FHH, 189–197.
3. Wiebe, *The Search for Order*, 158.
4. WJ, May 28, 1881, 169.
5. Mann, *Yankee Reformers in the Urban Age*, 73–99.
6. Charles W. Elliott, "Woman's Work and Woman's Wages," *North American Review*, 135 (1882), 146–161.
7. JWH, "The Industrial Value of Women," *North American Review*, 135 (1882), 437.
8. Ibid., 439.
9. Ibid., 442.
10. Quoted in the New York *Times*, Oct. 18, 1884.
11. Ibid., Dec. 12, 1884.
12. Ibid.
13. WJ, Jan. 17, 1885, 20.
14. JWH, report of the New Orleans Exposition, HPSL.
15. JWHD, Jan. 13, 1885, HPHL.
16. WJ, Jan. 31, 1885, 34.
17. REM, 397.
18. R&E, 2:105–106.
19. R&E, 2:106–107, speech at the formal opening of the Woman's Department, in papers on the New Orleans Exposition, HPSL.
20. Joy J. Jackson, *New Orleans in the Gilded Age: Politics and Urban Progress* (Baton Rouge: Louisiana State University Press, 1969), 206.

21. New York *Times,* Feb. 26 and Jan. 7, 1885; R&E, 2:109; *Congressional Record,* 48th Cong., 2d sess., 16:3 (Feb. 26, 1885), 2212–2213.
22. For a discussion of the southern question and woman suffrage see Kraditor, *The Ideas of the Woman Suffrage Movement,* 163–218.
23. JWHD, June 30, 1885, HPHL.
24. Quoted in R&E, 2:109.
25. Quoted in New York *Times,* May 11, 1885.
26. JWH, report of New Orleans Exposition, HPSL.
27. Quoted in WJ, Apr. 25, 1885, 134.
28. WJ, Dec. 12, 1885, 396.
29. WJ, Nov. 28, 1885, 380.
30. For JWH's series of articles, "Industries of Women," see WJ, Nov. 28, 1885–Oct. 2, 1886.
31. WJ, July 16, 1870, 217.
32. Merk, "Massachusetts and the Woman Suffrage Movement," 230.
33. WJ, June 16, 1888, 191.
34. JWHD, Apr. 17, 1888, HPHL.
35. Clipping from the New Orleans *Times* [1895], JWHS, v. 5, p. 2, HPSL.
36. JWHD, Jan. 7, 1893, HPHL.
37. The above discussion of the shift to municipal suffrage is largely derived from Merk, 60–62, and Kraditor, 45.
38. Merk, 60–62. JWH supported school suffrage on the same grounds as municipal suffrage, WJ, May 28, 1881, 173.
39. WJ, Mar. 5, 1892, 76.
40. Merk, 68.
41. Interview with JWH in San Francisco by the *Post,* clipping in JWHS, v.2, HPSL.
42. Merk, 240.
43. WJ, May 5, 1888, 140.
44. JWHD, Feb. 17, 1890, HPHL.
45. Wiebe, *The Search for Order,* 44–75.
46. JWHD, Mar. 1, 1889, HPHL.
47. Quoted in WJ, May 30, 1891, 170.
48. JWH to Ednah Dow Cheney, Sept. 24, 1889, HPHL.
49. JWH to Ednah Dow Cheney, Feb. 27, 1889, HPHL.
50. O'Neill, *Everyone Was Brave,* 87.
51. REM, 390.
52. Clipping from the Springfield *Republican,* Nov. 4, 1897, JWHS, 4:20, HPSL.
53. O'Neill, 87.

15

Mine Eyes Have Seen the Glory

1. Queen Victoria was born on May 24, 1819.
2. Quoted in WJ, Oct. 2, 1909, 157.
3. Thomas Wentworth Higginson to JWH, Feb. 5, 1907, HPHL.
4. Quoted in WJ, Sept. 25, 153.

5. *Sunday Inter-Ocean,* June 4, 1899, clipping in JWHS, v. 4, HPSL.
6. JWH to Laura Richards, June 19, 1891, HPHL.
7. JWH to Louisa Crawford Terry, July 8, 1893, Chanler Papers, Houghton Library, Harvard University.
8. JWH to Laura Richards, Aug. 10, 1893, HPHL.
9. Henry Adams, *The Education of Henry Adams* (Modern Library ed.), 338.
10. JWHD, Oct. 29, 1896, HPHL.
11. JWHD, Jan. 1, 1899, HPHL.
12. JWHD, Dec. 15, 1898, HPHL.
13. William Palmer Wesselhoeft to JWH, Nov. 2, 1899, HPHL.
14. A rare statement of JWH's financial situation was inserted in a letter to Laura Richards, written in the last days of 1899. It shows Julia's income to have consisted of $2,200 from Uncle John Ward's legacy and $2,000 in rent from the property in South Boston. Out of this, $1,408 had to go for taxes and the mortgage on her Beacon Street house. This left her $2,792 to live on — adequate but hardly affluent. It would be roughly comparable to $16,750 today. JWH to Laura Richards, Dec. 9, 1899, HPHL.
15. JWH to Laura Richards, Aug. 21, 1896, HPHL.
16. Thomas Wentworth Higginson, *Carlyle's Laugh and Other Surprises* (Boston: Houghton Mifflin, 1909), 302–305.
17. Mary Thatcher Higginson, ed., *Letters and Journals of Thomas Wentworth Higginson* (Boston: Houghton Mifflin, 1921), 231.
18. R&E, 2:332–333.
19. John Higham, *Strangers in the Land,* 88.
20. Ibid., 71–72.
21. Ibid., 96–105.
22. William Lloyd Garrison to JWH, Jan. 28, 1897, HPHL.
23. For Julia's ideas on immigration and immigrants, see her "Aliens in America" (1891), HPLC, folder #12; "Who Would Be Free Must Himself Strike the First Blow," WJ, May 28, 1881, 172; "The Power of the Gospel," clipping in JWHS, v. 5, HPSL; and JWHD, June 3, 1891, HPHL.
24. Higham, 234–243.
25. JWH, *To the Friends of Russian Freedom,* pamphlet in JWHS, 3:130, HPSL; and WJ, Feb. 4, 1905, 19.
26. JWH to George Frisbie Hoar, May 19, 1896, HPHL.
27. Harold Faulkner, *Politics, Reform and Expansion, 1890–1900* (New York: Harper, 1959), 226; for JWH's appeal, see WJ, Aug. 28, 1897, 273.
28. JWHD, May 2, 1898, HPHL.
29. Clipping in JWHS, 4:37, HPSL.
30. JWH to Maud Howe Elliott, Dec. 25, 1898, Harris Collection, John Hay Library, Brown University.
31. WJ, Feb. 23, 1895, 61.
32. JWH to Ednah Dow Cheney, Aug. 25, 1900, HPHL.
33. REM, 1–2.
34. WJ, Sept. 28, 1907, 153.
35. JWH, "Religious Progress in the Last Two Generations," *Christian Register,* Apr. 2, 1908, clipping in JWHS, 4:210, HPSL.
36. JWHD, Apr. 2–May 10, 1908, HPHL.

37. The original manuscript is in HPHL; see also R&E, 2:377.
38. Quoted in WJ, June 4, 1910, 92.
39. JWH's letter, which was published in *The Times* (London), is quoted in WJ, Aug. 1, 1908, 121.
40. *Outlook* 90 (1908): 58.
41. WJ, May 22, 1909, 81.
42. WJ, Oct. 15, 1910, 169.
43. The unpublished manuscript is in the possession of the author.
44. JWHD, June 23 and Sept. 21–22, HPHL; R&E, 2:409.
45. W. W. Bailey to a friend, June 18, 1909, Elliott Collection, John Hay Library, Brown University.
46. R&E, 2:412–413.
47. WJ, Oct. 29, 1910, 183.

Selected Bibliography

Manuscript Sources

Most of Julia Ward Howe's unpublished papers are to be found in three repositories:

The Howe Papers, Houghton Library, Harvard University (referred to as HPHL). The largest collection, it includes letters both to and from Julia and her husband; Julia's diaries, 1863–1910 (an occasional volume is missing); manuscripts of her poems, plays and speeches; and a quantity of juvenile material. The collection also includes ten boxes of uncatalogued, miscellaneous pieces of all kinds.

The Julia Ward Howe Papers, Schlesinger Library, Radcliffe College (referred to as HPSL). Letters and a variety of other papers are included, but the most valuable items are nine scrapbooks of clippings, which she began compiling in the 1850's but which are most useful for the 1880's onward. Some of the clippings are articles by her; others are articles about her; still others are articles of interest to her; most of them pertain to the woman's movement of the late nineteenth century.

The Julia Ward Howe Papers, Library of Congress (referred to as HPLC). The collection contains a great many essays, speeches and sermons, and a few letters and poems.

Smaller collections of her papers are in the Sophia Smith Collection, Smith College; the John Hay Library, Brown University; the Boston Athenaeum; and the Boston Public Library.

A number of her letters are in private collections. Mrs. Frances Howard, a great-granddaughter, has a few letters that Julia wrote in her teens. The Richards family has copies of her letters to her brother Sam, to her sisters, and to her daughter, Laura Richards. I was informed at the time these were loaned to me by her granddaughter, Rosalind Richards, that the originals were all in Houghton. It turned out, however, that not all of them are in the Howe Papers there and have had to be cited as copies. In my own collection are some papers of Rosalind Richards'. These contain reminiscences of Julia Ward Howe in her old age as well as short sketches of other Bostonians.

Selected Bibliography

𝓝𝓝

Other manuscript collections that proved useful include the papers of Samuel Ward (1786–1839), Julia's father, and those of the younger Samuel Ward (1814–1884), Julia's brother, in the New York Public Library; the New England Woman's Club Papers and the Saturday Morning Club Papers in the Schlesinger Library, Radcliffe College; the Longfellow and Sumner Papers in Houghton Library, Harvard University.

Julia Ward Howe's Published Works

At Sunset. Boston: Houghton Mifflin, 1910. A book of poetry.

From the Oak to the Olive: A Plain Record of a Pleasant Journey. Boston: Lee and Shepard, 1868. A description of a journey to Europe in 1867.

From Sunset Ridge: Poems Old and New. Boston: Houghton Mifflin, 1898.

Hippolytus, in *America's Lost Plays,* edited by Barrett H. Clark (Bloomington: Indiana University Press, 1963–1965) 16:77–128. This play, written in the 1850's, was produced for the first time after JWH's death in 1911.

Is Polite Society Polite? Boston: Houghton Mifflin, 1895. A collection of essays.

Later Lyrics. Boston: J. E. Tilton, 1866. A book of poetry.

Margaret Fuller. 1883. Reprint: Westport, Conn.: Greenwood Press, 1970.

Modern Society. Boston: Roberts Brothers, 1881.

Passion Flowers. Boston: Ticknor & Fields, 1854. Her first book of poetry.

Reminiscences. Boston: Houghton Mifflin, 1899. Referred to as REM.

Trip to Cuba, A. Boston: Ticknor & Fields, 1860.

Words for the Hour. Boston: Ticknor & Fields, 1857. Her second book of poetry.

World's Own, The. Boston: Ticknor & Fields, 1857. JWH's first play had a short run in Boston and New York.

A few of Julia's early poems as well as one by her mother, Julia Cutler Ward, can be found in:

Griswold, Rufus Wilmot, ed. *The Female Poets of America.* Philadelphia: Carey and Hart, 1849.

She also published a number of poems and articles in the *Atlantic Monthly.* Unsigned letters of hers can be found in the New York *Tribune,* beginning in September, 1859. She published articles regularly in the *Woman's Journal.* Here also can be found reports of her speeches at suffrage conventions, hearings and the like. She also wrote for the *Galaxy* and other periodicals. I have included only those sources I found most valuable.

Julia also served as the editor of a number of periodicals. More often than not, she contributed articles of her own as well:

Boatswain's Whistle. Boston: National Sailor's Fair, 1864, Nos. 1–10. A journal published daily for the duration of the fair, it contained articles, poems and works of fiction by Julia and other popular New England writers.

Northern Lights. Boston, 1867. An illustrated magazine containing articles, poems and works of fiction. It lasted only three months.

Woman Suffrage Bazaar Journal. Boston, 1866. Suffrage bazaars were held in Boston for a number of years in the 1880's and a journal was published daily for the duration of each bazaar.

She also edited a number of collections of essays on a variety of subjects. The following is of special interest:

Sex and Education. 1874. New York: Arno, 1972. The work is essentially a reply to Edward Hammond Clarke's *Sex in Education,* cited below.

Other Sources

The works I found particularly useful for studying the woman's movement of the nineteenth century, and especially Julia Ward Howe's part in it, are marked with an asterisk (*).

Works by other members of the Howe family that proved most valuable were those by Maud Howe Elliott, Florence Howe Hall, and Laura E. Richards.

Ahlstrom, Sydney E. *A Religious History of the American People.* New Haven: Yale University Press, 1972.

Albion, Robert Greenhalgh. *The Rise of the New York Port, 1815–1860.* New York: Scribner's, 1939.

Albrecht, Robert C. "The Theological Response of the Transcendentalists to the Civil War." *New England Quarterly* 38 (1965): 21–34.

Austin, James C. *Fields of the Atlantic Monthly: Letters to an Editor, 1861–1870.* San Francisco: Huntington Library Press, 1953.

Austin, Warren. "The Concord School of Philosophy." *New England Quarterly* 2 (1929): 199–233.

Baker, Paul R. *The Fortunate Pilgrims: Americans in Italy, 1800–1860.* Cambridge: Harvard University Press, 1964.

Boyer, Richard O. *The Legend of John Brown: A Biography and a History.* New York: Knopf, 1973.

Brooks, Van Wyck. *The Flowering of New England, 1815–1865.* New York: Dutton, 1935.

————. *Dream of Arcadia: American Writers and Artists in Italy, 1760–1915.* New York: Dutton, 1958.

————. *New England, Indian Summer, 1865–1915.* New York: Dutton, 1940.

————. *The World of Washington Irving.* New York: Dutton, 1944.

Chapman, John Jay. *The Selected Writings of John Jay Chapman.* Edited by Jacques Barzun. New York: Doubleday Anchor Books, 1959. Contains an excellent short essay on Julia Ward Howe.

*Clarke, Edward Hammond. *Sex in Education; or, A Fair Chance for Girls.* Boston: J. R. Osgood, 1874.

Commager, Henry Steele, ed. *Theodore Parker: An Anthology.* Boston: Beacon Press, 1960.

————. *Theodore Parker: Yankee Crusader.* Boston: Beacon Press, 1947.

*Cott, Nancy, F. *The Bonds of Womanhood: "Woman's Sphere" in New England, 1780–1835.* New Haven: Yale University Press, 1977.

Selected Bibliography

אב

Crawford, Mary Caroline. *Romantic Days in Old Boston: The Story of the City and of Its People During the Nineteenth Century.* Boston: Little, Brown, 1910.

Donald, David. *Charles Sumner and the Coming of the Civil War.* New York: Knopf, 1961.

*Douglas, Ann. *The Feminization of American Culture.* New York: Knopf, 1977.

Elliott, Maud Howe. *The Eleventh Hour in the Life of Julia Ward Howe.* Boston: Little, Brown, 1911.

————. *This Was My Newport.* Cambridge: The Mythology Co., 1944.

————. *Three Generations.* Boston: Little, Brown, 1923.

————. *Uncle Sam Ward and His Circle.* New York: Macmillan, 1938.

*Flexner, Eleanor. *Century of Struggle: The Woman's Rights Movement in the United States.* 1959. Rev. ed.: Cambridge: Harvard University Press, 1975.

Fredrickson, George M. *The Inner Civil War: Northern Intellectuals and the Crisis of the Union.* New York: Harper & Row, 1965.

*Fuller, Margaret. *Woman in the Nineteenth Century.* Boston: John P. Jewett, 1855.

Furnas, J. C. *The Road to Harpers Ferry.* New York: Sloane, 1959.

*Hall, Florence Howe, ed. *Julia Ward Howe and the Woman Suffrage Movement.* Boston: Dana Estes, 1913. Referred to as FHH.

————. *Memories Grave and Gay.* New York: Harper, 1918.

————. *The Story of the Battle Hymn of the Republic.* New York: Harper, 1916.

Haller, John S., and Robin M. *The Physician and Sexuality in Victorian America.* Urbana: University of Illinois Press, 1974.

Handlin, Oscar. *Boston's Immigrants: A Study in Acculturation.* New York: Atheneum, 1968.

Hatvary, George Egon. "Horace Binney Wallace: A Study in Self-Destruction." *Princeton University Library Chronicle* 25:137–149.

*Hays, Elinor Rice. *Morning Star: A Biography of Lucy Stone.* Harcourt Brace & World, 1961.

Higginson, Thomas Wentworth. *Cheerful Yesterdays.* 1899. Reprint: New York: Arno, 1968.

*————. *Common Sense About Women.* Boston: Lee & Shepard, 1882.

Higham, John. *Strangers in the Land: Patterns of American Nativism, 1860–1925.* New York: Atheneum, 1971 (reprint of 2nd ed., 1955).

Hone, Philip. *The Diary of Philip Hone, 1828–1851.* Ed. by Allan Nevins. 2 vols. New York: Dodd, Mead, 1927.

*James, Edward T., ed. *Notable American Women, 1607–1950: A Biographical Dictionary.* Cambridge: Harvard University Press, 1971.

*Kraditor, Aileen S. *The Ideas of the Woman Suffrage Movement, 1890–1920.* New York: Columbia University Press, 1965.

Longfellow, Fanny Appleton. *Selected Letters and Journals . . . 1817–1861.* Ed. by Edward Wagenknecht. New York: Longman Green, 1965.

Lyman, Susan Elizabeth. *The Story of New York: An Informal History of the City from the First Settlement to the Present Day.* 1964. Rev. ed.: New York: Crown, 1975.

*Mann, Arthur. *Yankee Reformers in the Urban Age.* Cambridge: Harvard University Press, Belknap Press, 1954.

Mead, Edwin D. *Julia Ward Howe's Peace Crusade.* World Peace Foundation Pamphlet, ser. 4, no. 7 (October, 1914).

Selected Bibliography

𝒵𝒩

Memorial Exercises in Honor of Julia Ward Howe. Boston: City of Boston Printing Department, 1911.

*Merk, Lois Bannister. "Massachusetts and the Woman Suffrage Movement." Ph.D. dissertation, Harvard University (1958; revised 1961).

*O'Neill, William L. *Everyone Was Brave: A History of Feminism in America.* Chicago: Quadrangle Books, 1969.

Pivar, David J. *Purity Crusade: Sexual Morality and Social Control, 1868–1900.* Westport, Conn.: Greenwood Press, 1973.

Richards, Laura E., and Maud Howe Elliott. *Julia Ward Howe, 1819–1910.* 2 vols. Boston: Houghton Mifflin, 1916. Referred to as R&E.

Richards, Laura E., ed. *Letters and Journals of Samuel Gridley Howe.* 2 vols. Boston: Dana Estes, 1906, 1909.

———. *Samuel Gridley Howe.* New York: Appleton-Century, 1935.

———. *Stepping Westward.* New York: Appleton, 1931.

———. *Two Noble Lives: Samuel Gridley Howe, Julia Ward Howe.* Boston: Dana Estes, 1911.

———, ed. *The Walk with God.* New York: Dutton, 1919. Selections from the writings of Julia Ward Howe.

———. *When I Was Your Age.* Boston: Estes & Lauriat, 1894.

*Rossi, Alice S., ed. *The Feminist Papers: From Adams to Beauvoir.* New York: Columbia University Press, 1973.

Schwartz, Harold. *Samuel Gridley Howe, Social Reformer, 1801–1876.* Cambridge: Harvard University Press, 1956. Referred to as HS.

*Smith-Rosenberg, Carroll. "The Female World of Love and Ritual: Relations between Women in Nineteenth Century America." *Signs: Journal of Women in Culture and Society* 1 (1975): 1–29.

Snyder, Edward D. "The Biblical Background of the Battle Hymn." *New England Quarterly* 24 (1951): 231–238.

Solomon, Barbara Miller. *Ancestors and Immigrants.* Cambridge: Harvard University Press, 1956.

*Stanton, Elizabeth Cady, et al. *History of American Woman Suffrage.* 2 vols. Rochester, 1881.

Tharp, Louise Hall. *Three Saints and a Sinner: Julia Ward Howe, Louisa, Annie and Sam Ward.* Boston: Little, Brown, 1956.

Thomas, Lately. *Sam Ward, King of the Lobby.* Boston: Houghton Mifflin, 1965. Referred to as SW.

Tryon, Warren S. *Parnassus Corner: A Life of James T. Fields, Publisher to the Victorians.* Boston: Houghton Mifflin, 1963.

Tyack, David B. *George Ticknor and the Boston Brahmins.* Cambridge: Harvard University Press, 1967.

Tyler, Alice Felt. *Freedom's Ferment: Phases of American Social History from the Colonial Period to the Outbreak of the Civil War.* New York: Harper & Row, 1962.

Wagenknecht, Edward. *Longfellow: A Full-Length Portrait.* New York: Longmans Green, 1955.

Wells, Anna Mary. *Dear Preceptor: The Life and Times of Thomas Wentworth Higginson.* Boston: Houghton Mifflin, 1963.

*Welter, Barbara. "The Cult of True Womanhood, 1820–1860." *American Quarterly* 18 (1966): 151–174.

Selected Bibliography
𝔥𝔑

Whitehill, Walter Muir. *Boston: A Topographical History.* Cambridge: Harvard University Press, 1968.

Wiebe, Robert H. *The Search for Order, 1877–1920.* New York: Hill and Wang, 1967.

Wilson, Edmund. *Patriotic Gore: Studies in the Literature of the American Civil War.* New York: Oxford University Press, 1962.

The *Woman's Journal,* first published in Boston in 1870, was very useful for tracing the history of the American Woman Suffrage Association and provided numerous articles on suffrage and other matters relating to women in the nineteenth century.

Acknowledgments

The credit for inspiring me to write a biography of Julia Ward Howe in the first place goes to Martin Duberman, who literally challenged me to begin.

In the preparation of this book I have, of course, contracted numerous debts. My warm thanks go first of all to the librarians past and present at the Houghton Library of Harvard University and the Schlesinger Library of Radcliffe College, who went out of their way to be helpful. They include Rodney Dennis, Carolyn Jakeman, Marty Shaw, Patricia King and Eva Mosely. In addition I would like to express my gratitude to the librarians of the Manuscript Room at the Library of Congress; the John Hay Library, Brown University; the Sophia Smith Collection, Smith College; the Boston Public Library; and finally, the Boston Athenaeum.

A number of Howe and Ward descendants have shown their support and encouragement by keeping me supplied with clippings, photographs and other information, and by allowing me to see family letters and other manuscripts. My thanks to Julia Ward Stickley, Frances Howard, Eleanor Hall Saunders, Rosalind Richards, Laura E. Wiggins, Winthrop Aldrich and Laura Chanler White.

William Catton, Norman Pettit, Mary Grant and my husband, Nicholas, historians all, read the manuscript and gave me

304

Acknowledgments

אא

detailed and valuable commentary. Jeremy Felt and Harold Schultz provided encouragement and creative suggestions, as did numbers of other people.

I am also indebted to my editor Upton Brady and my copyeditor Jean Whitnack, who have both been tireless in their efforts to improve the manuscript.

Lastly, I want above all to thank my husband and my four daughters, Mary, Sarah, Susannah and Rebecca, for allowing Julia Ward Howe to become a member of our family.

D.P.C.

Index